Repre~~sent~~

G000123376

Figure 1 Rodney M. Gilbert, Co-Founder of AdvantageArts, in the Thomas H. Kean Theatre at Drew University, 2016, photographed by Bill Cardoni, photo courtesy of Bill Cardoni.

Represent!

New Plays for Multicultural Youth

Edited by

LISA S. BRENNER and CHRIS CERASO

Foreword by Dominique Morisseau

methuen | drama

LONDON · NEW YORK · OXFORD · NEW DELHI · SYDNEY

METHUEN DRAMA
Bloomsbury Publishing Plc
50 Bedford Square, London, WC1B 3DP, UK
1385 Broadway, New York, NY 10018, USA
29 Earlsfort Terrace, Dublin 2, Ireland

BLOOMSBURY, METHUEN DRAMA and the Methuen Drama logo are trademarks of
Bloomsbury Publishing Plc

This collection first published in Great Britain 2021

Cover design: Louise Dugdale
Cover image © Lynne Delade. Kenneth Haynes IV, Dazine Austin, Emma Barakat,
and Lilibeth Miranda, with AdvantageArts at Drew University (2018; 2016; 2015).

Bloomsbury Publishing Plc does not have any control over, or responsibility for, any
third-party websites referred to or in this book. All internet addresses given in this book were
correct at the time of going to press. The author and publisher regret any inconvenience caused
if addresses have changed or sites have ceased to exist, but can accept no responsibility for
any such changes.

A catalogue record for this book is available from the British Library.

A catalog record for this book is available from the Library of Congress.

ISBN: PB: 978-1-3501-7187-9
        ePDF: 978-1-3501-7188-6
        eBook: 978-1-3501-7189-3

Typeset by RefineCatch Limited, Bungay, Suffolk
Printed and bound in Great Britain

To find out more about our authors and books visit www.bloomsbury.com
and sign up for our newsletters.

*This anthology is dedicated in fond memory and
with deep gratitude
to
Rodney Maurice Gilbert
Artist, Teacher, Activist, and Mentor*

Contents

Illustrations

Cover images

Kenneth Haynes IV, Dazine Austin, Emma Barakat, and Lilibeth Miranda, with AdvantageArts at Drew University (2018; 2016; 2015). Photography by Lynne Delade, photos courtesy of Lynne Delade.

Contributors

Keith Josef Adkins (*Playwright, Ghosts of Skunk Hollow; Gunshots at 2 p.m.*) is a playwright and screenwriter. Keith's plays have been seen at Cincinnati Playhouse, St. Louis Rep, Rattlestick, the National Black Theatre, among others. He's been commissioned by the Apollo Theater, the Public Theater, New York Theater Workshop, and Mark Taper Forum. He's the recipient of the Helen Merrill Playwriting Award, Teen Spirit Award, and Samuel French's Impact and Activism in the Theater Community Award. Publishers include Humana Festival's Complete Plays, Playscripts, *48 Hours in Harlem's* 10 Minutes Plays. TV writing includes Netflix's *Outer Banks*, Starz's *P-Valley*, ABC's *For the People*, CBS's *The Good Fight*. Keith earned his M.F.A. from the University of Iowa and is the artistic director of The New Black Fest.

Lisa S. Brenner (*Co-Editor*) has worked as a playwright and dramaturg in New York, Philadelphia, and New Jersey, and has directed many of the plays in this collection. She holds a PhD in theatre from Columbia University and has studied with seminal artists Augusto Boal, Anne Bogart, Moisés Kaufman, and Holly Hughes. She is a past editor of *Theatre Topics*, an official journal of the Association for Theatre in Higher Education; the editor of the book *Playing Harry Potter: Essays and Interviews on Fandom and Performance* (Mcfarland); and the co-editor of *Katrina on Stage: Five Plays* (Northwestern University Press). Her documentary-based play *Katrina: the K Word* (co-written with Suzanne Trauth) has been produced on campuses in fourteen states. She is also the co-editor of *Applied Theatre With Youth: Education, Engagement, Activism* (Routledge, 2021).

Chris Ceraso (*Co-Editor; Playwright, Marathon and Mucilage: A Contemplation on an Appellation*) has written for stage, film, TV, and radio. His plays have been performed at the Ensemble Studio Theatre, Chester Theatre, Lexington Conservatory Theatre, and the New York Theatre Workshop New Directors Festival, among others. Publishers include Samuel French and Plays for Living. His award-winning documentary, *Passing Over* (co-written and produced with Michael Ceraso) has been seen on many PBS stations; he was a staff writer for NBC's *Another World*. As the "Teen Dean" of New York's renowned 52nd Street Project, he adapted eight Shakespeare plays for performance by the Teen Acting Ensemble and co-authored a book on the subject, published by Dramatists Play Service. He is also the co-editor of *Applied Theatre With Youth: Educaion, Engagement, Activism* (Routledge, 2021).

Paris Crayton III (*Playwright, The Aftermath*) is an award-winning playwright, actor, and director. He was one of ArtsATL "30 under 30" and an Atlanta Journal Constitution "Artist to Watch." Creative Loafing ATL named him 2014's "Best Local Playwright." Critics have called him "a powerful dramatist" and praised him as "one of the most important emerging playwrights of our time." His plays have been presented and/or workshopped by The Lark, Classical Theatre of Harlem, Aurora Theatre, Clark University, Working Title Playwrights, Stage Door Players, Rising Sage Theatre, 3 Hill Productions, Atlanta Black Theatre Festival, Beth Marshall Presents, Indianapolis Fringe Festival, and more. He is an Artistic Associate with NewYorkRep. He directed *The Aftermath* and *Southwestern High* for Advantage Arts.

Evelyn Diaz Cruz (*Playwright, Homecoming Dance*; *Stare and Compare*) holds an MFA in playwriting from the University of California, Los Angeles. She is originally from the Bronx, New York, and resides in San Diego. Her body of work is decidedly Latina-centric and has been produced at the University of San Diego, The Centro Cultural de la Raza in San Diego, City Heights Performance Annex in San Diego, Drew University, and in New York, including performances at Teatro LATEA and multiple staged readings at the Repertorio Español. She is the co-editor of *Applied Theatre With Youth: Education, Engagement, Activism* (Routledge 2021).

Chisa Hutchinson (*Playwright, This Time with Feeling; 777*) has been widely produced and commissioned, at the National Black Theatre, Second Stage Theatre, Atlantic Theatre Company, South Coast Rep, Keen Company, Primary Stages, and the Neo-Futurists among many others. Her most recently produced play, a top-rated audio drama called *Proof of Love*, is available on Audible. She has been a member of the Lark Play Development Center and a New Dramatists Fellow, and is the recipient of numerous honors and awards. Her publishers include Dramatists Play Service and Playscripts. She has written frequently for young performers and is currently working on an adaptation of *Oliver Twist* for Disney with Ice Cube.

Cassandra Medley (*Playwright, Southwestern High*) is the recipient of numerous grants and awards, including the Going to the River Lifetime Achievement Award and the Audelco August Wilson Playwriting Award, Cassandra's plays have been produced by the Ensemble Studio Theatre, Diverse City Theatre, Molelo Theatre, and the People's Light Theatre. She taught playwriting for many years at Sarah Lawrence College. Her work has been widely published by Broadway Play Publishing, Dramatists Play Service, Smith and Krause, and Applause books among others.

Nina Angela Mercer (*Playwright, Charisma at the Crossroads*) is an interdisciplinary artist, dramaturg, and scholar, Nina's work has been shared at The Woolly Mammoth for DC's Fringe, Rutgers University, The Warehouse Theatre, Schomburg Center for Black Culture, National Black Theatre, New Federal Theater at Henry Street Settlement's Abrons Arts Center, Anacostia Arts Center, and the Nuyorican Poets Cafe. Her work is published in *The Killens Review of Arts and Letters*; *Black Renaissance Noire*; *Continuum: The Journal of African American Diaspora Drama, Theatre and Performance*; *Performance Research Journal*; and the anthologies *Black Girl Magic* and *Are You Entertained: Black Popular Culture in the 21st Century*.

Dominique Morisseau (*Foreword*) is the author of *The Detroit Project (A 3-Play Cycle)* which includes: *Skeleton Crew* (Atlantic Theater Company), *Paradise Blue* (Signature Theatre), and *Detroit '67* (Public Theater, Classical Theatre of Harlem, and NBT). Additional plays: *Pipeline* (Lincoln Center Theatre); *Sunset Baby* (LAByrinth Theatre); *Blood at the Root* (National Black Theatre); and *Follow Me to Nellie's* (Premiere Stages). She is also the Tony-nominated book writer for Broadway musical *Ain't Too Proud—The Life and Times of the Temptations* (Imperial Theatre). Dominique served as Co-Producer on the Showtime series *Shameless* (three seasons) and is a recent MacArthur Genius Grant Fellow.

Nilaja Sun (*Playwright, No Child . . .*) is the author and original performer of *No Child . . .* The recipient of over twenty awards including an Obie, two Outer Critics

Circle Awards, two NAACP Theatre Awards, and a Lucille Lortel Award, she is an actor, playwright, and teaching artist who has worked in New York City public high schools for two decades. *No Child . . .* has now been licensed and performed in theatres and schools across the nation. TV/film credits include: *Madam Secretary*, *30 Rock*, *Law and Order: Special Victims Unit*, and *The International*. Raised in the Lower East Side of New York City, Nilaja is a Princess Grace Award winner and recently received an honorary doctorate of the arts from her alma mater, Franklin and Marshall College.

David Lee White (*Playwright, The Bottom Line*) has had plays produced at Passage Theatre (where he was the Associate Artistic Director), Dreamcatcher Rep, and several others. His show *This Trenton Life* (an oral history show created with Trenton area youth) was the subject of an Emmy-nominated broadcast on PCK Media's *State of the Arts*. In 2016, he was commissioned by the New Jersey Performing Arts Center to write the play *Fixed*, based on interviews with people dealing with bipolar disorder. With composer Kate Brennan, he has created the musicals *ALiEN8* and *Clean Slate* which have been workshopped with McCarter Theater's education program, Ignition Arts, and Drexel University.

Pia Wilson (*Playwright, Snap the Sun*) is a Sundance Fellow, a Public Theater Emerging Writers Group member, and a Playwriting Fellow with the New Jersey State Council on the Arts. Pia is also the recipient of an NJPAC Stage Exchange commission and Verdone Writing Award, among other honors and accolades. Her plays have been developed and produced at Classical Theatre of Harlem, Work/Space Productions, Horse Trade Theater Group, the Public Theater, Looking Glass Theatre, and the Red Room. She is also a fiction writer and screenwriter.

Preface

Lisa S. Brenner and Chris Ceraso

This book is based on a singular premise: in the words of our late colleague Rodney Gilbert, "The magical world of theatre becomes even more magical when you can see yourself" in it (quoted in Hutchinson & Gilbert, 2017: 167). Growing up in Newark, NJ, Rodney attended local theatre productions featuring black artists like Esther Rolle, Tony Fargas, and Woody King Jr. He viewed theatre as a possible career path because he saw and heard people who looked and spoke like him on stage. Years later, in addition to becoming a professional actor and director, Rodney became a teacher, passing on the importance of being seen, of having your identity celebrated rather than dismissed. He explained:

> Because it's painful to be different. And there aren't a lot of roles where you can be you. And I noticed it when I've had Asian students, where I gave them works from Asian American playwrights and [their acting was] totally different than anyone's other work that I gave them. I have that with African American students who've grown up in predominantly white neighborhoods who come to college and they want to do monologues from *Our Town*, and then I give them August Wilson. (167)

The plays in this anthology offer young multicultural actors the opportunity to perform characters who share their backgrounds, whose relationships and environments resemble their own. As Rodney put it, this book is an effort "to get the narrative to the table where everyone can hear it" (164). While the characters' struggles are universal—loss of loved ones, peer pressure, existential questions about the meaning of life, the desire to achieve one's dreams—they are grounded in a specific social reality drawn from authentic experiences of young people in Newark, NJ.

The imperative to bring young performers and audiences into a richer sense of self and community through theatre has become a common goal of today's educational and community-based theatre programs; yet we face a body of dramatic literature for young people that is often limited to "one size fits all" offerings. Given the overwhelming power of today's social media to allow young people to express their self-reflective voices and largely uncensored experiences, the popularity of commercial shows like *Dear Evan Hansen*, *Be More Chill*, and *Harry Potter and the Cursed Child* is not surprising. However, these works, in their supposed appeal to mass market strategies, once again represent predominantly white voices, both in terms of authorship and representation. Characters of other backgrounds tend to exist only in a world of color-blind casting rather than speaking to their distinct heritage. "Color-blind" or "non-traditional" casting admittedly offers some additional opportunities for non-white actors to perform; nevertheless, these opportunities are still limited both in number and in scope. As Daniel Banks asserts in his influential essay "The Welcome Table," "To erase color is to erase identity and legacy; to recognize and appreciate our differences is to know and honor one another's histories and stories" (2019: 15).

Theatre artists and educators can help change this paradigm by developing alternatives to the structures of commercial theatre. In 2018, Pulitzer Prize-winning playwright Quiara Alegría Hudes charged educators to look at the type of plays produced in their schools or studied in their classrooms: "Does your mainstage season, syllabus, and/or curriculum reinforce dominant cultural values, and in particular, appearance-based and presentation-based casting hierarchies? Do looks, class markers, accents, and presentation afford students more or less cachet when it comes to casting departmental productions?" (2019: 7). Lack of content representing multicultural youth ignores their lived experiences and unique cultural heritages; at worst, it perpetuates stereotypes and inequities that are frequently embedded in many familiar classic and modern plays for teens and young adults. This book is meant to offer an alternative. Not only are the characters expressly written for actors of diverse cultural and racial backgrounds, but many of the plays feature strong parts for female or gender-fluid actors. The worlds created by these writers are dramatic and comic, satirical and earnest, touchingly real and amusingly surreal. Furthermore, this anthology, which contains plays of a variety of lengths, allow educators and directors to choose works that fit the ambitions and resources of their specific programs.

Creating more equitable representation on stage also invites more diverse audiences into that world. One way that theatres can make audiences feel more welcome is by producing plays written by people with whom they share a culture and a history. Again, in the words of Rodney Gilbert, "We need that authentic voice . . . If people hear it, they will come. . . . They need to see it because they understand it. I want to reach out and include and represent those people" (165). The plays in this collection, for instance, packed houses at Drew University, mostly thanks to audience members who had traveled from Newark to support the work. This anthology of plays therefore aims to expand whose stories are portrayed, who gets to tell those stories, who gets to depict them, and to whom they are being conveyed. As a result, productions of these plays (whether in theatres or in schools or university campuses) can foster community.

The plays included here, however, did not happen overnight. Produced between 2012 and 2019 by AdvantageArts at Drew University, and arranged here in the order that they were produced over those years, they are the result of a collaboration between Drew's Department of Theatre and Dance and the Newark Public Schools' Marion A. Bolden Student Center. In 2010, the editors of this volume, together with Rodney Gilbert, were charged with creating an applied theatre class that could join our theatre students with Newark high school students in a mutually beneficial experiential learning process: the Drew students could hone theatre skills while developing the ability to mentor and guide young people, while the Newark students would undergo theatre training that could allow them to speak firsthand about their lived experience and to express their personal truths. The youth in our program hailed from many cultural and racial backgrounds including Black (some born in the U.S.; others, first-generation immigrants from African nations and Jamaica), Latinx, Asian, Middle Eastern, and Portuguese. Our classroom burst with the characteristic enthusiasm, laughter, and salutary tears of many youth theatre programs. We played theatre games, adapted fairy tales, improvised, and created original work in the classroom exploring social justice themes and regularly presented the results of our work to appreciative audiences at both Drew's campus and in Newark.

In addition to offering acting and playwriting lessons, AdvantageArts incorporated movement and dance, often led by Kimani Fowlin, head of the dance program at Drew, who joined the Advantage Arts faculty in 2015 and served as choreographer and co-director of several plays in this volume. Kimani brought the perspective that "the beauty and importance of this program is that it introduces students to art at a pre-professional collegiate level . . . [and] creates professional opportunities that can be life-changing for these Newark students" (Fowlin 2020). She quickly became part of the leadership team, always seeking out opportunities for our talented Newark AdvantageArts students to perform at Drew—whether as part of our department's dance show or the Rodney M. Gilbert Salon (a showcase in collaboration with the Educational Opportunity Scholars program).

As our ambitions developed, so did the generous support of Newark's Victoria Foundation and of private donors, allowing us to expand into year-round programming. During the academic year, the program focused on building the high schoolers' writing and performance skills. Over the last eight summers, however, we were able to include a month-long intensive focusing on theatre production. Students could perform—plus assist with design, technology, research, and stage management—in a professionally written play, commissioned from accomplished playwrights from diverse backgrounds who have spent some significant part of their careers working closely with young people in urban settings. The writers conducted workshops with the Newark students, held discussions, and explored potential characters and themes through games, exercises, and writing prompts. They then wrote plays expressly for these students,[1] responding with great skill in a variety of styles: intimate, outrageous, comic, dramatic, and mysterious. *Homecoming Dance*, for example, was inspired by a moving poem written by a young man from Newark about the recent passing of his beloved grandmother. He was cast as the lead in the production and reflected that he "resonated with the character in a way that I didn't' see coming. I say this because certain aspects of who he is and his life are exactly how mine is going . . . someone who knows me exceptionally well was just as dumbfounded at the end of the play as I was due to the fact of how similar it was to my being and life itself."[2] It is worth noting here that this young man, who started work with us as a shy, hesitant performer delivered a demanding leading role with grace, power, and real emotional depth (see Fig. 3 on p. 105).

The plays address such themes as racial and cultural identity; ancestry and assimilation; bullying and self-empowerment; disenfranchisement and alienation; parental pressure to over-achieve; loss and gain of self; youth activism; and the very real perils of daily school life in an era of gun proliferation. In addition to providing a resource for theatre practitioners, this collection also serves as a resource for educators, even those outside of traditional theatre classes. These plays can be studied and discussed as works of art, just as students are accustomed to studying standard plays from Shakespeare to Arthur Miller, by examining theme, characterization, setting, language; or as a means of exploring current events, social studies, history, etc. through a more engaging, interactive pedagogy.

To aid in this learning, we have provided background information on each play provided by the playwrights, as well as custom-designed lesson plans to delve deeper into the plays' content and form. Modeled after aesthetic education theories developed by Lincoln Center Education (formerly Lincoln Center Institute) and the Manhattan Theatre Club Education Program, among others, these exercises ask students to grapple with and respond to the plays' central themes and questions through artistic expression—improvisations, theatre games, writing prompts, mural creation, movement, etc.—forging connections between the worlds on stage and off. In this process, students enter the work through their prior knowledge and personal experience, thus fostering a sense of ownership, intimate understanding, and recognition that results in the realization of material learning rather than its mere acquisition.

We are adamant that AdvantageArts would not and should not have been created without Rodney's direction and a clearly identified and willing community partner in the Newark public school system. While some Drew students and AdvantageArts staff helm from Newark themselves—and several may identify with the race, class, gender/sexual expression, and disabilities of our community participants—as members of the university, we are conscious of working with an underserved population where we are predominantly outsiders from a resource-privileged setting. Rodney was a unique leader, both a highly respected and trusted figure in Newark (where he was born and raised) and a long-time faculty member at Drew, who was able to connect these two worlds. Rodney enlisted the talent and energy of Newark theatre artists Michele Morgan and Tobias Truvillion, who helped to build this program. When Rodney unexpectedly passed away in 2017, AdvantageArts faced a great challenge to continue. Thankfully, others from each community stepped up to help, such as Newark teaching artists (in alphabetical order): Tiolinda Azzizi, Paris Crayton III, Misty Easler, Keesha Green, Horace Jackson, Malik Whitaker, and M. Print Arts; and Drew graduates who became teaching artists: Philipe Abiyouness, Emma Barakat, Alcides Costa, Najah Johnson, Nathan Keiller, Michele Taliento, Stephanie Weymouth, and Alicia Whavers (who became our Managing Director). There are numerous additional Drew students, alumni, and staff members (see below) who have given their time, creativity, and talents to AdvantageArts—many of whom in turn changed their career paths to become teachers and/or to work directly in Applied Theatre. For the past ten years, our program has been housed at the Marion A. Bolden Student Center, an afterschool facility in Newark, where we were fortunate to work with several administrators, including Antoinette Baskerville-Richardson (current President of the Newark Board of Education) and Sarah Cruz.

Most importantly, this book would not be possible without the many open-hearted, creative student participants in our programs. We would also like to acknowledge the various authors who diligently labored to bring these plays to fruition. We thank them for their fierce work, both on this book and in life. Thank you as well to our funders over the years—including the Victoria Foundation, the Casement Fund, Dr. Paul Drucker, the Neuberger-Berman Foundation, and Bringing Theory to Practice—and to the Drew staff and administrators who supported these endeavors. We hope these plays help people to be seen and heard, to laugh, cry, think, and rejoice together, as we have in producing them.

—For Rodney Gilbert, Rest in Power

Additional Thanks

Photography: Lynne Delade
Additional Drew students and alumni who helped produce these plays:
Beatrice Awobue, Ashley Backe, Andrew Binger, Jasmin Casiano, Madison Couture, Emily Deuchar, Madeline Emile, Vivienne Golde, Dallas Haines, Maliik Hall, Ruby

Hankey, Everton Johnston, Billie Krishawn, Izzy Lawrence, Elizabeth Linkewitz, Alexander Logrono, Alizé Martinez, Cristina Martinez, Chloe Martins, Zandalee Montero, Haley Pilkington, Eva Serene Portman, Ciana Proto, Jennifer Rose, Sandra Sanchez-Silva, Jaye Santoro, MJ Santry, Aaron Sartorio, Shakur Tolliver, Joe Treimanis.

Administration and Support:
Amy Koritz and the Office of Civic Engagement; Drew University Department of Theatre and Dance; Cordelza Haynes and the Educational Opportunities Scholars program; the Drew Office of Advancement; the Drew CLA Dean's Office; Tanya Bennett, Kirsten Trambley, Elias Ortega-Aponte, and the Drew School of Theology's Justice Ministry Education Program; Andrew Binger, Kareem Willis, and Yendor Productions; Jonathan Golden and The Arts of Respect, Andy Elliott, Sunita Bhargava, Wendy Kolmar and Drew Summer College.

A word about language: Following established editorial practice at the time of this writing, we have chosen to capitalize "Black" when in reference to race, but not "white" (see Baquet and Corbett, 2020).

Notes

1. The first play we produced, *No Child . . .* being an exception; while Nilija Sun did spend time with the students in our program, her play was originally written based on her experiences as a teaching artist in the Bronx, NY. One other, *Marathon and Mucilage*, originally written for the New York's 52nd Street Project, was revised and adapted specifically for our ensemble.
2. Reprinted with permission from the class journal of C.J. Moten.

Works Cited

Banks, Daniel (2019) "The Welcome Table: Casting for an Integrated Society," in *Casting a Movement: The Welcome Table Initiative*, Claire Syler and Daniel Banks, eds. London and NY: Routledge: 12–30.

Baquet, D. and Corbett, P. "Uppercasing 'Black.'" The *New York Times*. June 30. nytimes.com. Accessed 16 Sept. 2020. https://www.nytco.com/press/uppercasing-black/

Fowlin, Kimani. Personal Communication. Email. May 15, 2020.

Hudes, Quiara Alegría and Gabriella Serena Sanchez (2019) "Pausing and Breathing: Two Sisters Deliver the ATHE 2018 Conference Keynote Address." *Theatre Topics* 29(1): 1–13.

Hutchison, Chisa & Gilbert Rodney (2017). "Shoestrings: A Conversation with Chisa Hutchinson and Rodney Gilbert." *Theatre Topics* 27(2): 163–168.

Foreword

Dominique Morisseau

I was in college, University of Michigan, the Theatre Department. I was an aspiring Black woman actress getting my BFA in Theatre Performance. I was from Bliggity Black Detroit. Ann Arbor was predominately white. It was forty-five minutes west of home and in a vastly different world. Michigan (U of M) was a predominately white institution, what folks are now calling PWIs. We didn't have these acronyms when I was in school, we just felt it. Everywhere. This idea that somehow we were now "othered." Coming from a city where everyone who looked like me was running everything, from city government to school boards to hospitals to factories, this was a shock. Not only to my body politic and identity, but also to my ideologies and ways of understanding systems.

Michigan was electric with activism at this time. Affirmative Action was currently in place to ensure "diversity" among student enrollment, and it was being threatened by dissenters, lawsuits, and even active students who somehow believed the presence of students of color to be a hindrance to their own academic success. The word "diversity" was in every mailing. Every course term. Every student organization. Students would don shirts that had the expression, "Black at Michigan." This was before hashtags. There is now a continuation of this idea among Michigan's more recent Black students. It's called, #BBUM (Being Black at the University of Michigan). We come from a long line of Black artists who have studied at Michigan and felt erased from the overall pedagogy of their arts programs. Before us, there was BAM (Black Action Movement), not to be confused with the nationwide BAM (Black Arts Movement) that was happening at the same time. You get the point. Defiance was everywhere. We were obsessed with defending our right to get an education at Michigan without harassment, marginalization, or hostility.

At this same time, I was getting burnt out in the theatre department. We were only studying plays by dead white men. Some of them were cool. Never let it be said that I didn't sometimes have an affinity for a Tennessee Williams lament or a Shakespeare sonnet, but they absolutely did not make my world go round. None of them were in my skin or my bones. None of those plays and playwrights activated my heart shakra or blood memory. And yet, I felt that I was supposed to be feeling something if I was ever going to be considered a good actress. That my resistance to narratives with arcs that didn't include me was somehow my failure, instead of my acute awareness to the injustices that white male pedagogical training created for a young Black woman artist.

Something quickly awakened in me. I recognized that if I was going to continue to pursue my degree within this narrow curriculum, I would have to disrupt the white gaze that was suffocating me. If my professors were not going to make playwrights of color a necessity, then I was going to have to do it myself. I was going to not only study Black theatre in every elective, I was going to study it independently of my training program. I was reading anthologies of plays edited by Woodie King Jr. and Sydne Mahone. I read Cheryl West and Pearl Cleage and Nubia Kai and Rhodessa Jones and Aishah Rahman. These were plays by Black women. I read Maria Irene Fornes, a Latinx woman. I read

Ed Bullins and Charles Fuller and OyamO – who was one of my only three Black professors at the school. And with the fulfillment I had in exploring aspects of myself in their writing, I decided that I was going to have to write my way into visibility at my school. Though I had only written poetry and essays, and perhaps a few short stories by this point, it became extremely clear to me that it was time to write my first play.

It was called *The Blackness Blues, Time to Change the Tune – A Sister's Story*. Much in the fashion of Ntozake Shange's *For Colored Girls Who Have Considered Suicide / When the Rainbow Is Enuf*, my first play was a choreopoem. I had definitely been one of those colored girls considering suicide in my life, and particularly this second year of college, which had me vexed by the rejection of both my theatre department and my boyfriend back home in Detroit. I was in two abusive relationships. One with a young man who was making me doubt my value as a woman and an artist and a loving being in this world, and one with a theatre department that was doing the same. I had reached the point of no return with them both. Writing *The Blackness Blues* . . . , which I had titled after a song by the dynamic group Sounds of Blackness, both uplifted and liberated me. I was telling my unapologetic truth. I was being *me* in front of my entire department. My whole, Black, free self. Writing this play saved me from my own obscurity. I had broken up with my boyfriend. Received a scholarship to remain in school. And never looked back.

I always think of this story when I need to remember who I am. Whenever I am feeling defeated or frustrated with the artistic field in general, or my own life in particular, I think about what it felt like to have a story where I was centered. There is nothing, absolutely nothing more profound and life-affirming than seeing reflections of yourself. It's a cliché that is unrelenting. It's the stone-cold truth. Wherever we are missing from the narrative, we are witnessing our own erasure and insignificance. A theatre world owes its people better. Our art is the engine that keeps this sport alive. Without us, stages go bare and sunlight ceases to burn. There can be no theatre without all of us, in our many brilliant complexities. And we deserve to be represented, counted, and *centered*.

This is why *Represent!* is more than a collection of some of the nation's most brave, courageous, and rebellious writers. Many of these writers are my peers. I have watched their work stretch and grow and demand to be produced. These plays, just like the many of you who will read them, *matter*. They come from fellow writers who have also been actors, like myself. Writers who have also been directors and producers, like myself. Writers who have felt at times under-represented and silenced and erased. Their words have become protective shields and also weapons against the singular, narrow, oppressive binary white male gaze. They are calling upon readers and theatremakers of all backgrounds to see the necessity of our many varied cultural voices. When we are digesting each other's words and worlds, we will truly know one another more intimately as a human family. We will see ourselves in each other. And we will have a more inclusive field of playmaking.

This is the moment of you being amplified. This is your version of my second year of college, where perhaps you are on the brink of feeling invisible and are instead becoming *invincible*. Where you can hopefully find yourself and your truth in the language and poetics of Nilaja Sun and Chisa Hutchinson and Evelyn Diaz Cruz and Pia Wilson and Keith Josef Adkins and David Lee White and Cassandra Medley and

Nina Angela Mercer and Chris Ceraso and Paris Crayton III. They are writing for you because they are also writing for themselves. None of us is creating art in a vacuum. None of us is alone in our quest for liberation and value and purpose. We are each other's reflection, and we are here to represent ourselves, our families, our cultures, our world, and our many small and courageous truths.

It's your time to be heard. Go be unapologetic and bold. And most importantly, go be wholly, fully, freely . . . *YOU.*

peaceandlovedominiquemorisseau ☺

Synopses of Plays

No Child . . . (Nilaja Sun)   In this multi-award-winning drama, a teaching artist must learn to balance the frustrations and uncertainties of her own life and a broken public school system to bring a class of students at Malcolm X High together in an inspirational artistic achievement.

The Ghosts of Skunk Hollow (Keith Josef Adkins)   A group of jaded high school students on a class outing have a chilling encounter that causes them to drop their fronts and gives them a new appreciation for ancestral heritage.

Gunshots at 2 p.m. (Keith Josef Adkins)   When the sound of gunfire in the halls sends a class into lockdown, fearful assumptions reinforce their biases and lead them to target the outcast among them.

This Time with Feeling (Chisa Hutchinson)   Parental pressure to succeed drives an over-achieving Black candidate for student body president to a startling, violent act. Her peers and the press are left to ruminate on the tragedy and its meaning in the Black community.

777 (Chisa Hutchinson)   Number 777 arrives at a next life waystation with a group of wounded travelers awaiting their chance to assume a new identity. When 777 wins the lottery, his jealous companions don't understand his surprising choice.

Marathon and Mucilage: A Contemplation on an Appellation (Chris Ceraso)   A drowsy student in an ancient history class takes a dream journey into self-identity—complete with Egyptian cats, Hannibal's elephants, and the Oracle of Delphi—and wakes up with a new name.

Homecoming Dance (Evelyn Diaz Cruz)   A young man who strives to escape his hometown and his heritage rekindles his love of community and family through a mysterious encounter with an unusual teenager named Taina at the school dance.

Snap the Sun (Pia Wilson)   A group of city kids at a science camp in the country are led to question the fleeting nature of authentic experience as they attempt to capture a moment of beauty and true togetherness on a cell-phone camera.

The Bottom Line (David Lee White)   Racial tensions erupt when a white reporter, a life-long resident of the local community, invades the private grieving of an African-American family that recently lost a teenager to gun violence.

The Aftermath (Paris Crayton III)   Whodunnit? The truth is elusive and slippery prey for the authorities to capture in the wake of an uproarious food fight in the school cafeteria. Romance, rivalry, and ridicule are uncovered in multiple perspectives, leading to surprising revelations.

Charisma at the Crossroads (Nina Angela Mercer)   Charisma's dreams of becoming a fashion designer are put on trial before a nightmarish adult kangaroo court that only wants to consume the hopes and aspirations of youth. An interactive play with music and dance.

Southwestern High (Cassandra Medley)   A graduating senior and her local-celebrity aunt find mutual healing across their generational divide when a visit to old Southwestern High forces them to confront painful incidents of bullying that haunt them both.

Stare and Compare (Evelyn Diaz Cruz)   Two very different sisters—"Serena-the-Queen-ah," a social media influencer, and Angel, a community activist—take a deep dive into their personal values on a family trip to help hurricane survivors in Puerto Rico.

No Child . . .

Nilaja Sun

Background and Insights for *No Child* . . .

from Nilaja Sun

Notes on Casting

This play may be performed with one actor or with as many as sixteen actors. Regarding the playing of Ms. Tam: Please be sure she is played as Chinese-American. No accent needed.

Notes on Production

The play takes place in several locations but is best staged in a fluid style with lights and sounds suggesting scene changes.

No Child . . . was written and is set in 2005. Please feel free to contact me, the playwright, for any changes regarding technology or 2005 lingo that may seem foreign to the ears of your audience. I am open to making the language palatable for your community, within reason.

I, as an educator, understand if the need arises for any and all curse words to be edited/removed. The key is to be sure that the feeling of the curse words still remains. Feel free to contact me, and we can work through the editing and substituting of curse words in order to support the integrity of the students' words, tone, and intentions.

The Inspiration for This Play

I received a grant from the New York State Council of the Arts through Epic Theatre Ensemble to write a play about education. At the time, there were no stories in the theatre about teaching artistry, and so I decided to write the story of a fictitious school named Malcolm X High and infuse it with all of the many experiences I had teaching in New York City public schools.

During preview week of the initial production of No Child . . . at the Beckett Theatre, I began to realize that teachers were really affected by the play and its messages and started to support it by bringing their students, colleagues, and families. I, myself, was lucky to have really great teachers growing up who believed in me. No Child . . . is dedicated to those educators who deeply believe in their students and dedicate their time, attention, and lives to set them up for success.

Major Themes

Some of the major themes in No Child . . . have proven to be: equity in education, the importance of arts in education, educators who dare to care, and highlighting the intelligence and artistry of students from all racial, socioeconomic, and ethnic backgrounds.

No Child . . . Food for Thought

After you witness No Child . . ., *I hope you can think back to your own upbringing and schooling and honestly ask yourself how it affected your life for the better, or perhaps for the worse. Were you blessed to have a teacher or teachers who really made a difference in your life? Do you still have fond memories of stepping up to the chalkboard, waving to the crossing guard, or performing in the school play? How important are the arts in your life or in the lives of your children and in their schools? Would you fight to keep the arts in all schools?*

Entrance into the World of Theatre

I've always seen the people in my life as characters in a bigger story. I was lucky to have been raised in the very diverse neighborhood of the Lower East Side of Manhattan in the 1980s. Hip hop was being birthed on the streets, break dancers were poppin' and lockin' in schools, all on the same corners that Eastern European, Chinese, and Latino immigrants called home. How could I not have been inspired! I'd come home from Catholic school and perform endless character impressions to the enjoyment of my very loving and patient parents.

So, when I asked myself in college what I really wanted to do with my life, it was simple: tell stories. Why for the theatre? It's home. There is a charge, an electrical energy and an angelic presence in every theatre, on every stage, and whenever "places" is called that cannot be matched. No matter where I roam, I'll always come back home to the theatre.

No Child . . . was originally produced Off-Broadway at the Barrow Street Theatre (Scott Morfee and Torn Wirtshafter, Producers). It was commissioned, developed, and received its world premiere by Epic Theatre Ensemble in New York City in May 2006 with additional support from the New York State Council on the Arts and Jack Sharkey. It was directed by Hal Brooks; the set design was by Nardle Sissons; the costume design was by Jessica Gaffney; the lighting design was by Mark Barton; and the sound design was by Ron Russell. It was performed by Nilaja Sun.

Characters *(in order of appearance)*

Janitor Baron, *eighties, narrator*
Ms. Sun, *thirties, teaching artist*
Ms. Tam, *twenties, teacher*
Coca, *sixteen, student*
Jerome, *eighteen, student*
Brian, *sixteen, student*
Shondrika, *sixteen, student*
Xiomara, *sixteen, student*
Jose, *seventeen, student*
Chris, *fifteen, student*
Mrs. Kennedy, *school principal*
Security Guard, *any age*
Phillip, *sixteen, student*
Mrs. Projensky, *substitute teacher*
Mr. Johnson, *teacher*
Doña Guzman, *seventies, grandmother to Jose Guzman*

Place: New York.
Time: Now.

Scene One

School. Morning. **Janitor** *enters, mopping floor as he sings.*

Janitor

Trouble in mind.
I'm blue.
But I won't be blue always.
Cuz the sun's gonna shine
In my back door someday.

(*To audience.*) Hear that? Silence. Beautiful silence, pure silence. The kind of silence that only comes from spending years in the back woods. We ain't in the back woods (though I'm thinking 'bout retirin' there). It's 8:04 A.M.—five minutes before the start of the day. And, we on the second floor of Malcolm X High School in the Bronx, USA. Right over there is my janitor's closet, just right of the girls' bathroom where the smell of makeup, hair pomade, and gossip fills the air in the morning light. There's Mrs. Kennedy's room—she the principal. For seventeen years, been leading this group of delinquents—Oh I'm sorry, academically and emotionally challenged youth. She got a lot to work with! Seventeen feet below my very own, lay one-hundred-thousand-dollar worth of a security system. This include two metal detecting machines, seven metal detecting wands, five school guards, and three NYC police officers. All armed. Guess all we missing is a bomb-sniffing dog. Right over there's Ms. Tam's class, she one of them new teachers. Worked as an associate in the biggest investment firm in New York then coming home from a long dreary day at work, read an ad on the subway—ya'll know the ones that offer you a lifetime of glorious purpose and meaning if you just become a New York City teacher. Uh-huh—the devil's lair on the IRT. I adore Ms. Tam, she kind, docile, but I don't think she know what she got herself into. See, I been working here since 1958 and I done seen some teachers come and go, I said I seen teachers come and go. Ah! One more time for good luck, I seen teachers come and go and I do believe it is one of the hardest jobs in the whole wide world. Shoot, I don't gotta tell you that, y'all look like smart folk! The most underpaid, underappreciated, *underpaid* job in this crazy universe. But for some miracle, every year God creates people that grow up knowing that's what they gonna do for the rest of they life. God, ain't He sometin'! Now, you might say to me, "Jackson Baron Copeford the Third. Boy, what you doin' up dere on dat stage? You ain't no actor." That I know and neither are these kids you about to meet. (*He clears his throat.*) What you about to see is a story about a play within a play within a play. And a teacher (or as she likes to call herself—a teaching artist—just so as people know she do somethin' else on her free time). The kids call her Ms. Sun and in two minutes from now she gonna walk up them stairs towards the janitor's room and stop right at Ms. Tam's class. She gonna be something they done never seen before. Now I know what you're thinking: "Oh, Baron. I know about the public schools. I watch Eyewitness News." What I got to say to that? HUSH! You don't know unless you been in the schools on a day-to-day basis. HUSH! You don't know unless you been a teacher, administrator, student, or custodial staff. HUSH! Cuz you could learn a little somethin'. Here's lesson number one: Taking the 6 train, in eighteen minutes, you can go from Fifty-ninth Street, one of the richest congressional districts in the nation, all the way up to Brook Ave. in the Bronx, where Malcolm X High is, the poorest congressional district in the nation. In only eighteen minutes. HUSH!

Scene Two

Before class.

Ms. Sun (*on the phone, hallway*)   Mr. Pulaski! Hi, it's Ms. Sun from Bergen Street. 280 Bergen. Apartment four? Hey! Mr. Pulaski, thanks for being so patient, I know how late my rent is . . . By the way, how's your wife Margaret? Cool. And your son Josh? Long Island University. That's serious. Oh he's gonna love it and he'll be close to home. But yes, I apologize for not getting you last month's rent on time, but see the IRS put a levy on my bank account and I just can't retrieve any money from it right now. Well, it should be cleared by Tuesday but the real reason why I called was to say I'm startin' a new teaching program up here in the Bronx and it's a six-week-long workshop and they're paying me exactly what I owe you so . . . what's that? Theatre. I'm teaching theatre. A play actually. It's called *Our Country's Good* . . . Have you heard of it? Well it's about a group of convicts that put on a play . . . So the kids are actually gonna be doing a play within a play within . . . What's that? Ah, yes, kids today need more discipline and less self-expression. Less "lululala" and more daily structure like Catholic school during Pope Pious the Twelfth. On the flip side of the matter, having gone to Catholic school for thirteen years, I didn't even know I was Black until college. (*She roars her laughter.*) Sir? Sir, are you still there? (*Bell rings.*) I gotta go teach, sir. Are we cool with getting you that money by the twenty-fifth? How about the thirtieth? Thirty-first? I know, don't push it. You rock. Yes, I'm still an actor. No, not in anything right now. But soon. Yes, sir, happy Lent to you too, sir.

Scene Three

Classroom.

Ms. Tam   Ms. Sun? Come on in. I'm Cindy Tam and I'm so excited to have your program here in our English class. Sorry we weren't able to meet the last four times you set up a planning meeting but so much has been going on in my life. Is it true you've been a teaching artist for seven years? In New York City? Wow. That's amazing. I'm a new teacher. They don't know that. It's a *challenge.* The kids are really *spirited.* Kaswan, where are you going? Well, we're going to be starting in a few minutes and I would strongly suggest you not leave. (*Listens.*) OK, but be back in five minutes, um, Veronica, stop hitting Chris and calling him a motherfucker. I'm sorry, please stop hitting Chris and calling him a motherfucker. Thanks, Veronica. Sorry, like I said, very excited you're here. Where is everyone? The kids usually come in twenty to thirty minutes late because it's *so* early. I know it's only a forty-one-minute class but I've been installing harsher penalties for anyone who comes in after fifteen. After five? OK, we'll try that. Well, what we *can* do today is start the program in ten minutes and wait for the bulk of them to come in, eat their breakfast, and . . . You wanna start now? But there are only seven kids here. The rest of them will ask what's going on and what am I gonna say to each late student? (*Scared out of her wits.*) OK. Then, we'll start. Now. Class! Please welcome Ms. Sun. She's going to be teaching you a play, and teachng you about acting, and how to act and we're gonna do a play and it's gonna be fun.

Coca   Fun? This is stupid already. I don't wanna act. I wanna do vocabulary.

Jerome   Vocab? Hello, Ms. Sun. Thank you for starting the class on time. Since we usually be the only ones on time.

Brian   Niggah, you ain't never on time.

Jerome   Shut up, bitch motherfucker.

Ms. Tam   Jerome, Brian? What did I tell you about the offensive language?

Jerome   Yo, yo. We know. Pork fried rice wanton coming up.

Ms. Tam   I heard that, Jerome.

Jerome   Sorry, Ms. Tam.

Brian (*accent*)   Solly, Ms. Tam.

Ms. Tam   Go on, Ms. Sun!

Beat.

Ms. Sun   Ah, well, I'm Ms. Sun and I will be with you all for the next six weeks and by the end of those glorious weeks, you would have read a play, analyzed the play, been cast in it, rehearsed it, and lastly performed it. It's gonna be a whirlwind spectacle that I want you to start inviting your parents and friends and loved ones to come see . . . What's that? No, it's not *Raisin in the Sun* . . . No, it's not *West Side Story*. It's a play called *Our Country's Good*.

Coca   Ew. This is some patrionism?

Ms. Sun   Patriotism? No. It's a play based in Australia in 1788 and it's written by a woman named Timberlake Wertenbaker.

Brian   Yo, Justin Timberlake done wrote himself a play. "Gonna rock yo' body. Today. Dance with me."

Ms. Tam   Brian, focus?

Brian   "People say she a gold digga, but she don't mess with no broke niggas."

Ms. Tam   Brian! Put down the Red Bull.

Brian   Beef fried rice.

Ms. Tam   Brian.

Brian   Vegetable fried rice.

Jerome   Ay yo! This some white shit. Ain't this illegal to teach this white shit no mo'?

Ms. Sun   Are you done?

Jerome   Huh?

Ms. Sun   Are you done?

Jerome   What?

Ms. Sun   With your spiel? With your little spiel?

Jerome   Yeah.

Ms. Sun   Because I'm trying to tell you what the play is about and I can't when you keep on interrupting.

Jerome   Oh my bad. Damn. She got attitude. I like that.

Shondrika   I don't. What's this play about anyway?

Ms. Sun   Well, what's your name?

Shondrika   Shondrika.

Ms. Sun   Well, Shondrika . . .

Shondrika   Shondrika!

Ms. Sun   Shondrika?

Shondrika   Shondrika!

Ms. Sun   Shondrika!

Shondrika   Close enough.

Ms. Sun   Ah-hah . . . *Our Country's Good* is about a group of convicts.

Xiomara   What are convicts?

Jerome   Jailbirds, you dumb in a can. Get it? (*Laugh/clap.*) Dominican! Dominican!

Ms. Sun   . . . And they put on a play called *The Recruiting Officer.* You'll be reading . . .

Coca   We gotta read?

Jerome   Aw hell no.

Ms. Tam   Yes, you'll be reading, but you're also gonna be creating a community.

Jerome   Ay yo! Last time I created a community the cops came.

Latecomers enter.

Ms. Tam   Kaswan, Jose, Jennifer, Malika, Talifa, Poughkeepsie, come on in, you're late. What's your excuse this time, Jose?

Jose   Sorry, miss. But that faggot Mr. Smith was yelling at us to stop running to class. Fucking faggot.

Ms. Sun   ENOUGH!

Jose   Who? Who this?

Ms. Sun   Hi. I'm Ms. Sun. Take your seats *now*. And as of today and for the next six weeks, when I'm in this classroom, you will not be using the word faggot or bitch or nigga or motherfucker or motherfuckerniggabitchfaggot. Anymore. Dominicans shall not be called and will not call each other dumb in a cans or *platanos*.

Coca   *Ah, y pero quien e heta? Esa prieta?*

Ms. Sun   *La prieta soy yo, senorita.*

Coca *is speechless.*

Brian   Shwimp fwy why! Shwimp fwy why!

Ms. Sun   We will respect our teacher's ethnicity.

Brian   Shwimp fwy why?

No one else laughs.

Ms. Sun   Ladies will not call each other heifers or hos.

Shondrika   Shoot! That's what I'm talkin' about.

Ms. Sun   We will start class on time. We will eat our breakfast beforehand. And from now on we are nothing but thespians.

Xiomara   Lesbians? I ain't no Rosie O'Donnell.

Ms. Sun   No, no! Thespian! It means actor, citizen, lover of all things great.

Xiomara   I love that hard cash that bling-bling.

Ms. Sun   Say it with me, class, thespian.

Xiomara (*bored*)   Thespian.

Ms. Sun   Thespian!

Jerome (*bored*)   Thespian.

Ms. Sun   Thespian!

Coca   Thespian, already, damn!

Ms. Sun   Now, let's get up and form a circle.

Shondrika   Get up? Aw hell no!

Jose   Miss, we not supposed to do exercises this early.

Ms. Tam   Come on, guys, stand up. Stand up.

Coca   Miss, this is mad boring.

Ms. Sun   Boredom, my love, usually comes from boring people.

Brian   OOOOOOOOOOOOH!

Coca (*dissed*)   What's that supposed to mean?

Brian   That's O.D., yo! Oh she played you, yo!

Jerome   Ay yo, shut yo trap. Miss, I could be the lovable and charming leading man that gets all the honies' numbers?

Ms. Sun   We'll see.

Jerome   Miss, can I get your number? (*Beat.*) Nah, I'm just playing. Let's do this, yo. Get up.

They get up.

Ms. Sun   OK, thank you . . .

Jerome   Jerome!

Ms. Sun   Jerome. Great circle! Let's take a deep breath in and out. In . . .

Brian   Ohm! Nah! I'm just playing. Keep going. Keep going. Keep going. Keep going.

Ms. Sun   . . . and out . . . In . . .

Coca   I'm hungry. What time it is?

Ms. Sun   . . . and out . . . stretch with me, will you? Now, who here has ever seen a play?

No one raises their hand . . . but **Chris**.

Ms. Sun   Really? Which show?

Chris   *Star Wars.* It was a live reenactment.

Ms. Sun   Was it in a theater?

Chris   Yeah. We all wore outfits and costumes and acted alongside the movie.

Jerome   Damn, Chris, you like SupaDupaJamaicanNerdNegro.

Chris   And for that, I zap you. (*To Ms. Sun.*) You really gonna make us act onstage?

Ms. Sun   Yup.

Chris   I'm scared.

Ms. Sun   Yeah, well guess what? Before I walked in here, even with all my acting and teaching experience, I was scared and nervous too, but you get over it once you get a feel for the audience and you see all of your parents and your friends and your teachers smiling at you. Did you guys know that public speaking is the number one fear for all humans—even greater than death?

Jerome   What? They ain't never lived in the hood.

Jose   But, miss, you should be scared of this class, cuz we supposed to be the worst class in the school.

Ms. Tam   It's true. They are.

Ms. Sun   Really, well, in the past thirty-five minutes, I've met some pretty amazing young adults, thinkers, debaters, thespians . . .

Brian   Lesbians.

Ms. Sun   Keep breathing! (*Bell rings.*) Oh no, listen, read Scenes One through Five for the next time. Thanks, guys, you are great.

Ms. Tam   Wow. That was amazing. You're really great with the kids. (*Beat.*) Just to let you know. They're probably not going to read the play and they are probably going to lose the handout and probably start to cut your class and their parents probably won't come to the show. Probably. OK, bye.

Ms. Sun   Bye. (*She watches her leave.*) For all our sake, Ms. Tam, I hope you're probably wrong.

Scene Four

School hallway.

Mrs. Kennedy   Ms. Sun, hi, Mrs. Kennedy—the principal, so glad to meet you. Sorry about the attendance. Ms. Tam is a new teacher and we need all these kids to pass five Regents exams in the next two months. The pressure's on. Let me know when you'll be needing the auditorium. There are four schools in this building and it's like fighting diseased lions to book a night in it. But, you're priority. We've given you one of the most challenging classes. But I believe in them. I believe in you. Tyesha, can I have a word?

She walks off. **Security Guard** *stops.* **Ms. Sun**

Security Guard   Y'ave pass ta leave. I said do you have a pass to leave? Oh, you a teaching artist? Oh. Cuz you look like one a them. Well, excuse me for livin'! (*To other guards.*) Just trying to do mi job. I don't know the difference 'tween the teachers, teaching artists, parents, Board of Ed people, and these animals comin' in here. I don' know da difference. Just tryin' to do mi job. (*To Student.*) Girl, girl! Whatcha t'ink dis is? You can't go in wifoot goin' tru da detector. I don' care if you just walked out and now you come back in. Rules are rules. Put ya bag in and yo wallet and your selfish phone.

(*Beep.*) Go back. Ya belt.

(*Beep.*) Go back. Ya earrings.

(*Beep.*) Go back. Ya shoes. Don't sass me!

(*Beep.*) Go back. Ya hair . . . t'ings.

(*Beep.*) Go back. Ya jewelry. Oh, oh I don' have time for your attitude. Open your arms, spread your legs. Oh, oh I don' care about your science class. Should know betta' than to just waltz in 'ere ten minutes 'fore class. Got ta give it one whole hour. Lemme see yo I.D. Don't have? Can't come in. Excuse?! What ya name is? Shondrika Jones! I don' care about ya Regents. Go, go, go back home. Next time don' bring all dat bling and don' bring all dat belt and don' bring all dat sass. Who ya t'ink ya is? The mayor of New York City? Slut! (*To another student*). Boy, boy, don't you pass me!

Light shift.

Janitor (*to audience*)   Your tax dollars at work! As Ms. Sun makes her way back me on the train, she thinks to herself.

Scene Five

Subway car.

Ms. Sun   What will these six weeks bring? How will I persuade them to act onstage? (*Beat.*) Why did I choose a play about convicts? These kids aren't convicts. The kids in Rikers are convicts. These kids are just in tenth grade. They've got the world telling them they are going to end up in jail. Why would I choose a play about convicts? Why couldn't I choose a play about kings and queens in Africa or the triumphs of the Taino Indian? This totally wouldn't jive if I were white and trying to do this. How dare I! Why would I choose to do a play about convicts?

Scene Six

Classroom.

Jerome   Because we treated like convicts every day.

Ms. Tam   Jerome, raise your hand.

Jerome (*raises hand*)   We treated like convicts every day.

Ms. Sun   How do you mean?

Shondrika   First, we wake up to bars on our windows.

Coca   Then, our moms and dads.

Shondrika   You got a dad?

Coca   Yeah . . . so? Then our mom tells us where to go, what to do, and blah, blah, blah.

Jerome   Then, we walk in a uniformed line towards the subways, cramming into a ten-by-forty-foot cell (*laughs*) checking out the fly honies.

Brian   But there ain't no honies in jail, know what I'm saying?

Jerome   Unless, you there long enough, what, what!

Ms. Sun   Then, class, you'll walk into another line at the bodega at the corner store, to get what?

Xiomara   Breakfast.

Ms. Sun   And what's for breakfast?

Xiomara   Welch's Orange and a Debbie snack cake.

Ms. Sun   Exactly, then what?

Shondrika   Then, we go to school.

Chris   . . . Where a cool electronic object points out our every metal flaw.

Jerome   Damn, Chris, you read way too much sci-fi!

Shondrika   Then we go to a class they tell us we gotta go to, with a teacher we gotta learn from and a play we gotta do.

Ms. Sun   And now that you feel like prisoners . . . open to page twenty-seven. Phillip says, "Watkin: Man is born free, and everywhere he is in chains." What *don't* people expect from prisoners?

Jose   For them to succeed in life . . .

Ms. Sun   But, in the play . . .

Coca   They succeed by doing the exact opposite of what people expect.

Ms. Sun   And so . . . how does that relate to your lives?

Shondrika   Shoot, don't nobody expect us to do nothing but drop out, get pregnant, go to jail . . .

Brian   . . . or work for the MTA.

Xiomara   My mom works for the MTA, nigga. Sorry, miss . . . *negro.*

Shondrika   So, dese characters is kinda going through what we kinda going through right now.

Ms. Sun   Kinda, yeah. And so . . . Brian . . .

Brian   By us doing the show, see what I'm saying, we could prove something to ourselves and our moms and her dad and Mrs. Kennedy and Ms. Tam that we is the shi . . . shining stars of the school, see what I'm saying?

Ms. Sun   Great, turn to Act One, Scene Six. Can I have a volunteer to read?

She looks around.

Shondrika   Shoot, I'll read, give me this: "We are talking about criminals, often hardened criminals. They have a habit of vice and crime. Habits . . ."

Jose   Damn, Ma, put some feeling into that!

Shondrika   I don't see you up here reading, Jose.

Jose   Cuz you the actress of the class.

Shondrika (*realizing she is the "actress" of the class*)   "Habits are difficult to BREAK! And it can be more than habit, an I-nate–"

Ms. Tam (*correcting*)   Innate . . .

Shondrika   See, Ms. Tam, why you had to mess up my flow? Now I gotta start from the beginning since you done messed up my flow.

Class sighs.

Brian   Aw. Come on!

Ms. Tam   Sorry, Shondrika.

Shondrika   Right. "Habits are difficult to break. And it can be more than habit, an innate tendency. Many criminals seem to have been born that way. It is in their nature." Thank you.

Applause.

Ms. Sun   Beautiful, Shondrika. And is it in your nature to live like you're a convict?

Shondrika   No!

Ms. Sun   Well, what is in your nature? Coca?

Coca   Love.

Ms. Sun   What else? Chris?

Chris   Success. And real estate.

Ms. Sun   Jose, how about you?

Jose   Family. Yo. My brother and my *buela.*

Ms. Sun   Brian?

Brian   And above all, money, see what I'm sayin', know what I mean, see what I'm saying?

Ms. Sun   Yes, Brian, we see what you're saying . . . and now that you know that you actually *can* succeed, let's get up and stretch!

Coca   Get up? Aw hell no!

Jose   This is mad boring.

Xiomara   I just ate. I hate this part.

Jerome   Can I go to the bathroom?

Bell rings. Light shift.

Janitor   Not so bad for a second class. Although, due to discipline issues, attention problems, lateness, and resistance to the project on the whole, Ms. Sun is already behind in her teaching lesson. And, the show is only four weeks away. Let's watch as Ms. Sun enters her third week of classes. The show must go on! (I'm good at this. I am!)

Scene Seven

Classroom.

Coca   Miss. Did you hear? Most of our class is gone for the day . . . They went on an important school trip. To the UniverSoul Circus. There's only five of us here.

Ms. Sun   That's OK, Coca. We'll make due with the five of us, including Ms. Tam.

Ms. Tam (*tired*)   Ewww . . .

Ms. Sun   So, we will start the rehearsal section for *Our Country's Good.* We have the lovely Xiomara as Mary Brenham.

Xiomara (*deep voice*)   I don't want to be Mary Brenham, I want to be Liz . . . the pretty one.

Ms. Sun   I think I can make that happen. Chris as the Aborigine.

Chris   It's good.

Ms. Sun   And Phillip as . . . Phillip as . . . Ralph! Phillip, do me a favor, go to page thirty-one and read your big monologue about the presence of women on the stage.

Phillip (*inaudibly*)   "In my own small way in just a few hours I have seen something change. I asked some of the convict women to read me some lines, these women who behave often no better than animals."

Pause.

Ms. Sun   Good, Phillip, good. Do me a favor and read the first line again but pretend that you are speaking to a group of a hundred people.

Phillip (*inaudibly*)   "In my own small way in just a few hours I have seen something change."

Ms. Sun   Thank you, Phillip. You can sit down now.

She goes to work on another student.

No, Phillip, get back up. Someone is stealing your brand new . . . what kind of car do you like, Phillip?

Phillip (*inaudibly*)   Mercedes LX 100, limited edition.

Ms. Sun   That! And, you have to, with that line there, stop him from taking your prized possession. Read it again.

Phillip (*inaudibly*)   "In my own small way I have seen something change."

Ms. Sun   Now open your mouth . . .

Phillip (*inaudibly but with mouth wide*)   "In my own small way . . .

Ms. Sun   Your tongue, your tongue is a living breathing animal thrashing about in your mouth—it's not just lying there on the bottom near your jaw—it's got a life of its own, man. Give it life.

Phillip (*full on*)   "In my own small way I have seen something change!"

The bell rings.

Ms. Sun   That's it. That's it. Right there . . . (*She is alone now.*) God, I need a Vicodin.

Scene Eight

School. Night.

Janitor   It may not look it, but this school has gone through many transformations. When I first arrived at its pristine steps, I marveled at the architecture . . . like a castle. Believe it or not, there were nothin' but Italian kids here and it was called Robert Moses High back then. Humph! See, I was the first Negro janitor here and ooh that made them other custodians upset. But I did my job, kept my courtesies intact. Them janitors all gone now . . . and I'm still here. Then came the sixties, civil rights, the assassination of President Kennedy right there on the TV, Vietnam. Those were some hot times. Italians started moving out and Blacks and Puerto Ricans moved right on in. Back then, landlords was burning up they own buildings just so as to collect they insurance. And, the Black Panthers had a breakfast program—would say "Brotha Baron! How you gonna fight the MAN today?" I say "With my broom and my grade D ammonia, ya dig?" They'd laugh. They all gone, I'm still here. Then came the seventies when they renamed the school Malcolm X after our great revolutionary. I say, "Alright, here we go. True change has got to begin now." Lesson number two: Revolution has its upside and its downside. Try not to stick around for the downside. Eighties brought Reagan, that goddamn crack ('scuse my cussin') and hip-hop. Ain't nothing like my Joe King Oliver's Creole Jazz Band but what you gonna do. And here we come to today. Building fallin' apart, paint chipping, water damage, kids running around here talking loud like crazy folk, half of them is raising themselves. Let me tell ya, I don't know nothing about no No Child, Yes Child, Who Child What Child. I do know there's a hole in the fourth-floor ceiling ain't been fixed since '87, all the bathrooms on the third floor, they all broke. Now, who's accountable for dat? Heck, they even asked me to give up my closet, make it into some science lab class cuz ain't got no room. I say, "This my sanctuary. You can't take away my zen. Shoot, I read *O* magazine." They complied for now. Phew! Everything's falling apart . . . But these floors, these windows, these chalkboards—they clean . . . why? Cuz I'm still here!

Scene Nine

Classroom.

Coca   Miss, did you hear? Someone stole Ms. Tam's bag and she quit for good. We got some Russian teacher now.

Mrs. Projensky   Quiet Quiet Quiet Quiet Quiet Quiet Quiet. Quiet!

Ms. Sun   Miss, Miss, Miss. I'm the teaching artist for . . .

Mrs. Projensky   Sit down, you.

Shondrika   Aw, snap, she told her.

Mrs. Projensky   Sit down, quiet. Quiet, sit down.

Ms. Sun   No, I'm the teaching artist for this period. Maybe Miss Tam or Mrs. Kennedy told you something about me?

Jerome (*shadowboxes*)   Ah, hah, you being replaced, Russian lady.

Ms. Sun   Jerome, you're not helping right now.

Jerome   What?! You don't gotta tell me jack. We ain't got a teacher no more or haven't you heard?

He flings a chair.

Jerome   We are the worst class in school.

Mrs. Projensky   Sit down! Sit down!

Ms. Sun   Guys, quiet down and focus. We have a show to do in a few weeks.

Coca   Ooee, I don't wanna do this no more. It's stupid,

Chris   I still want to do it.

Jerome   Shut the fuck up, Chris.

Jose   Yo man, she's right. This shit is mad fucking boring yo.

Coca   Yeah!

Xiomara   Yeah!

Brian   Yeah!

Shondrika   Yeah!

Coca   Mad boring.

Jerome   Fuckin' stupid.

Mrs. Projensky   Quiet! Quiet! Quiet!

Ms. Sun   What has gotten into all you? The first two classes were amazing, you guys were analyzing the play, making parallels to *your* lives. So, we missed a week when *you* went to go see, uh . . .

Shondrika   UniverSoul Circus.

Ms. Sun   Right! But, just because we missed a week doesn't mean we have to start from square one. Does it? Jerome, Jerome! where are you going?

Mrs. Projensky   Sit down, sit down, you! Sit down!

Jerome   I don't gotta listen to none of y'all.

He flings another chair.

I'm eighteen years old.

Brian   Yeah, and still in the tenth grade, nigga.

He *flings* a *chair.*

Ms. Sun   Brian!

Jerome   I most definitely ain't gonna do no stupid-ass motha fuckin' Australian play from the goddamn seventeen-hundreds!

Ms. Sun   Fine, Jerome. You don't wanna be a part of something really special? There are others here who do.

Jerome   Who? Who in here want to do this show, memorize your lines, look like stupid fucking dicks on the stage for the whole school to laugh at us like they always do anyhow when can't none of us speak no goddamn English.

Ms. Sun   Jerome, that's not fair, no one is saying you don't speak English. You all invited your parents . . .

Coca   Ooee, my moms can't come to this. She gotta work. Plus the Metrocard ends at seven.

Xiomara   My mom ain't never even been to this school.

Jerome   That's what I'm sayin'! Who the fuck wanna do this? Who the fuck wanna do this?

Ms. Sun   I'll take the vote, Jerome, if you sit down. Everyone sit down.

Mrs. Projensky   Sit down!

Ms. Sun   Thank you, ma'am. OK, so, who, after all the hard work we've done so far building a team, analyzing the play in your own words (that is not easy, I know), developing self-esteem *y coraje* as great thespians . . .

Brian   Lesbians.

Ms. Sun   Who wants to quit . . . after all this?

She looks around as they all raise their hands . . . except for **Chris**.

Ms. Sun   I see.

Chris   Miss. No. I still wanna do the show.

Jerome   That's cuz you gay, Chris. Yo, I'm out! One. Niggas.

Pause. **Ms. Sun** *is hurt.*

Ms. Sun   OK . . . Well . . . Ms?

Mrs. Projensky   Projensky.

Ms. Sun   Ms. Projensky.

Mrs. Projensky   Projensky!

Ms. Sun   Projensky.

Mrs. Projensky   Projensky!

Ms. Sun   Projensky!

Mrs. Projensky   Is close.

Ms. Sun   Do they have any sample Regents to take?

Mrs. Projensky   Yes, they do.

Ms. Sun   Great. I'll alert Mrs. Kennedy of your vote.

Phillip (*audibly*)   Ms. Sun?

Ms. Sun   Yes, Phillip, what is it?

Phillip   Can I still do the show?

Beat.

Scene Ten

Principal's office.

Mrs. Kennedy   So they voted you out? Well, Malcolm X Vocational High School did not get an eight-thousand-dollar grant from the Department of Education of the City of New York for these students to choose democracy now. They will do the show. Because I will tell them so tomorrow. If they do not do the show, each student in IOF will be suspended and *not* be able to join their friends in their beloved Six Flags trip in May. The horror. Look, I understand that they consider themselves the worst class in school. News flash—They're not even close. I know that they've had five different teachers in the course of seven months. I also can wrap my brain around the fact that 79 percent of those kids in there have been physically, emotionally, and sexually abused in their tender little sixteen-year-old lives. But that does not give them the right to disrespect someone who is stretching them to give them something beautiful. Something challenging. Something Jay-Z and P. Diddy only *wish* they could offer them. Now, I will call all their parents this weekend and notify them of their intolerable behavior as well as invite them to *Our Country's Good.* Done. See you next Wednesday, Ms. Sun?

Ms. Sun   Yes, yes. Thanks! Yes! . . . Uh, no, Mrs. Kennedy. You won't be seeing me next Wednesday. I quit. I came to teaching to touch lives and educate and be this enchanting artist in the classroom and I have done nothing but lose ten pounds in a month and develop a disgusting smoking habit. Those kids in there? They need something much greater than anything I can give them—*they need a miracle* . . . and they need a miracle like every day. Sometimes, I dream of going to Connecticut and teaching the rich white kids there. All I'd have to battle against is soccer moms, bulimia, and everyone asking me how I wash my hair. But, I chose to teach in my city, this city that raised me . . . and I'm tired, and I'm not even considered a "real" teacher. I don't know how I would survive as a real teacher. But they do . . . on what, God knows. And, the worst thing, the worst thing is that all those kids in there are *me*. Brown skin, brown eyes, stuck. I can't even help my own people. Really revolutionary, huh?

It seems to me that this whole school system, not just here but the whole system is falling apart from under us and then there are these testing and accountability laws that have nothing to do with any real solutions and if we expect to stay some sort of grand nation for the next fifty years, we got another thing coming. *Because we're not teaching these kids how to be leaders.* We're getting them ready for jail! Take off your belt, take off your shoes, go back, go back, go back. We're totally abandoning these kids and we have been for thirty years and then we get annoyed when they're running around in the subway calling themselves bitches and niggas, we get annoyed when their math scores don't pair up to a five-year-old's in China, we get annoyed when they don't graduate in time. It's because we've abandoned them. And, I'm no different, I'm abandoning them too. (*Beat.*) I just need a break to be an actor, get health insurance, go on auditions, pay the fucking IRS. Sorry. Look, I'm sorry about the big grant from the Department of Ed but perhaps we could make it up somehow next year. I can't continue this program any longer, even if it is for our country's good. Bye!

Light shift.

Janitor (*sings*)

> I'm gonna lay. Lay my head
> On some lonesome railroad line.
> Let that 2:19 train—

Scene Eleven

Outside of school.

Ms. Sun (*sings*)

> Ease my troubled mind—

Jerome   Ms. Sun?

Ms. Sun   Hi. Jerome.

Jerome You singing? (*Beat.*) We were talking about you in the cafeteria. Had a power lunch. (*He laughs.*) Most of us were being assholes . . . sorry . . . bad thespians when we did that to you.

Ms. Sun You were the leader, do you know that, Jerome? Do you know that we teachers, we have feelings. And we try our best not to break in front of you all?

Jerome Yeah, I know, my mom tells me that all the time.

Ms. Sun Listen to her, sweetheart, she's right. (*Beat.*) Look, the show is off. I'll be here next year, and we'll start again on another more tangible play, maybe even *Raisin in the Sun.* Now, if you'll excuse me, I have an audition to prepare for.

She turns to leave.

Jerome Ms. Sun, "The theatre is an expression of civilization . . ."

Ms. Sun What?

Jerome I said, "The theatre is an expression of civilization. We belong to a great country which has spawned great playwrights: Shakespeare, Marlowe, Jonson, and even in our own time, Sheridan. The convicts will be speaking a refined, literate language and expressing sentiments of a delicacy they are not used to. It will remind them that there is more to life than crime, punishment. And we, this colony of a few hundred, will be watching this together. For a few hours we will no longer be despised prisoners and hated gaolers. We will laugh, we may be moved. We may even think a little. Can you suggest something else that would provide such an evening, Watkin?" (*Beat.*) Thank you.

Ms. Sun Jerome, I didn't know . . .

Jerome . . . that I had the part of Second Lieutenant Ralph Clark memorized. I do my thang. Guess I won't be doing it this year though. Shoot, every teacher we have runs away.

Beat.

Ms. Sun Listen, Jerome, you tell all your cafeteria buddies in there, OK, to have all their lines memorized from Acts One and Two and be completely focused when I walk into that room next week—that means no talking, no hidden conversations and blurting out random nonsense, no gum, and for crying out loud, no one should be drinking Red Bull.

Jerome Aight. So you back?

Ms. Sun . . . Yeah, and I'm bad.

She does some Michael Jackson moves.

Jerome Miss, you really do need an acting job soon.

Light shift.

Janitor Things are looking up for our little teaching artist. She got a new lease on life. Got on a payment plan with the IRS. Stopped smoking, ate a good breakfast, even took the early train to school this mornin'.

Scene Twelve

Classroom.

Coca   Miss, did you hear? We got a new teacher permanently. He's kinda . . . good!

Mr. Johnson   What do we say when Ms. Sun walks in?

Shondrika   Good morning, Ms. Sun.

Mr. Johnson   Hat off, Jerome.

Jerome   Damn, he got attitude! (*Beat.*) I like that!

Ms. Sun   Wow, wow. You guys are lookin' really, really good.

Mr. Johnson   Alright, let's get in the formation that we created. First, the tableau.

Ms. Sun (*intimate*)   Tableau, you got them to do a tableau.

Mr. Johnson (*intimate*)   I figured you'd want to see them in a frozen non-speaking state for a while. Oh, Kaswan, Xiomara, and Brian are in the auditorium building the set.

Ms. Sun (*intimate*)   Wow. This is amazing. Thank you.

Mr. Johnson   Don't thank me. Thank Mrs. Kennedy, thank yourself, thank these kids. (*To class.*) And we're starting from the top, top, top. Only one more week left. Shondrika, let's see those fliers you're working on.

Shondrika   I been done. "Come see *Our Countrys Good* cuz it's for your *own* good."

Ms. Sun   Beautiful, Shondrika. Let's start from the top. (*Sound of noise.*) What's all that noise out in the hallway?

Brian   Ay, yo. Janitor Baron had a heart attack in his closet last night. He died there.

Coca   What? He was our favorite . . .

Jerome   How old was he, like a hundred or something?

Shondrika   I just saw him yesterday. He told me he would come to the show. He died all alone, ya'll.

Long pause.

Ms. Sun   Thespians, I can give you some time . . .

Jerome   Nah, nah we done wasted enough time. Let's rehearse. Do the show. Dedicate it to Janitor Baron, our pops, may you rest in peace.

Ms. Sun   Alright, then, we're taking it from the top. Chris, that's you, sweetheart.

Chris   "A giant canoe drifts onto the sea, clouds billowing from upright oars. This is a dream that has lost its way. Best to leave it alone."

Light shift.

Janitor   My, my, my . . . them kids banded together over me. Memorized, rehearsed, added costumes, a small set, even added a rap or two at the end—don't tell the playwright! And, I didn't even think they knew my name. Ain't that something? I think I know what you saying to yourselves: I see dead people. Shoot, this is a good story, I wanna finish telling it! Plus, my new friend up here, Arthur Miller, tells me ain't no rules say a dead man can't make a fine narrator. Say he wish he thought of it himself. Meanwhile, like most teachers, even after-hours, Ms. Sun's life just ain't her own.

Scene Thirteen

Ms. Sun *'s apartment. Night.*

Ms. Sun (*on phone*)   Hi. This is Ms. Sun from Malcolm X High. I'm looking for Jose Guzman. He's a lead actor in *Our Country's Good* but I haven't seen him in class or after-school rehearsals since last week. My number is . . .

Light shift. On phone:

Hi. This is Ms. Sun again from Malcolm X High. I know it's probably dinner time but I'm still trying to reach Jose or his grandmother, Doña Guzman . . .

Light shift. On phone:

Hi. Ms. Sun here. Sorry, I know it's early and Mrs. Kennedy called last night, but the show is in less than two days . . .

Light shift. On phone:

Hi. It's midnight. You can probably imagine who this is. Does anyone answer this phone? Why have a machine, I mean really . . . Hello, hello, yes. This is Ms. Sun from Malcom X High, oh . . . *Puedo hablar con*, Doña Guzman. Ah hah! Finally. Doña Guzman, ah ha, *bueno, Ingles*, OK. I've been working with your grandson now for six weeks on a play that you might have heard of. (*Beat.*) *Un espectaculo* . . . ah ha, *pero Ingles*, OK. I haven't seen him in a *week* and the show is in twenty-four hours *Mañana* actually . . . *Como?* His brother was killed. *Ave Maria, lo siento, señiora* . . . How? Gangs . . . no, no, *olvidate*, forget about it. I'll send out prayers to you *y tu familia. Buenas.*

She hangs up. Light shift.

Janitor   Chin up now!

Scene Fourteen

School auditorium.

Janitor   Cuz, it's opening night in the auditorium . . . I'm not even gonna talk about the logistics behind booking a high school auditorium for a night. Poor Mrs. Kennedy became a dictator.

Mrs. Kennedy   I booked this auditorium for the night and no one shall take it from me!

Janitor The stage is ablaze with fear, apprehension, doubt, nervousness, and, well, drama.

Mr. Johnson   Anyone seen Jerome?

Ms. Sun   Anyone seen Jerome?

Coca   His mom called him at four. Told him he had to babysit for the night.

Ms. Sun   But he's got a show tonight. Couldn't they find someone else? Couldn't he just bring the brats? Sorry.

Mr. Johnson   What are we going to do now? His part is enormous.

Phillip   Ms. Sun?

Ms. Sun   What, Phillip?

Phillip   . . . I could do his part.

Ms. Sun (*with apprehension*)   OK, Phillip. You're on. Just remember . . .

Phillip   I know . . . someone is stealing my Mercedes LX 100 Limited Edition.

Ms. Sun   And . . .?

Phillip   . . . Let my tongue be alive!

Doña Guzman   *Doña Guzman, buenas. Buenas. Doña Guzman.* The *abuela de Jose.*

Ms. Sun   Jose, you made it. I'm so sorry about your brother.

Jose   Yeah, I know. Where's my costume at? *Buela, no ta allí.*

Doña Guzman   *Mira pa ya, muchacho.* We had very long week *pero* he love this class. He beg me, "Mami, mami, mami, Our Country Goo, Our Country Goo, Our Country Goo." What can I do? I say yes. What I can do, you know.

Ms. Sun   Oh *senora.* It's parents like you . . . thank you. *Muchissima gracias por todo.* Sit, sit in the audience *por favor.*

Mrs. Kennedy   Ms. Sun, everyone is in place, there are about seventy-five people in that audience, including some parents I desperately need to speak to. We're glad you're back. Good luck!

Shondrika   Miss, you want me to get the kids together before we start?

Ms. Sun   Yeah, Shondrika, would you?

Shondrika   Uh huh.

Janitor   Now, here's a teacher's moment of truth. The last speech before the kids go on!

Ms. Sun   Alright. This is it. We're here. We have done the work. We have lived this play inside and out. I officially have a hernia.

Coca (*laughing*)   She so stupid. I like her.

Ms. Sun   We are a success . . . no matter what happens on this stage tonight. No matters which actors are missing or if your parents couldn't make it. I see before me twenty-seven amazingly talented young men and women. And I never thought I'd say this but I'm gonna miss you all.

Shondrika   Ooh, she gonna make me cry!

Ms. Sun   Tonight is your night.

Coca   Ooee, I'm nervous.

Phillip   Me too.

Ms. Sun   I am too. That just means you care. Now let's take a deep breath in and out. In . . .

Brian   OHM! Nah, I'm just kiddin'. Keep going. Focus. Focus.

Ms. Su   . . . and out. In and out.

Shondrika   Miss, let's do this for Jose's brother and Janitor Baron.

Ms. Sun   Oh, Shondrika, that's beautiful. OK, gentlemen, be with us tonight! PLACES.

Light shift.

Chris   A giant canoe drifts out onto the sea, best to leave it alone.

Coca   This hateful hary-scary, topsy-turvy outpost. This is not a civilization.

Xiomara   It's two hours possibly of amusement, possibly of boredom. It's a waste, an unnecessary waste.

Phillip   The convicts will feel nothing has changed and will go back to their old ways.

Jose   You have to be careful. OH DAMN.

Nervously, he regains his thought.

You have to be careful with words that begin with IN. It can turn everything upside down. INjustice, most of that word is taken up with justice, but the IN turns it inside out making it the ugliest word in the English language.

Shondrika   Citizens must be taught to obey the law of their own will. I want to rule over responsible human beings.

Phillip   Unexpected situations are often matched by unexpected virtues in people. Are they not?

Brian   A play should make you understand something new.

Shondrika   Human beings—

Xiomara   —have an intelligence—

Brian   —that has nothing to do—

Jose   —with the circumstances—

Coca   —into which they were born.

Chris   THE END.

Raucous applause. Light shift.

Janitor   And the show did go on. A show that sparked a mini-revolution in the hearts of everyone in that auditorium. Sure, some crucial lines were fumbled, and some entrances missed and three cell phones went off in the audience. But, my God, if those kids weren't a success.

Scene Fifteen

Backstage.

Coca   Miss, I did good, right? I did good? I did good. I did my lines right. I did my motivations right. l did good, right. I did good? I did good? I did good? (*Assured.*) I did good. I did good. I did good. Oh, miss. l been wantin' to tell you. You know I'm pregnant right? . . . Oh don't cry . . . Damn. Why do everyone cry when I say that? No, I wanted to tell you because my baby will not live like a prisoner, like a convict. I mean we still gotta put the baby-proof bars on the windows but that's state law. But that's it. We gonna travel, explore, see somethin' new for a change. I mean I love the Bronx but there's more to life right? You taught me that. "Man is born free" right . . . I mean, even though it's gonna be a girl. (*Beat.*) I know we was mad hard so thank you.

Jose   Miss? I don't know but, that class was still mad boring to me.

Phillip (*audibly*)   Ms. Sun?! I wanna be an actor now!

Security Guard   O, O! We gotta clear out the auditorium. You can't be lolly-gagging in here. Clear it out. Clear it out. Clear it out! By the way, I never done seen dem kids shine like they did tonight. They did good. You did good. Now, you got ta clear it out!

Ms. Sun (*to herself*)   Jerome . . . Jerome. (*Beat.*) "And we, this colony of a few hundred, will be watching this together, and we will no longer be despised prisoners and hated gaolers. We will laugh, we may be moved. We may . . ."

Jerome (*gasping*)   ". . . even think a little!"

Ms. Sun   Jerome? What are you doing here?

Jerome (*panting*)   Mom came home early. Told me to run over here fast as I could . . .

He realizes.

I missed it. I missed it all. And I worked *hard* to learn my lines.

Ms. Sun   Yes, you did, Jerome. You worked very hard.

Long beat.

Jerome   You gonna be teaching here again next year?

Ms. Sun   That's the plan. But, only tenth-graders again. Sorry.

Jerome   Oh no worries. I'm definitely gonna get left back for you. Psyche . . . Lemme go shout out to all them other thespians. You gonna be around?

Ms. Sun   No, actually I have a commercial shoot early tomorrow morning.

Jerome   Really, for what?

Ms. Sun (*slurring*)   It's nothing . . .

Jerome   Aw, come on you could tell me.

Ms. Sun   Really, it's nothing.

Jerome   Lemme know. Lemme know. Come on lemme know.

Ms. Sun   It's for Red Bull, damnit. Red Rull.

Jerome   Aight! Ms. Sun's finally getting paid.

Light shift.

Scene Sixteen

Janitor   And on to our third and final lesson of the evening: Something interesting happens when you die. You still care about the ones you left behind and wanna see how life ended up for them. Ms. Tam went back to the firm and wound up investing 2.3 million dollars towards arts in education with a strong emphasis on cultural diversity. Phillip proudly works as a conductor for the MTA. Shondrika Jones graduated *summa cum laude* from Harvard University and became the first black woman mayor of New York City. Alright now. Jose Guzman lost his life a week after the show when he decided to take vengeance on the blood that killed his brother. Jerome. I might be omnipresent but I sure as heck ain't omniscient. Some of the brightest just slip through the cracks sometime. Do me a favor—you ever see him around town, tell him we thinkin' about him. And Ms. Sun. Well, she went on to win an NAACP Award, a Hispanic Heritage Award, a Tony Award, and an Academy Award. She was also in charge of restructuring of the nation's No Child Left Behind law *and* lives happily with her husband, Denzel Washington. His first wife never had a chance, poor thang. She still comes back every year to teach at Malcolm X High; oh, oh, oh, recently renamed Saint Tupac Shakur Preparatory. Times—they are a-changin'!

He grabs his broom and sings. Lights shift as he walks towards a bright light offstage.

Trouble in mind,
it's true
I had almost lost my way

Offstage light brightens as if the heavens await. He knows to walk "into" it.

But, the sun's gonna shine in my back door someday
That's alright, Lord. That's alright!

End of play.

Suggested Exercises for Educators and Teaching Artists
for *No Child* . . .

Before reading or seeing the play

- Classroom Exercise:

  Create a group mural to explore the question of what makes someone a good teacher. Give students either an index card or Post-it™ note (a small piece of paper with a re-adherable strip of glue on its back) and a marker. Have the students answer this question by listing three characteristics. Have the students tape their cards to a large mural paper.

  Next, divide the students into pairs (either choose pairs ahead of time, or perhaps ask the students to work with someone in the class they know the least). Ask the students to create a two-person frozen image with their bodies. The image should include two people: a teacher, who has one of the attributes listed on the mural, and a student. One at a time, have each pair show their image to the class. They should hold the image for five sections. Then, each person in the sculpture speaks a single, improvised line of text from the perspective of the characters (teacher and student).

  Finally, break into groups of four (have a pair join another pair). Half of the groups should once again choose a word from the mural and imagine a character of a teacher who has this characteristic (perhaps they discuss what this person might be like). The second half should create a teacher character who has the opposite of the chosen characteristic (its antonym). Next, each small group should invent the circumstances of an improvisation in which the teacher responds to a problem or classroom conflict. One person in the group should portray the teacher, while the others can be students in the class and/or other people at the school (a parent, the principal, etc.).

  Alternate performances of the improvisation between the positive and negative attributes.

- Classroom Exercise 2:

  Break the class into small groups of five. Let the group choose one actor to portray a "guest teacher" who will be with the class for a limited amount of time and wants the class to accomplish an arts project of some sort (let the group choose the project).

  Note: use the board from the first exercise to choose *both* positive and negative traits for the teacher: be sure not to choose opposing traits that flatly contradict each other (i.e., "patient" and "impatient"), but that might reasonably be found in one person (i.e., "caring" and "stern"). Give the group some time to discuss and debate the realistic possibilities.

Improvisation: The Teacher's first day in class. The others in the group take varying stances: the one who is thinks the project is boring; the one who thinks the project is interesting; the one who wants to challenge or defeat the teacher; the class clown who takes the opportunity to show off. Time the improv; at the end of five minutes, the Teacher must decide on three class rules or procedures that will move the project forward (cancelling is not an option).

• Homework Assignment:

Ask students to research the phrase "No Child Left Behind" and write a one-page summary (What does it mean? Who initiated it?) and a one-page response (What has been its effect on education since its inception? How does it, or similar policies in your area, impact your own life?)

After reading or seeing the play

• Classroom Exercise:

Ask the students to do a freewrite about an incident at their school. Give them five to ten minutes to write; encourage them to keep writing the whole time without censoring themselves. Once the time is up (wherever they get to is fine), ask the students to rewrite the description of the incident from the perspective of an objective observer. This could be a person or an object that is witnessing the event but is not involved in it. Ask for up to three volunteers to read their second version out loud to the class. As a class, discuss: what is the effect of telling the story from that perspective? How does the story change?

Discuss: How might the story of *No Child*... have been different if it had been told to us by others in the play, i.e., by Ms. Tam or by one of the students in the class?

• Classroom Exercise:

As a class or in small groups, discuss the ways that various adults in the play treat the students and how this affects how the students in the play see themselves. How do expectations for students influence what they can achieve?

Next, ask each student to write a letter to themselves outlining a goal that they would like to accomplish by the end of the year and explaining why. What do they hope to achieve? Have the students put their letter in an envelope and address the envelope to themselves. Collect all of the letters. Return them to the students on the last day of school.

Ghosts of Skunk Hollow

A ten-minute play

Keith Josef Adkins

Background and Insights for *Ghosts of Skunk Hollow*

from Keith Josef Adkins

Notes on Casting

All of the characters should be cast with African-American and/or Afro-Latinx (identified) actors.

Notes on Production

The director and cast may modify any inappropriate language as well as replace slang with the latest word/phrases.

The Inspiration for This Play

I was inspired to write this play by my love of genealogy and unknown African-American history. I was also interested in seeing teenagers participate in a conversation about legacy, history, and their accountability for their own futures. I was interested in the idea of honoring where and who one comes from.

Major Themes

- *Legacy*
- *Generational wealth*
- *Pride*

Food for Thought

I hope the play inspires debates around communal and family responsibility and the importance of understanding and honoring our family histories. And if not, why not?

Entrance into the World of Theatre

I became interested in storytelling of all types at an early age. I was fortunate to have a family who loved to tell stories and re-enact everyday situations. However, I fell in love with theatre because of the immediacy and the urgency of it all. Nothing can compare to the experience of putting a production together with a team of artists and then share that collaboration with a live audience (that changes every night). Something about theatre and its ability to change the hearts and minds of the artists involved and the audience is one of the best gifts to humanity.

Characters

Jamal, *eighteen years old, smart, a leader, likes to have fun*
Arial, *eighteen years old, smart, not very focused, attitude*
Andrea, *eighteen years old, smart, somewhat quiet but no pushover*
Rae, *eighteen years old, smart, inquisitive, and observant*
Dennis, *eighteen years old, smart, comic relief*

Place: *Palisades Interstate Park (the former site of Skunk Hollow).*
Time: *Noon.*

Playwright's Note: Skunk Hollow is the oldest known free African-American community in the state of New Jersey. It was established as early as 1806 and nearly deserted by the year 1910.

Lights up on a park trail. **Jamal** *stands reading from a historical pamphlet as a disinterested* **Arial** *and an interested* **Andrea** *stand nearby.*

Jamal (*holding pamphlet*)   Skunk Hollow was the oldest African-American community in all of New Jersey. A free community.

Arial   Free? What's that mean? They didn't have to pay?

Jamal   Not slaves. Free from slavery. As early as the year 1806.

Arial   Okay. You don't have to get all twisted about it. I'm just asking.

Jamal   This says it was a prosperous African-American community too. That means they owned their homes and stuff.

Andrea   Jamal, you know you got to be specific. Mister Hendricks did not bring us on this field trip to come back with some notes about "stuff."

Jamal   Why do you all keep slicing my flow? I'm dropping knowledge, pick that ish up and keep it going.

Andrea   We're listening, Jamal.

Jamal   Now, this says the Black residents initially called this place The Mountain, but it was renamed by whites as Skunk Hollow because of a plant called Skunk Hollow that grew nearby. Wow. The area was not good for farming because of all of the rocks, but the Black people purchased it anyway. They liked the isolation. To be away from prejudice and policing.

Andrea   When was this again? You said it too fast.

Arial   Andrea, I know you are not taking more notes.

Jamal   She should take notes. Everything I say is gold. What!

Arial   Everything you say is booty.

Jamal   My booty is gold, baby. My booty is gold!

Andrea   Arial, you know how Mister Hendricks drops those pop quizzes, and this got pop quiz written all over it.

Arial   A bunch of Black people living near the Palisades? In the 1800s? Not here for it!

Jamal   Not just Black people. Our New Jersey ancestors.

Andrea   Yeh. We live in the state. We should know its history. Especially when it's about people who looked or lived like us.

Arial   You know this is dumb, right?

Jamal   How is learning about your state's history dumb? The more knowledge you have of self, the stronger you step through life. The less mistakes you make.

Arial   Who are you? Malcolm X?

Jamal   Jamal X. And you have permission to share on all platforms.

Arial   I'm not interested in Black history or New Jersey.

Andrea   Why did you sign up for this field trip if you didn't want to come?

Jamal   Yeh, Andrea. Why did you sign up if you didn't want to partake in the historical partakings?

Arial   Korean barbecue for lunch at So Moon Na Jip. Act like you ain't heard.

She screams.

Jamal   Yo! What's your problem, yo?! Stop screaming!

Arial *attempts to pull something from inside the back of her shirt.*

Andrea   Girl, what is wrong?

Arial   It's crawling down my back. Oh my God! It's in my shirt!

Jamal *and* **Andrea** *stand by slightly entertained.*

Jamal (*laughing*)   There's one's in your hair, too!

Andrea   That *was* funny.

Arial   It felt like a finger. On my back. It felt like somebody's finger was going up and down my back.

Andrea   Girl, you are o'd-ing.

Arial   I know what I felt. I know what a finger feels like.

Jamal   Arial . . . Yo . . . Snap back. Some kind of tree worm fell into your shirt. It was not a finger. Alright? It was a tree worm and now it's gone. Alright?

Arial   Whatever.

Dennis *and* **Rae** *enter.*

Rae   What was all the screaming? Did somebody die?

Jamal   Arial had a spider in her shirt.

Rae   Sounded like it was killing you. You okay?

Arial (*attitude*)   No.

Dennis   Yo, whatever y'all do, don't use those Porta Potties™. Smelled like fifty people just rolled up in there and shit for twenty days, non-stop.

Andrea   That's nasty, Dennis.

Dennis   What? You don't believe me. Go take a whiff yourself. Smelled like zombie central up in that piece.

Rae   Have you seen Mister Hendricks?

Jamal   No. He's not at the van?

Rae   We didn't see him.

Dennis We looked in, under, and inside the van. Rae even looked in the glove compartment.

Rae I did not. Don't be stupid.

Dennis You know Mister Hendricks is about as big as my hand. Dude vanished.

Andrea He's got my phone. I was supposed to call my moms when we got here.

Jamal Didn't he say to meet him at the park ranger headquarters in ten minutes?

Dennis Oh, that's right. He sure did.

Jamal And that's a ten-minute walk, too. So, we should head out soon.

Arial Let's go now. I am not here for all of this fresh air and bug life.

Rae Wait. We need to do a group selfie.

Arial We *need* to go.

Jamal We already did a group selfie at the van, Rae.

Andrea I'm selfied out.

Dennis Yo, I'm down for a selfie. I never get tired of looking at my handsome face. It don't get no sexier than this.

Rae As much as we all never tire of your face, this is about Skunk Hollow. Documenting this ancestral field trip. Our Jersey ancestors.

Jamal I'm down with the documentation. No doubt.

Rae (*pulling out camera*) Everybody. Come on!

Everybody gathers for the selfie and poses.

In five, everybody say, "Skunk Hollow." One, two . . .

Before **Rae** *can finish the count, something makes a noise in the trees behind them.*

Jamal What was that?

Dennis You mean "who" was that? I heard somebody. Sounded like a voice.

Andrea It did.

Arial Stop playing around.

Jamal I'm not playing. We all just heard that.

Arial Why dudes always have to default into juvenile behavior? It's stupid.

Dennis Because we're still juvenile.

Something makes another noise.

Jamal Did you hear that?

Rae I did.

Andrea   Me too. I heard something.

Arial   Look, I want to leave, now.

Dennis   Was that some kind of animal?

Jamal   Maybe it was a bird or something.

Andrea   It would have to be eight foot tall to sound like that.

Dennis   Yeh. Ten feet tall.

Jamal   Look, let's be serious right now. Whatever that was, it was an animal of some kind. This is nature, there are animals. Right? Think about it. We're burnt up right now because we're from the city and anything that's not a car horn is strange to us. It was an animal of nature.

Everyone nods in agreement.

Arial   Are we leaving or not?

Rae *notices something on the ground.*

Rae   What's that?

She points to what looks like a piece of a headstone.

Andrea   Where?

Rae (*pointing*)   There. Can't you see it?

Jamal   That's a rock, B.

Rae   That is not a rock.

Andrea *gets closer.*

Arial   Why are you getting closer to it?

Dennis   Yo, is it moving? Don't touch if it's moving. The shit is moving.

Andrea   It is not moving. It's a headstone.

Jamal   Whose headstone?

Andrea   I can't read it.

Dennis   Move. I got twenty-twenty vision in both eyes, yo.

Andrea   I can read, fool.

Dennis   B, who are you calling a fool?! I don't appreciate people calling Black dudes fools. It hurts our feelings and it's just wrong.

Jamal   Yo! What's the name on the headstone?

Rae *moves in to look.*

Rae   James Sisco. Or Jane Sisco.

Arial Stop lying.

Rae Why would I lie? It says it right here. Sisco.

Dennis Yeh, it does say Sisco.

Jamal What do you care that it says Sisco? That headstone was not there a minute ago. Did you see it, Andrea?

Andrea No, I didn't see it before until Rae pointed it out.

Jamal How did it all of sudden appear? A headstone? A fricking headstone?

Arial That's my mom's name.

Dennis What?

Rae Are you for real, Arial?

Dennis Like in moms, pops, family unit type moms?

Arial Yes. My mom is a Sisco. I mean, her mom was a Sisco. Granny. Why are you doing this?

Andrea Doing what?

Arial Is this some of kind of prank? You know how you're always pranking, Jamal.

Denni He does prank a lot. Dude, you do prank a lot.

Jamal Why would I prank anybody by putting a headstone in the middle of Palisades Park? I know I'm ranking top five in our class and I got a gift in science and mathematics that is unmatched, but headstones aren't in my scholastic repertoire.

They hear a noise again behind the tree. Then another noise behind another tree.

Jamal Did you all hear that? *Did* you all hear that?!

Andrea I heard it.

Rae Me too.

Dennis That's definitely not an animal. It sounded like a voice, didn't it?

Jamal Yes. A man's voice.

Dennis We should go.

Jamal I'm game. Let's get out of here!

*They start to leave, but **Rae** stops them.*

Rae We should stay.

Arial What? Are you puffing that smoke? Stay here with this? No!

Jamal Rae, we need to find Mister Hendricks. He doesn't even know where we are.

Andrea I'm with Jamal.

Dennis   Me, three.

Jamal   Dude, you're always "me three-ing."

Dennis   Would you prefer it another way?

Rae   Whatever that is, it's not angry. It's not trying to scare us.

Jamal   I'm going to be real with you, Rae. I'm a little scared.

Dennis   Me three.

Rae   We need to stay and honor them.

Arial   Honor who? Some dead ancestors?

Rae   Yeh, why not?

Andrea   I don't know, Rae. This doesn't sound Christian.

Dennis   Andrea, you don't even go to church.

Andrea   That doesn't mean I'm not Christian, Dennis.

Jamal   We got to do something. We're all feeling the energy, right?

Rae   This is sacred ground. People like us used to live here, laugh, cry, love . . .

Dennis   Okay, okay. I'm with you, I'm with you.

Arial   Something's in those trees and we got no business here.

Rae   I think it's our ancestors. Your ancestors.

Arial   Why are you saying mine? There's got to be a million Siscos in the world.

Rae   Where's your family from, Arial?

Arial   I don't know. I don't care.

Rae   What about you, Jamal?

Jamal   My dad's father was born in Newark, I know that for sure. And his dad was from Bergen County. My mom's fam is from Jersey by way of North Carolina.

Dennis   All of my grandparents are from the Caribbean, but we all cut from a similar colonial experience, right?

Andrea   Somebody's been listening to Mister Hendricks.

Dennis   Don't hate a brother who retains the knowledge.

Rae   My mom is from New Jersey. Don't know about my dad. I think his dad was Puerto Rican.

Arial   I want to go.

Rae   Let's hold hands. In a semicircle. We got to do this. Come on.

She extends her arms. Everybody else grabs hands. Except **Arial**.

Arial   Y'all need to stay away from vaping. Seriously.

Jamal   Arial, it was hard for these people to live at the time they did. They were free black folks, who could *still* be kidnapped and sold into slavery. They chose here because they didn't have many options. So, they made the best of it. And you, you could be one of their descendants. Even if you're not, you need to ask yourself, is your life any different? Do you have some of the same obstacles? Don't you all look at me like that. You know I drop knowledge. Arial, we owe them. They're speaking to us right now. We got to honor them.

Arial *joins the group.*

Andrea   Can we at least say "Amen" at the end? It'll make me feel better.

Rae   Yes. Let's just say the ancestors' names out loud.

Dennis   I don't have their names. Where am I supposed to get the names?

Andrea   Such a fool.

Jamal   Open your pamphlet to page two.

Dennis *follows instructions.*

Jamal   Treadwells.

Rae   Johnsons.

Dennis   Cartwrights.

Andrea   Thompsons.

Arial   . . . Siscos.

Rae   We honor you. We are your future and we won't let you down.

Andrea   Amen.

Dennis   Yo, now can we go?

Jamal   Let's do that jet speed!

They all leave except for **Arial**. *She looks around and then: A noise is heard.*

Arial   I'm sorry . . . and thank you. Thank you for everything.

End of play.

Suggested Exercises for Educators and Teaching Artists
for *Ghosts of Skunk Hollow*

Before reading or seeing the play

- Class Exercise:

  Create an improvisation with five characters on a school outing. In advance of the improvisation, the teacher should determine the location and the assignment for the outing. Create index cards with the following character traits, each written out on a separate card: too cool for school, the peacemaker, the show-off, prankster, the teacher's pet. Ask for volunteers to participate; assign each volunteer a card. Instruct the students to act out the scene, with each performer adhering to the attribute of their card. As a group, the characters must complete or abandon the assignment by the end of the improvisation.

  Note: If you have more than five people who want to participate, you can do more than one round of the improvisation. An improvisation with more than five people at a time people becomes unwieldy.

- Homework Assignment:

  Ask students to research a place in their community that is connected to their ancestry or the history of their community. The students should then create a dialogue between themselves and the ancestors, or a series of monologues (one talking to the ancestor and one with the ancestor talking back). Ask students to consider: What would you want to ask them about their lives? What do you think they would have to say about your life? What advice might they have for people in the present?

  Note: This can be done as an individual assignment, or as a small-group assignment.

After reading or seeing the play

- For Discussion:

  Break the class into small groups. Have each group discuss: What is the importance of honoring one's family history? Which characters in the play seem to agree with that position? Which characters do not? What are their reasons or excuses? Why do the characters agree to do the final ritual? What does Arial mean when she says "Thank you for everything" at the end of the play?

  Note: Have the students write down their answers (one student can be the group scribe and take notes). One student from each group should report the group findings.

- Creative Exercise:

  Ask each group to name three things for which they are grateful to their ancestors. Have students create a group mural of the items named (with words and/or images).

Gunshots at 2 p.m.

A ten-minute play

Keith Josef Adkins

Background and Insights into *Gunshots at 2 p.m.*

Keith Josef Adkins

Notes on Casting

The characters in this play should reflect a standard urban high school. Ideally, the majority of the actors should be African-American, Latinx, and any other ethnicity you would find at an urban public high school.

Notes on Production

The director and cast can modify any inappropriate language as well as replace slang with the latest word/phrases.

The Inspiration for This Play

I was inspired to write this play by the number of school shootings in our country, but wanted to turn that on its head by focusing on the vilification of the culprits. I wanted to create a shooting situation and explore how we're quick to vilify the person we don't understand, the outsider. I wasn't interested in exploring empathy for persons like this; I was interested in the power of assumption and judgment.

Major Themes

- *The vilification of the other*
- *Fear*
- *The negative consequences of assumption*

Food for Thought

I hope the play inspires debates around the topics of fear, why we choose to judge others, and how far that judgment can escalate.

Entrance into the World of Theatre

I became interested in storytelling of all types at an early age. I was fortunate to have a family who loved to tell stories and re-enact everyday situations. However, I fell in love with theatre because of the immediacy and the urgency of it all. Nothing can compare to the experience of putting a production together with a team of artists and then share that collaboration with a live audience (that changes every night). Something about theatre and its ability to change the hearts and minds of the artists involved and the audience is one of the best gifts to humanity.

Characters

Neff, *seventeen years old, smart, a leader, fearless*
Marcos, *seventeen years old, smart, athletic, a bit arrogant, judgmental*
Oliver, *seventeen years old, smart, a bit of a follower*
Deanne, *seventeen years old, smart, a bit shy*
Anthony, *seventeen years old, smart, fearless, appears intimidating but gentle*

Place: A high school History class.
Time: 2 p.m.

Lights up on **Neff**. *She stands at the classroom door, listening to something outside the room. Three other students,* **Marcos, Deanne,** *and* **Oliver**, *sit at their desks, a bit nervous, a bit on guard.*

Marcos   What do you see? You see anything? People? Blood? Those screams came from the west hallway. Neff, I'm talking to you!

Neff *waves her hand for him to be quiet.*

Marcos   Why are you waving at me?

Neff   Because you're talking, and I need you to shut up.

Marcos   You got to see something. We just heard a round of ammunition and about ten people scream.

Oliver   Sounded like all of Mrs. de Silva's pre-calculus class. That's about fifteen right there. I know I heard Monica. She has a high-pitched voice and she screams the same way. She's got one of those crazy-somebody-just-tickled me screams.

Marcos   Dude . . . now is not the time to go frantic over some girl you're crushing on.

Oliver   Nobody's going frantic over a girl I'm crushing on. I'm making an observation. I'm allowed to observe. I have that constitutional right.

Deanne   You do.

Marcos   Neff! You got to see something. Didn't you just get new glasses?

Neff   Yes.

Marcos   Then put those babies on so you can see and tell us what's up!

Neff   Would you shut up for second? Be quiet!

They all go quiet. **Neff** *slowly opens the door.*

Marcos   Yo, don't open the door! Are you on that Diesel?!

Deanne (*very scared*)   Oh my God. Oh my God.

Oliver   Close the door, Neff! Are you crazy?

Marcos   Everybody knows you're Miss-A-Student and You're-Probably-Going-to-Yale-or-Whatever . . .

Neff   Spelman.

Marcos   Spelman, whatever . . . but right now you're acting real stupid!

The sound of what appears to be gunshots is heard as well as students' screams. **Neff** *closes the door and retreats to the back of the room with the others. Everyone is silent.*

Marcos   He's killing people. This mofo is killing everybody.

Neff   He? He who?

Marcos The dude that's shooting. Who the hell you think?

Neff We don't know who's out there. We have no idea about anything.

Deanne We don't even know if that's gunfire. Right? Could be firecrackers.

Marcos It is gunfire.

Deanne Sounds like firecrackers. Sounds like a whole bunch of firecrackers.

Oliver We know Mrs. de Silva's class screamed. I heard Monica. I know her voice. What if she's dead?

Neff Okay, okay. Everybody! Chill on that!

Oliver I'm chill.

Deanne Me too. I'm scared as hell, but I'm chill.

Neff Okay, good. We got to figure out something.

Marcos I've already figured it out. I'm crawling through that window in five seconds.

Neff And do what? Jump? We're on the sixth floor of this school.

Marcos I rather jump than get gunned down by some crazy mofo two months before I graduate. I'm going to Howard University just like my dad. I'm going to Howard and study my ass off and get me a corporate job and move to New Rochelle on the side where all the black celebs live and nothing's going to stop me.

Oliver I'm not jumping. I broke my ankle last summer racing my cousins. If I fall on my ankle, I could get permanent damage and walk with a limp for the rest of my life. The doctor said that. I'm not walking with a limp. I don't want to be the dude in school who walks with a limp.

Neff Nobody's jumping. You won't walk with a limp. We got to think of something else.

Marcos If dude comes in here with a semi-automatic, I'm jumping. Whether I get a limp or not.

Deanne Oh my God!

Neff Deanne, what's wrong?

Deanne (*having an epiphany*)   I saw Anthony with a gun.

Neff What?

Deanne Anthony. I saw him with something.

Marcos Anthony de Jesus?

Deanne No. Anthony Tillery.

Oliver T.T.?

Marcos   He doesn't go by T.T. any more. He goes by Anthony.

Oliver   I thought he still went by T.T.

Marcos   He doesn't go by T.T. They haven't called him T.T. since the ninth grade.

Neff   Would you all shut up! What did you see Deanne?

Marcos   It's Anthony. It's got to be Anthony.

Neff   Let her talk. Damn! What did you see?

Marcos   She saw him with an automatic that's what she saw. An automatic gunning down fools in the cafeteria.

Oliver   Wait a minute. I thought we weren't sure it was gunfire. I thought we were still considering firecrackers. Last year, Mike and them brought all those firecrackers to school.

Neff   Deanne, what did you see?

Deanne   I didn't really see a gun, but I saw Anthony walk in school with this big green bag.

Marcos   What kind of bag?

Oliver   Like a garbage bag? Like for sanitation?

Deanne   It was more like a garment bag. For clothes.

Neff   You saw him go through security with it?

Marcos   How did he get through security? He got an automatic through security?

Oliver   I can't even get my iPhone through security. And if this gangsta school let us have our iPhones, we could call nine-one-one and get some help.

Deanne   Security was dealing with that fight.

Marcos   Between Darius and Omar?

Neff   The Fluschette Brothers?

Deanne   Yes.

Oliver   They don't fight. They argue.

Marcos   Every morning at the same time. About the same thing. Something about their mother. Something about some lunch money.

Deanne   Anthony walked through during that. I was talking to Mrs. Jones. The secretary, not the guidance counselor. You know how I can't go to prom because my stupid job cut my hours so I can't pay for my dress?

Neff   Yeh. You've been telling everybody.

Deanne   I was telling Mrs. Jones.

Marcos   Yo! Could you zero in on dude and the bag and security?!

Deanne   Anthony stood at the stairwell for a second and just watched everything. Darius and Omar fighting, I mean. Then I saw him go into the boys' bathroom.

Oliver   With the garment bag?

Deanne   Yeh.

Marcos   Anthony is shooting everybody. Why is he shooting everybody?

Neff   We don't know it's him. We don't know if it's shooting.

Marcos   What do you mean 'we don't know'? Deanne just said she saw that demented kat walk into school with a garment bag full of artillery.

Oliver   And his last name is Tillery too. That's deep. Tillery, ar-tillery.

Neff   Deanne said she saw him walk through security with a garment bag. She didn't see any guns? Did you, Deanne?

Deanne   No, but . . .

Neff   Exactly.

Marcos   Anthony has always been a weird kat. You, me, everybody in this school knows that. He sits in the back of every class he's in and talks real loud, non-stop, all the time. Every teacher in the school has put him on detention. He has no friends.

Oliver   I don't think he takes a bath.

Neff   He does take a bath. Anthony smells better than most dudes in this school.

Marcos   I caught him a few times talking to himself in the bathroom. There are over one thousand students in this school, what reason would he have to talk to himself?

Neff   I don't know. Maybe because nobody listens to him.

Marcos   He's a demented kat. Dude doesn't bathe, change his clothes, and he talks to himself, that's all I need to know. And you saw him with the bag, right Deanne?

Deanne   Yes.

Marcos   Bruh came to school today to kill everybody because nobody loves him at home, or he thinks he's playing *State of Decay 2* and now he wants to blame everybody here and kill us.

The door slams. It's **Anthony**. *He's holding the garment bag.*

Anthony   The police are in front of the building. I never seen nothing like it. Mad people, mad police. Like an apocalypse. Like when Mister Hendricks taught us that chapter on slave rebellions and that kat Nat Turner went ballistic and had mad people trying to find him. It's like that out there. Mad crazy. Smoke is everywhere. Smells like the Fourth of July.

He turns to look out window of door.

I tried opening every door on this floor. All of them locked. Double-bolted. Yours and Mrs. de Silva's rooms were the only rooms open. I mean, I went to Mrs. de Silva's but it was so full of smoke, I didn't even want to go in there . . .

Oliver (*nervous*)   Did you see Monica? She's got a high-pitched scream.

Marcos (*to* **Oliver**, *quietly*)   Shut up.

Anthony   Mister Hendricks' door always had locking issues. I knew there was a chance it could be open and boom.

Neff (*cautious*)   Are you okay, Anthony?

Anthony   No, I'm not okay. Are you okay?

Marcos   She didn't mean that, man. She's just asking if everything's alright.

Anthony   If you think the school being surrounded by mad police, or that it smells like the Fourth of July out there, then, yo, you're even dumber than you look.

Marcos (*offended*)   What?!

Neff (*pacifying*)   Do they know who's doing it? Or what's going on?

Marcos (*to* **Neff**)   What?

Anthony   I don't think they know yet. Whoever it is, is pretty slick though. Genius even.

Oliver   Genius?

Anthony   To pull something like this off and still on the prowl? Still roaming the halls? Got everybody on freeze and pause? Genius. Hey, Deanne.

Deanne   Sup.

Anthony   Why do you all look scared as hell?

Marcos   Because some dude on a psychotic binge is putting bullets into everyone we know and have ever known. So yeh, we all a bit scared.

Anthony   Bullets? Word is somebody set off some firecrackers in the west hall and now the school's on lock.

Neff   So you think it's firecrackers?

Anthony   Yeh, that's what they're saying.

Marcos   Firecrackers? Some dude is out there . . .

Anthony   How do you know it's a dude?

Marcos   What?

Anthony   You said dude. How do you know it's a dude doing this? You seen him?

Marcos   I . . .

Neff   He doesn't know.

Anthony   Because that's pretty jacked up if you automatically put this on a dude. Like a dude is expected to do something like this. That it's inherent. Primal. We just wake up in the morning, walk into our school, and start trouble. Not to say brothers don't have it hard out there. Profiling, policing, according to local news we are allegedly stealing, raping, killing the country. It's enough to make you lose your mind. Some even have, but to assume a dude is gonna do something crazy just because . . .

Marcos   What's in the garment bag, Anthony?

Anthony   What? This thing?

Oliver   Yeh. What's in it?

Anthony   What do you think is in it? What would a person bring to school in a garment bag?

Oliver   I don't know.

Anthony   Oh, shit. Oh, shit! Oh shit!

Neff   Anthony?

Anthony   You all think somebody's in the school shooting people. And you think I'm the one doing it. You think I have guns and ammo in this garment bag. Is that what's up? You all think I'm naturally the one who would do this. I can't believe this. I can't believe this!

He knocks over a desk and then another.

Marcos   Yo, calm down. We don't think it's you.

Anthony   Oh, now you don't think it's me. Now that I'm all pissed off!

Neff   Anthony, come on, chill.

Anthony   How can I chill when everybody in this room believes I'm guilty. That I walked into school and wanted to do harm to everybody I know.

Neff   Anthony . . .

Deanne   Then what's in the garment bag?

Anthony   A gift for somebody.

Marcos   Then let's see it.

Oliver   Yeh. Open it.

Anthony   You want it open, you come open it, bruh!

Neff   Everybody calm down.

Anthony   Come on, punk-ass. Open the bag!

Everyone stands in silence.

Anthony   I didn't think so!

Marcos *rushes toward* **Anthony** *and knocks him down.*

Neff   Stop it!

Marcos   Grab the bag! Grab the bag!

Oliver *grabs the bag and opens it.* **Anthony** *pulls away from* **Marcos.**

Oliver   It's a dress.

Anthony   Get off of that. That has nothing to do with you!

Marcos   Dude is carrying around a dress?

Anthony   It's a gift for somebody.

Neff   Anthony, I'm sorry.

Marcos   Why are you walking around with a dress? Who did you get the dress for?

Anthony   Deanne.

Deanne   What?

Anthony   Yesterday. I overheard you telling someone you couldn't go to the prom because your job cut your hours and you didn't have enough for the dress you wanted. I got you the dress.

Oliver   Wow. Foot all in my mouth.

Anthony   I know you're not feeling me, Deanne, but that doesn't mean I can't look out for you, does it?

Neff   That's really sweet, Anthony.

Anthony   I don't want anything from you, Deanne. And I know we got smoke in the hallways and mad police out front, I just wanted to give this to you.

He hands her the dress.

Deanne   Thank you. Nobody has ever—

Marcos   Naw, I'm not here for it! What about the gunshots? What about the lockdown?

Voice of Principal on Intercom   Ladies and gentlemen! The firecracker culprits have been detained. You'll be able to leave your classrooms very shortly. Thanks for your patience.

End of play.

Suggested Exercises for Educators and Teaching Artists for *Gunshots at 2 p.m.*

Before reading or seeing the play

- Classroom Exercise:

    Ask the students to do a freewrite for five minutes. We recommend using a pencil and paper and encouraging students to write without stopping, without censoring themselves (let them know that this paper will not be collected). The freewrite should be in response to the following prompt: Recall a time when you felt you were misjudged, or you misjudged someone else.

    Once the five minutes are done (regardless of how complete the writing is), ask the students to circle the most vivid or interesting words (to them) in their freewrite. The student should then use those words to inspire a poem (it doesn't have to rhyme) expressing their feelings at the time of the misjudgment. Ask volunteers to share these poems.

- Classroom Exercise:

    In class, play the party game "Killer":
    Have the class stand in a circle, facing away from each other so that they can't see into the center (push chairs and desks back if necessary). Have them close their eyes for good measure. As you (the teacher) walk unobserved in the inside of the circle, circumscribing the whole class, explain that you will eventually secretly touch one person on the shoulder. That person will be the designated secret "killer."

    Have everyone turn back to face one another in the circle. Explain the rules: At your prompt, the class will begin to mill around the room, as if they are at a party. There are two ways to play (perhaps let the class choose which way):

    1. They *must* make eye contact with each other as they pass.
    2. They *must* shake hands with each other as they pass.

    One of them is the killer who is at the party to kill. The killer will kill by one of these two modes:

    1. If you choose option one above, they will subtly wink at a victim as they pass.
    2. If you choose option two above, they will subtly scratch the palm of a victim's hand with one finger during a handshake.

    Tell the class: "You will never know when the killer will strike. They may pass you by innocently once, twice, three times, and then, suddenly, you will see the wink/feel the finger, of death." Instruct the victims *not to die immediately* if they have been stricken, but to greet *two more people* first. Then, they should die the most dramatic and loudest death imaginable, falling to the floor and remaining there until the round ends. Classmates should run to the dying person's aid and ease them to the floor as gently as possible.

As the bodies pile up, the game continues until someone still "alive" believes that they can identify the killer. "*J'accuse!*" they may cry (or not). If they are correct, the game ends with the killer's exposure (the killer must be honest). If the accuser is wrong, they must perish immediately. The game continues until the killer is caught. Play as many additional rounds as you like.

Discuss: What did it feel like to be constantly suspicious of others? How did you identify who you were suspicious of? How did it feel for suspicion to be cast on you?

Why do you think people suspected you?

After reading or seeing the play

- Classroom Exercise:

  As a class, identify the various "misjudgments" in the play? How do the students' fears exacerbate their misjudgment? How and why did preconceptions of the presumed perpetrator influence the classroom's attitudes, assumptions, and actions?

- Homework/Classroom Assignment:

  Prepare two to four news stories for your class about conflict between various parties. Divide the class into small groups and give each group copies of one of the stories. Have the students identify any misjudgments or assumptions between or about the people involved in their story. Each group should then discuss: How does misjudgment influence people's behavior towards one another in the story? Have each group create a group sculpture with their bodies depicting the misjudgment. Each group member should be a part of the sculpture.

  Next, one at a time, each group should present their sculpture to the rest of the class. The class should give each sculpture a title that identifies the misjudgment (the sculpture makers can relax at this point but encourage them to remember their image). The group that created the sculpture should wait to speak until after the class has weighed in. They can then offer any insights or share their intentions. They should then recreate their original sculpture but invite a volunteer to manipulate the sculpture to depict an ideal image in which this misjudgment is corrected. Ask the group to hold the frozen image for five seconds (the sculpture makers can relax at this point but encourage them to remember their image). The group that created the sculpture should wait to speak until after the class has weighed in. The rest of the class should observe and discuss: What does this image look like? Where are each of the characters or images in physical relation to one another? What would they title this ideal image?

  Next, ask the group, in a count of eight, to move from image one to image two. Ask the audience (the rest of the class who is watching) to describe out loud what changed physically from image one to two (note changes in levels, physical contact, proximity, eye contact, body language, etc.). What needed to happen to make this change? How does that translate to possible actions we could take in real life?

This Time with Feeling

A short play

Chisa Hutchinson

Background and Insights for *This Time with Feeling*

from Chisa Hutchinson

Notes on Casting

All the speaking characters we see are Black. Different types of Black. All are high-school aged except for Ms. Davis and the interviewer.

Notes on Production

Feel free to find substitutes for the curse words if you reeeeeally must. Update slang where necessary.

The Inspiration for This Play

Students are under waaaaay more pressure these days than I ever was. Suicide rates among teens have been going up at least ten percent each year since 2012. Don't even get me started on school shootings. It's just a lot.

Major Themes

The need for more thoughtful treatment of young people and the need for more effective coping mechanisms for pressure and stress. Incidentally, race and the role it plays in one's inclination to "crack" are also up in here.

Food for Thought

I'd like to get people thinking about the stigmas and assumptions surrounding mental health. Also the presumed correlation between wealth and well-being, as well as the one between poverty and violence.

Entrance into the World of Theatre

A really bad-ass drama teacher named Mr. Pridham is responsible for my theatre habit. He was incredibly encouraging and determined to expose me to as many different kinds of theatre as possible, but really the most valuable thing he gave me was the recognition of the need for more representation of POC on stage. (He took me to see August Wilson debate Robert Brustein on the issue of color-blind casting and that was it for me.)

Meanwhile, I also write screenplays, but nothing beats that live connection when you're trying to get audiences to plug into the plight of particular characters.

Characters

Morgan, *seventeen*
Ms. Davis, *her mother*
Chelsea *and* **Danny**, *teenagers*
Interviewer

Place: The Davis home, and a high school auditorium.
Time: Now.

Standing center and facing us is **Morgan**, *seventeen with a young Black Republican look about her. She's pretty put together—each relaxed hair optimally placed, orthodontically enhanced smile, maybe some pearl earrings—but it's clear she's probably not the most popular kid in the lunchroom. And also there's a sign hanging from her neck that reads in big, bold, black letters, "LOSER." When she speaks, she speaks very much in spite of it.*

Morgan Good morning peers, teachers, administrators . . . friends. For those of you who don't know me, my name is Morgan Davis and I want to be your next Student Body President.

From a seat in the front row someone heckles her:

Ms. Davis Boooooooriiiing.

Morgan *pauses for a moment, and proceeds with some trepidation, but without directly acknowledging the interjection.*

Morgan You're probably thinking, What makes you so special? What can you offer that the other candidate ca—

Ms. Davis You don't know what I'm thinking, bitch . . .

Morgan *pauses once again, allowing her eyes to land on the source of the heckling.*

Ms. Davis Don't look at me! I'll cut you! I'll totally fuck your shit up!

Morgan Mom. It's private school. Nobody talks that way.

Ms. Davis They may not talk that way, but trust me, they're thinking that way.

Morgan I just don't think the interjections are necessary since everyone at Pingry abides by the social contract that prohibits public death threats.

Ms. Davis And I just don't think you understand that I'm only trying to help you not be so deathly dull. I'm trying to motivate you to be a little more . . . animated. A little animation never killed anyone.

Morgan Can I at least lose the sign?

Ms. Davis Sweetheart, we've talked about this. You need a visual indicator. When you see my eyes wandering down to the sign, it means that you're just not interesting enough to take my attention off the fact that I think you're a loser.

Morgan Seriously?

Ms. Davis Well not me, per se, but everybody else. I mean, you did lose the Vice Presidency last year to a cheerleader. A cheerleader, further, who misused "then" on her campaign posters. Chelsea Gregory: Better THEN the Rest? Are you kidding me? Frankly, I don't know which is more pathetic, her grammar, or the fact that you lost in spite of it. And you can't even play the race card on that one, because she's Black, too. Barely. But still. Maybe I should've named you Chelsea. It's perky. People like perky. (*Beat.*) Look: the sign will give you strength if you can ignore it. If you can get me to ignore it. And anyway, we're just practicing. It's not like I'm making you wear it tomorrow.

Morgan *begins to remove the sign.*

Morgan   Whatever. I'm taking it off. It's stupid.

Ms. Davis (*scary forceful*)   NO. Leave it.

Morgan *stops mid-motion, leaves the sign where it is.*

Ms. Davis   Now start over. This time with feeling.

Morgan *bucks up, begins again.*

Morgan (*a bit hyper*)   Good morning, peers! teachers! administrators! friends!

Ms. Davis   I said "with feeling," not on coke. Although frankly, a little coke might do you some good. (*Beat.*) Again.

Morgan (*down several notches*)   Good morning, peers, teachers . . .

Ms. Davis   Now you're back where you were.

Morgan (*up a couple notches*)   . . . administrators . . . friends! My name is Morgan Davis and I want to be *your* next Student Body President!

Ms. Davis   What was that?

Morgan (*deflating*)   What?

Ms. Davis   "YOUR next Student Body President!" Why the weird emphasis?

Morgan   . . . I just want to . . . I dunno . . . appeal to their sense of ownership of the whole . . . student government . . . choosing . . . thing . . .

Ms. Davis   Well, don't. When cheerleaders do it, it appeals maybe. But when you do it, it just makes you sound like you're trying to sell used cars. (*Beat.*) Again.

Pause.

Morgan (*remarkably composed*)   Good morning, peers, teachers, administrators . . . friends. For those of you who don't know me, my name is Morgan D—

Ms. Davis   Try "I'm Morgan Davis" there.

Morgan   I'm Morgan Davis and I want to be your *next* Stu—

Ms. Davis   Why do you insist on emphasizing random words?

Morgan   I want to be your next Student Body President. Now, you may be thinking, What makes you so special? What can you offer that the other candidate can't? Well, since the function of student government is—

Ms. Davis   Oh God, now you're going to tell us about the function of student g—are you even going to acknowledge the fact that you lost last year anywhere in this speech? Because if you don't, it'll just look like you're in denial or have selective amnesia or something.

Morgan   Actually, I was just about to mention the shortcomings of last year's student government and talk about how things might've been better if I'd been elected, how things will be better if I am elected.

Ms. Davis   So you're basically about to attack the most popular kids in school?

Morgan   ... Well, how else am I supposed t—

Ms. Davis   You know, to be so smart ... Jesus. Don't make this about their weaknesses, Morgan, make it about your strengths! You know what? Forget it. Just ... (*exasperated sigh*) just let me see the speech.

Morgan *just looks at her mother for a moment.*

Ms. Davis   Give it to me.

Morgan *very deliberately tears up the speech and tosses it up.*

Ms. Davis   Oh, that's mature.

Morgan (*facetious*)   I know, right? Why on earth would I do that?

Ms. Davis   You're cracking, Morgan. You have to be stronger than this.

Morgan   Why do you have to be so ... hard all the time, Mom?

Ms. Davis   Because that's the only way I can seem to get you to do anything! Now stop being a whiny little bitch, suck it up and try again.

Morgan   I am trying. You're—

Ms. Davis   Try harder. (*Beat.*) From the top. From memory. Maybe not having that paper to hide behind and having to improvise a little will loosen you up. Go.

Morgan (*on the verge*)   Good morning, peers, teachers, administrators ... friends. For those of you who don't know me, I'm Morgan Davis and I want— (*Big ol' beat.*) Do you love me? Like at all?

Ms. Davis   What?

Morgan   Do you love m—

Ms. Davis   No, I heard you. I was just stalling to give myself a moment to figure out how to respond to such a dumb question.

Morgan   Well ...?

Ms. Davis   You're my daughter. Of course.

Morgan   Then say it.

Ms. Davis   I just did.

Morgan   No. Say, "I love you, Morgan."

Ms. Davis   I'm not going t—

Morgan   Say, "I love you even when you lose, Morgan. Maybe even because you lose—over and over again—but you keep trying anyway. I love you even though you're not a thing like me. Even though you look just like your father and every time I look at you, I remember that he left me. I love you even though you make mistakes and aren't a cheerleader and probably won't become Student Body President or get into Yale because whatever, you're just an upper-middle-class token with no struggle to brag about in a college essay, just some background color, an extra who people would walk right through if it weren't for the basic laws of physics." Say it!

Silence.

Mom? Say it.

Pause.

Ms. Davis   Whom.

Morgan   What?

Ms. Davis   It's "whom people would walk right through if it weren't for the basic laws of physics." Jesus. You're as bad as Chelsea. Now if you're done with your little tantrum . . . from the top, please.

Silence as the lights change. **Morgan** *changes too. She removes that sign, for starters. Her face becomes stony. Her body relaxes. She becomes eerily poised as six chairs appear in a row behind her, five of which are occupied by her* **Peers***. A moment.*

Morgan   Good morning, peers, teachers, administrators. Friends. I'm Morgan Davis. Some of you don't know me. Some of you should, but don't. Many of you may remember me only as that girl who had the audacity to run against Chelsea Gregory last year for the vice presidency. And look how that turned out, right? Now here I am. At it again. Yeah. (*Beat.*) I had a whole speech prepared about making student government less perfunctory. For those of you who missed that vocabulary lesson, that means more effective. I was going to talk about the importance of student advocacy in all aspects of student life: curriculum, disciplinary issues, the hiring of new faculty, even the food in the dining hall. I was going to point out how all Chelsea and the gang did last year was blow a big chunk of the treasury on a bouncy castle for Field Day. I was going to suggest that if you want your student government to do more for you, that you vote for me. But that's all moot. For a couple of reasons. First, you don't give a shit about effectiveness. You care more about cleavage. And cars. And who's hooking up with whommmm. You care more about social validation, about upping your status, if only via one little vote. You're like, "Hell yeah, I voted for Chelsea. And she won. That makes me a winner too." You all just want to back a winner, even if that winner's a total retard who's only interested in the latest advancement in the world of cosmetics and what protein shake her boyfriend is chugging these days. So. There's that. The other reason? Last night, after lying awake for hours, feeling preemptively humiliated over my future performance in this election, I had a revelation. I had a revelation, and I went into my mother's bedroom and, to share my revelation with her, I woke her with a knife across her miserable throat. I slit my mother's throat. Yeah, I know. You're like, "OMG, is she serious?" Well, I assure you: I am. And if you'd rather not take the word of a loser like me, maybe you'll believe the policemen who, at any moment, will come barging through those doors to arrest me. You see, as you were all gathering here, I was making a call to let them know that there'd been a murder at my house, and when they discover my mother's body—which they've no doubt done by now—they'll also find a note explaining why I did what I did and letting them know where to find me. Which is to say here. With all of you. Don't worry, this isn't Columbine. I'm no danger to you. You all are sooooo beyond the point. And the point is, I could never be your Student Body President. For so many reasons, but chief among them, I'll be too busy serving 25-to-life. But I want you to know—and this is the most important part, so please pay attention—I need you to know that even though I'm about to spend decades, possibly the rest of my natural life, in an 8-by-8 cell—I Googled the dimensions—I'm going to be freer than I've ever been. Freer than all of you. And as a bonus? After today, not one of you will ever, ever forget me.

A noise from the back of the auditorium. **Morgan** *looks up toward it.*

Good morning, officers. Here I am.

Lights down on **Morgan**. *Then lights up on two students,* **Chelsea** *and* **Danny**, *being interviewed by a* **Reporter** *we don't see.*

Chelsea (*so, so very earnest*)   I mean . . . it's tragic. Her poor mom. She's dead. That's like . . . permanent. Extremely permanent. There's just no reason for anything that extreme. Ever. Don't get me wrong, we all wanna kill our moms sometimes, but you don't like . . . actually do it. You know? I mean who does that? It's cray. It's literally cray. She's just . . . cray. There's literally no other word for it.

Danny   Um . . . there's . . . actually a lot of other words for it: insane, psychotic . . .

Chelsea   Anyway . . .

Danny (*overlapping*)   Disturbed, unhinged . . .

Chelsea (*overlapping*)   The thing that really freaks me out the most is that she seemed to be obsessed with me.

Danny (*overlapping*)   Sociopathic . . .

Chelsea   I mean, half that creepy speech she made was about me.

Danny (*still overlapping*)   Demented, deranged . . .

Chelsea   It could have just as easily been my throat she slit, you know?

Danny   Delusional . . .

Chelsea   That's how much she like . . . what's that word . . .?

Danny   Out of her mind . . .

Chelsea   Resented! She resented me so bad, you could like . . . smell it. It was the saddest smell ever. Like dead flowers.

Danny   Potpourri is made out of dead flowers. And people buy it specifically because it smells good.

Chelsea   Dead puppies, then. Anyway, I'm just really shaken up by the whole thing.

Interviewer   And you? What's your take on this whole tragedy?

Danny   Me? Um . . . I guess I'm just shocked.

Chelsea (*horning in*)   'm in total shock, too. It's like you hear about stuff like this on Facebook or whatever, but you just don't think it's going to happen to you, you know?

Danny   Good thing it didn't happen to you, then, huh?

Chelsea   Um . . . hello. I was there.

Danny   So was the janitor but it's not like he had to mop up any blood or anything.

Chelsea   Whatever.

Danny   Whatever. Anyway, I was saying . . . it's a shock. I didn't see it coming. (*Beat.*) Not the violence part necessarily. This place is a pressure cooker. Something was bound to explode sooner or later. But it's usually like . . . white people. You know? Black, as a general rule, don't crack.

Interviewer   So . . . you're shocked because the perpetrator is uh . . . a person of color?

Danny   I mean . . . yeah. Look at the really infamous school shootings: Columbine, Littleton, Sandy Hook, that guy who shot up that sorority in Cali. All white.

Chelsea   Um . . . and cray. White didn't have anything to do with it.

Danny   Look, we got our crazies, too, but ours don't go picking gunfights with unarmed six-year-olds.

Chelsea   Yeah, only because they can't afford guns.

Danny   Wow. Wow. That is actually the most accidentally smart thing I've ever heard you say. You're right! A lot of mentally ill Black people probably can't afford lunch, let alone an assault rifle. They certainly can't afford the fancy meds and the treatment that would help them get well and maybe become productive members of society, the same meds and treatment that most of these angry, entitled, well-off white kids are opting out of. I'm guessing that even in their unstable state, crazy Black people still recognize the urgency of a problem like starvation or the effect freezing temperatures might have on an unsheltered body. And either they focus on solving those problems or they die. And looka that—boom!—they can't be that dangerous kind of crazy because ain't nobody got time for that. They're putting all their energy into survival. But what happens to someone who's crazy, well-fed, safely housed, and generally comfortable? They don't have anything to keep them focused. They don't have anything to do other than fuck shit up.

Chelsea   I don't think you can say that on the—

Danny   That's what you choose to focus on right now? Really? I'm having a revelation over here . . .

Chelsea   You don't have to get upset. I was ju—

Danny   I am upset! I am! You know why? Because there doesn't seem to be . . . a good way to be. Either you're poor and struggling with all the problems that come along with that, or you're rich and you have no sense of what a real problem is and lose your shit entirely over stuff like student government or some girl who rejected you.

Chelsea   Oooor you could be a happy, healthy middle-class person. Like me.

Danny   You're only happy because you don't know any better. And you got a BMW for your seventeenth birthday. The middle class is dead.

Chelsea (*a misguided apology for privilege*)   Psh. 3 series. That's barely a BMW.

Danny (*gesturing to* **Chelsea**)   And this, America, is what we're striving for. Why we work so hard to get into the best schools, get the best grades, to land the best jobs and get promoted and promoted and promoted until we lose our sense of real purpose and get so far from our roots, we forget what the ground felt like. And Black America: this is what hundreds of years of fighting oppression and injustice have come to. All that sacrificing and marching and scraping and scratching for opportunity just so we could wind up crazy and homicidal like the white people. I'm feeling some kinda way about this. I am shaking my damn head.

He is, in fact, shaking his damn head. **Chelsea** *is watching him now like she might almost get what he's getting at.*

Danny   There's my mom. I'm gonna go thank her for working two jobs. Excuse me.

He walks away, leaving a stunned and unsettled **Chelsea** *in his wake. She looks like she's piecing something together.*

Chelsea (*mostly to herself*)   Ohmagah. He's like . . . poor. I had no idea.

End of play.

Suggested Exercises for Educators and Teaching Artists for *This Time with Feeling*

Before reading or seeing the play

- Classroom Exercise:

  The following is a modification of Story Circles: O'Neal, J. (2011) "Story Circle Discussion Paper," Junebug Productions, Junebugproductions.org. Retrieved May 22, 2020, https://www.junebugproductions.org/story-circle (see for more detailed instructions).

  Divide students into pairs. Have each pair share a story for two minutes per story (you should time them) in which they felt under pressure to succeed in order to favorably represent their identity, family, or community? The "listener" should not interrupt the "storyteller," but rather actively listen. After the first person shares, the listener should now become the storyteller. Next, give the students two minutes to ask each other questions about their stories: What other information are they curious about?

  Ask the students to choose one of the stories with which they want to work. They can flip a coin if they can't or don't want to decide which story to choose. Have them write a short, two-person scene based on the story. Who are the characters? Where are they? What is the conflict between the two? The scene should end with the "protagonist" (the leading character who feels the pressure) at a high point of frustration; in other words, the conflict is not resolved. Read all of the scenes out loud to the class.

After reading or seeing the play

- Follow-up to Classroom Exercise:

  Return to the scenes written in the above exercise. Have the class vote on one or two scenes with which to continue working. Have the original pair again act out the voted upon scene. If a student does not wish to act, you can ask for a volunteer to play the role. Next, discuss possible resolutions to the scene in which the protagonist's frustration is addressed or relieved. Which of these suggestions leads to the most promising, realistic, and healthy outcome for the protagonist? Why? What would have to change in order to achieve this outcome?

  Alternate Exercise: Instead of discussing possible resolutions, allow students to test these options on their feet. Perform the scene again, allowing a student to substitute for the original actor playing the protagonist. The substitute could the person who suggested a possible resolution; if they do not wish to act, ask for a volunteer from the class to act out this suggestion. The "substitute" should come up on stage, and the original actor playing the protagonist should return to the audience. Improvise the scene again with the substitute actor trying out their tactic. Once the tactic has been tried, freeze the scene and discuss with the class: Was the tactic realistic (something that they believe could actually happen)? Was the tactic effective is helping the protagonist respond to the judgment in a productive manner? Who might the protagonist call upon to support them? You can play as many rounds of these improvisations as time allows, discussing the consequences of each tactic.

Note: The above exercise is a modification of Augusto Boal's Forum Theatre. For more information see Boal, Augusto (1993) *Theatre of the Oppressed*. New York: Theatre Communications Group.

• Research Assignment:

How do culture, race, and class impact attitudes about and access to mental health care? Read the following articles (or other applicable scholarship) and let them be the basis for a class discussion or further research:

Gordon, Dan (2016) "Discrimination Can Be Harmful to Your Mental Health." UCLA Newsroom. January 13. Accessed June 8, 2020. https://newsroom. ucla.edu/stories/discrimination-can-be-harmful-to-your-mental-health

Shushansky, Larry (2017) "Disparities Within Minority Health Care." National Alliance on Mental Illness (NAMI). July 31. Accessed June 8, 2020. https://www.nami.org/Blogs/NAMI-Blog/July-2017/Disparities-Within-Minority-Mental-Health-Care

777

A short play

Chisa Hutchinson

Background and Insights for 777

from Chisa Hutchinson

Notes on Casting

Actors of color, please and thank you. No color-blind casting. Characters are all ages nineteen–twenty-two.

Notes on Production

Not many set requirements. Feel free to find substitutes for curse-words (though that's not ideal) and update slang where needed.

Inspiration for this Play

I wrote this play because I finally got to a point in my life where I wouldn't want to trade places with anyone else and want that for others.

Major Themes

Self-acceptance is major. It's an exploration of identity in general and especially sexual orientation, nationality, race, and gender.

Food for Thought

I hope folks see this play and question their assumptions about what brings happiness. Also to get folks thinking about why some populations struggle more than others (or really why society sees fit to heap struggle on those populations), why some identities are inherently harder to inhabit than others.

Entrance into the World of Theatre

A really bad-ass drama teacher named Mr. Pridham is responsible for my theatre habit. He was incredibly encouraging and determined to expose me to as many different kinds of theatre as possible, but really the most valuable thing he gave me was the recognition of the need for more representation of POC on stage. (He took me to see August Wilson debate Robert Brustein on the issue of color-blind casting and that was it for me.)

Meanwhile, I also write screenplays, but nothing beats that live connection when you're trying to get audiences to plug into the plight of particular characters.

Characters

773
774
775
776
777
Administrator

Place: A waiting room.
Time: Now.

A very bright waiting room. There is a row of four chairs, currently occupied by **Number 773, Number 774, Number 775, Number 776.** *They all look a little anxious. They all clutch little squares of paper. In walks an* **Administrator** *with a clipboard.*

Administrator   Number 773!

773 *stands, looks at the other three for courage. One of them gives her/him a nod like, "Go getcha life."*

Administrator   Okay. Let's go. Gotta get there before the window closes.

773 *follows the* **Administrator** *offstage. A bright light shines from the direction in which they've just exited and then a sound like a swoosh.*

The offstage light fades. Silence.

In wanders **Number 777,** *looking a little unsure clutching at a square of paper.*

He nods at the other people in the waiting room. They nod back.

777 *sits in the now empty chair.*

775   They tell you how you got here?

777   Car accident. Pretty brutal.

775   Aw man. How old were you?

777   Nineteen.

774, 775, & 776   Ooo . . .

774   That's rough. I thought I got a raw deal. I was twenty-two. At least I got to have a margarita without looking over my shoulder.

777   What happened to you?

774   Alcohol poisoning.

777   Hm. (*To* **775**.) You?

775   Got stabbed leaving a club. "You gay faggot!" That's what he kept saying. You gay faggot!" If I wasn't bleeding out in a parking lot, I maybe could've thought of a witty way to point out how stupid that sounded. Something like, "Department of Redundancy Department!"

776   Oh my God.

775   Yea, that's what I kept saying. "Oh my God!" Huh. Who knew, right?

774   The Hindus, apparently.

775   Yeah. Guy at the front desk told me the perp's gonna get his in prison, though, so that kinda makes me feel better. How'd you go?

776   . . . I'd rather not talk about it.

775   Oh, that means you died doing something really stupid.

774   Ooo! Twenty questions time! Was it on a dare?

776   No.

774   Did it involve a car?

776   No.

775   Electricity?

776   No.

774   Sex?

776   No!

775   Was it something someone else did to you?

776   . . . No.

775   Were you alone?

776 *doesn't respond.*

775 (*snaps fingers*)   Suicide! You committed suicide. See? Stupid.

777   Way to judge.

774   Oh my God, really? How? Why?

776   Sleeping pills and moscato.

774   Mmm, moscato . . .

776   And the why . . . that's . . . complicated.

775   More complicated than "You gay faggot"? Because that shit's com-*plex.*

776 (*visibly irritated now*)   Can we please not talk about why I wanted to commit suicide? I mean I did kill myself to get away from it, so can we just assume that it was really bad and move on? Please?

The others mutter apologies. Silence.

775   The weather here's not what I was expecting.

774   I know, right?

775   Very grey. Kinda dismal.

Pause.

776   I wonder who I'm gonna be next.

774   I know, right?

775   I hope I get a real family this time. Like one that won't disown me over some shit I can't help.

776   I wanna be born into a rich Persian family. But like, in America. Like Shahs of Sunset. Their families are mad tight. They got real strong culture and tan skin and good hair, but they still get to make fun of white people.

775   So do Latinos.

774   Yeah, but how many rich Latinos you know?

775   Touché.

776   I wanna be Beyoncé's next baby.

775   Despite the odds that you might wind up looking like Jay-Z?

776   I'd take those odds for the bajillion dollars I'd inherit.

An amused 777 laughs a little.

776   Just sayin'.

775 (*to 777*)   Who do *you* want to be next?

777   . . . Me.

775   Yeah, you.

777   No, that's my answer. I wanna be me.

774, 775, & 776 *all look skeptical.*

775   Okay, you can cut the love-thyself crap. We're all dead here. You don't have to impress anybody. We won't even remember we had this convo in a few minutes. Who would you be *really*?

777   Really. I'd be me. I actually got to be pretty happy with who I was.

775   But you weren't always, right?

777   Of course not. Who's always happy with themselves?

776   Beyoncé.

The **Administrator** *returns.*

Administrator   774, you're on deck!

774   Oh wow, that was fast.

Administrator   Hey, are you 777?

777   Yeah, that's me.

Administrator   Well, then . . .

Suddenly alarm bells go off and fun lights flash.

Congratulations! You're the luckiest customer of the day!

The alarm and the lights cut out.

That means you get to choose your next vessel. Here . . .

*The **Administrator** hands 777 a list from the clipboard and a pen.*

Administrator   These are the next available ten. All different types. Just check the box of the one that appeals most and that, my friend, will be where you spend your next lifetime, m'kay?

774   Damn. That coulda been me if I'da just held my liquor a little longer.

775   For real.

777   Seriously? I get to choose?

Administrator   Keep up. That was like seven sentences ago. Yes, you get to choose. Choose wisely. But you only have until your number gets called, so you also have to choose fast, m'kay? (*Beat.*) 774, you ready?

774   I guess.

*The **Administrator** leads 774 offstage into the growing light. As they go . . .*

774   Do you know what *my* next vessel's gonna be?

Administrator   Yup.

774   Can you tell me what it is?

Administrator   Nope.

The light grows bright and then: swoosh. 775 and 776 turn to look at 777.

775   Oh, you have got to be kidding me! Mr. Wouldn't Wanna Be Anyone But Me gets to choose who he's gonna be?

777 shrugs like, "I don't know what to say." 776 snatches the list to get a look.

776   Well shit, man, let's have a look at your choices . . .

775 muscles in to get a look.

775   Ooo . . . that's some prime life material right there. Looka that one: French male, white, two parents, father in finance, makes over 800,000 Euros a year . . . I don't know what that is in dollars, but I'm sure it's more than enough . . .

776   Huh. It never occurred to me that I might not be reborn an American.

775   Yeah, that's very American of you. Are there any Americans on the list?

They check.

776   Here's one! American female, white—

775   Are there any American males? It's not really a good time to be a woman in America right now.

777   Come on, guys . . .

775   You don't have even a little bit of interest in choosing, for real?

777 Not really.

775 So then give your choice to me.

777 laughs a little.

775 I'm serious! You're just gonna waste it. At least I'll make it count. Plus, you have to admit, I got shafted big time in the last life.

776 Um . . . and I didn't?

775 We don't know if you didn't because you won't tell us why you offed yourself.

776 But I *offed* myself! That's more than enough! It's different when someone else comes along and ends your life, but as tragic as that is, it's way worse when stuff happens to you that makes you want to end your own.

775 I guess we'll just have to take your word for it.

776 You ever have anything happen to you that made you want to kill yourself? Because if not—

775 Sweetheart. I was a po', gay, Black male from Memphis. Of *course* shit happened to me that made me want to kill myself. But I never woulda done that. I never woulda been that ungrateful for my life.

777 So then you know what I'm talking about.

775 I mean, look: I get what you're saying and all, but that don't mean I ain't gonna jump at the chance for a better life. Sheeit. That's just more to be grateful for.

777 What's better?

775 (*sucks teeth*)   You know what better is. Stop playin'.

777 No, really? What does "better" look like?

775 Well, not poor. That's a good start.

777 So you want money.

775 Hell yeah, I want money!

777 Because rich people are happy, right?

775 . . . They got a better chance of being happy anyway.

776 Probably because they can afford all those prescription happy pills.

777 Yeah, that's probably it.

776 Money's no guarantee for happiness. In fact, if you're the kind of person money matters that much to, you're probably not gonna be happy no matter how much you have or what else you got going on.

775 (*to 776*)   Oooooooh no no no no no, you ain't gonna poke holes in my shit. You just want to make me look bad so he won't give the choice to me.

777 And you're trying to change the subject. Money. A good start. Okay. What else?

775 I'd want to be a man.

776 Hmph. What's wrong with being a woman?

775 There's nothing *wrong* with being a woman. Just like there's nothing *wrong* with being poor. It's just *easier* to be a man.

777 I don't know. I always thought I would've had an easier time if I'd been a woman.

775 Yeah, a lot of gay guys do. Which brings me to my next requirement: straight. I'd need to be straight.

777 Okay, first of all: I never said I was gay.

775 (*sarcastically*) Oh, I'm sorry. I must've been misled by the mascara.

777 Okay, well, second: what's wrong with being gay?

775 *just looks at* **777** *like, "Really?"*

777 Who did you ever hurt being gay? What damage did you do?

775 Um . . . I broke up my whole family for starters.

777 How did you do that?

775 Hell*oooooo*! They didn't approve of my being gay.

777 Yeah, but what did *you* do? Because that sounds like their problem. Did you steal something, molest a niece, punch your mother in the neck in a fit of raging faggotry? What?

775 Okay, I see your point, but you have to admit: even if we don't *do* anything but offend people with our gayness, the way other people treat us is enough to make you wish you were born another kinda way. It would just be easier.

777 That ain't in your control, though.

775 It could be!

776 (*suddenly understanding*) He means none of it is in your control. How you're born, how people react to you, stuff that happens to you . . . none of that. You could be the richest, straightest, happiest man in the world and die in a plane crash because the pilot got a drinking problem.

777 Or get plowed by a truck on the New Jersey Turnpike. Like I did. Juuuust as I was beginning to really live. I'm sayin'. You can't control your circumstances. You can't control the things that happen to you. You can only control how you handle it. And me? I know I'm gonna be able to handle mine no matter what. I didn't live long and I sure didn't have it easy, but still managed to get me some happiness. So now I'm like, bring it. Whatever *it* is.

776 Yeah . . . okay. I get that.

775 (*to* **776**)   Whatever, now you're just trying to make yourself look good so he'll give the choice to you.

776   No. I don't want it.

775   . . . For real?

776   For real.

775   So then you gonna give it to me, right?

The **Administrator** *returns.*

Administrator   Number 775! You're up!

775   Wait! I'm . . . he's about to give me his choice! I get to choose my next vessel!

Administrator   Is that true, 777?

777   Sure. It'd just be wasted on me.

Administrator   Uuuuuh . . . well, this has never happened before . . . uh . . . I guess that means you're taking his place then. I need somebody to put in this vessel, makes no difference to me who, so . . .

777 (*standing*)   Okay, let's do this.

The **Administrator** *leads* **777** *out to the light.*

Administrator   You're an exceptional soul, my friend.

777   I know.

It's just **775** & **776** *now.*

775   Ha! I can't believe this shit! I get to choose my *life*! This is crazy . . .

775 *starts looking at the list again.* **776** *says nothing. Just sits there.*

775   And *you're* crazy. You know that, right? He probably woulda given it to you. You gave up too easy.

776 (*talking about something else*)   Yeah. I know that now.

775 (*looking at the list*)   Ooo! I could be the son of a surgeon . . . *ooo! Two* surgeons! That's a nice set-up.

776   My dad was a cardiologist.

775   Yeah?

776   Yeah. He was never home.

775   Oh.

Pause.

775   Is that why you killed yourself?

776   Doesn't even matter anymore. I'll get it right next time.

776 *smiles.* **775** *just looks at* **776** *like, "You're weird," and goes back to looking at the list.*

End of play

Suggested Exercises for Educators and Teaching Artists for 777

Before seeing or reading the play

- Classroom Exercise:

  In groups of four: Create a scene in a room in which characters face the promise of a new reality in which they are offered an opportunity, but with uncertain results. Brainstorm: What are the rules of this space? Who is in charge? Where do people go from here? How do you get here and how do you leave? Next, create a five-minute improvisation, in which each character should relay how and why they came there. Only one character gets to leave: who is it and why?

- Classroom Exercise:

  Brief discussion: Ask the students: "If given the opportunity to trade places with someone else, would you do it?" Why or why not?

  Break into small groups:

  Have the students write the names of various jobs, lifestyles, and career opportunities on index cards and place them in a hat or a box. Include the names of a few major celebrities or political figures just for fun (e.g., Beyoncé, Barack Obama, or the Queen of England).

  Have each member of the small group draw a card. In their own group, have them discuss the drawbacks and merits of switching places with the person on their own card. After each has spoken for themselves and their own card, see if anyone wants to trade for someone else's card. Encourage them to share with their group why they made the choices that they did.

After seeing or reading the play

- Classroom Exercise:

  Break the class into small groups of three. Each group should create a short play with three characters: the protagonist, a central character who is given the option to trade places with someone else; a character who encourages the protagonist to make the trade; and a character advocating that the protagonist keep the life they have. By the end of the play, the central character should make a decision. These plays can be improvisations (vs. scripted scenes), but give the groups time to rehearse them.

  Have each group perform their play for the class. Next, each group should discuss one of the other group's plays. Answer the following questions from the author of 777: "What brings happiness? Why do some populations struggle more than others (or really why does society see fit to heap struggle on those populations)?"

Marathon and Mucilage, a Contemplation on an Appellation

A short play in dream time

Chris Ceraso

Background and Insights into *Marathon and Mucilage: A Contemplation on an Appellation*

from Chris Ceraso

Notes on Casting

The more diverse the cast, the better. Ms. Gummm, Mother, and Father may be played by adult actors, but that's not necessary.

Notes on Production

The play should move with the logic, or illogic, of a dream. The atmosphere should be mysterious, surreal. Animal characters do not need animal costumes; the actors should look human, with animal characteristics.

The Inspiration for This Play

I originally wrote the play for an actor in New York's 52nd Street Project Teen Ensemble, and later adapted it for another actor in Drew University's AdvantageArts Program. The inspiration came from an interview in which the original actor told me that he had no name for many months after birth because his parents were waiting for him to tell them who he was.

Each actor for whom the play was conceived and reconceived had iconoclastic personalities out of synch with the traditional classroom. After decades of teaching artist work in high schools, I came to relate to the kid who was identified as the anarchist, the troublemaker or the silent class dropout. This kid would often come to startling creative life when presented with an opportunity to improvise or fantasize based on open questions and the relationships to those questions in their own mind. I think these young people carry Dionysian spirits.

Major Themes

Identity and coming-of-age: the search for self; the limits of "traditional" education; discovering one's path rather than following a charted course.

Food for Thought

What is true self-knowledge and where does it come from? Do we make our name or does our name make us? What can we learn from our dreams? What does studying the ancient world have to teach us?

Entrance into the World of Theatre

I loved movies when I was a boy, but I didn't see a live professional play until I was in high school. The play seemed real and not real at the same time. I loved the idea that a playwright could not only represent the world as we see it, but can create a world of their own imagining that an audience can believe in—maybe it looks like our world in part, maybe only sometimes, maybe not at all, but it seems to make sense for the time we are living in it.

I never stopped loving movies, so I also act in and write for movies and for TV, when I can. Most recently I started writing musicals. I enjoy visiting imagined places where I can see the complicated world in which we all live reflected back to us in truthful, if not necessarily realistic, ways. Hopefully, I return smarter, stronger, richer, and more able to share the "real" world as a compassionate and joyful person.

Marathon and Mucilage: A Contemplation on an Appellation was originally dreamed up and performed at the 52nd Street Project, New York, in 2008. It was directed by Reggie Flowers. Many thanks to Gus Rogerson, Carol Ochs, Megan Cramer, George Babiak, John Sheehy, Liz Bell, Joanna Vidal, and to Kimani Lewis Ashley by whom it was first inspired.

Characters
(in order of appearance)

He
Ms. Gummm
Classmates
Learned Cat
Hannibal
Elephants
Oracle of Delphi
Theatre Audience
Mother
Father

Place: A classroom, and a flat, windy plain.
Time: The present.

A classroom. **"He"** *sits at a desk, dozing, as the teacher,* **Ms. Gummm**, *speaks. It appears that* **Ms. Gummm** *is floating in the air.*

Ms. Gummm   Meeeeeeeeew-cilage.

He   Where will I be tomorrow?

Ms. Gummm   Meeeeeeeeew-cilage.

He   Where will I be next year?

Ms. Gummm   Maaaaaarathonnnnn . . .

He   If everyone has a destiny?

Ms. Gummm   Maaarathon!

He   When will mine come clear?

Ms. Gummm   BATTLE!

He   Huh? Wha'?

Ms. Gummm   Eeeeeeeeew must eeeeeeeeewwwws meeeeeeeeew-cilage.

He   I'm sorry?

Ms. Gummm   If you want the facts to stick. Ewwwwww must eeeeeeeews meeeeeeeew-cilage.

He   Meeeeeeeeeeew-cilage?

Ms. Gummm   Meeeeeeeeeeew-cilage. If you want the facts to stick.

He   Stick?

Ms. Gummm   WAKE UP!

He   Damn! What was the question?

The **Classmates** *appear, popping out of nowhere; when present, they hang around, disappear, float away, dissolve into one person, or split into many. They look like frogs, but do not wear frog costumes.*

Ms. Gummm   The question, Sophocles, is why are you sleeping in my class again? Sophocles!

He   Huh?

Ms. Gummm   Have you done your research assignment, Aristotle?

He   Who? Oh, um . . . The Battle of Marathon was fought in, in . . . a long time ago, and,—uh . . . what was the question?

Ms. Gummm   The Battle of Marathon was fought in 490 BCE. A small but determined army of Athenian Greeks defeated a much larger Persian army on a flat windy plain outside of Athens, ensuring the rise of Ancient Athens as the model for democratic government . . . Where is your colllllllaaaaaaage, young man?

He   I . . . um—

Ms. Gummm   Did you make a colllllllaaaaagge, Achilles?

He   I . . . don't think I—

Ms. Gummm   The facts didn't stick, did they, Aeschylus?

He   Ms. Gummm, my name is . . .

Ms. Gummm   Yes, Demosthenes-Euripdes-Phidipides?

He   My name—

Ms. Gummm   Yes, what?

He   I think I—

Ms. Gummm   What, what, what? What's your name?

He   I—

Ms. Gummm   Have you forgotten your own name?

He   I . . . think I lost it when I was asleep.

Classmates (*frog-like*)   No-name, no-name, no-name, no-name . . .

Ms. Gummm   Classssss!

Silence.

This is a tragedy of Greek proportions! Not only has this young man been asleep for the duration of my lesson, but now it appears that he isn't really here at all!

He   But—

Ms. Gummm   Blllllllooooowwwww him away. He is nothing!

The **Classmates** *start to blow him away, literally.*

Ms. Gummm   Don't return until you have found a name that attaches to you! I want facts that stick! Meeeeeeeeew-cilage. . . . Eeeeeeeeeew must eeeeeeeewwwws meeeeeeew-ci-laggggggge.

The **Classmates** *have blown him to a flat windy plain.*

He

Where am I?
It's really flat here. And really windy. And really plain.
I'm on a flat, windy plain.
Oooooo-kay. So, that's where I am.

But *who* am I where I am?
Or *am* I where I *be*?
In other words: who is this guy called *me*?
If someone saw me, would they say, "Who's *He*?"
Or would I be invisible?

Very strange, very strange.
Don't feel quite at home on this here range.
But I know I must be *some*body, 'cause, check it out:
I figure I'm about five-eleven, two-oh-seven.   *(Note: suit this rhyme to the actor.)*
I've obviously been on the planet
For a little while, yo.
Long enough for my hair to grow,
Long enough for my feet to smell,
Long enough for my brain to swell
With questions,
About Life,
About Love,
About the Order of Creation:
Does everybody have a station?
Do we wave the flag of just one nation?
Who's running this show!?
My basis has officially become need-to-know,
'Cause dust is blowin' in my eyes,
And no one out here hears my cries!
Where, oh where do I fit in?!
Do I need these legs, or should I have a fin?!
AND WHY AM I RHYMING?!

He *holds his head.* A **Learned Cat** *passes by.*

He   Who are you?

Cat   Funny *you* should ask.

He   What are you doing here?

Cat   I'm a Learned Cat. (*Taps head.*) Very wise. Advisor to the ancient pharaohs.
You can find my picture in all the sacred, secret crypts of Egypt.

He   What are you doing *here*?

Cat   Crossing your path.

He   Isn't that bad luck?

Cat   Rude. What kind of cat do you take me for?

He   I can't really tell. You don't actually look like a cat. I mean, I only have your
word for it.

Cat   And that's not good enough for you? Also rude.

He   What kind of advice do you give?

Cat   What do you need?

He   I'm trying to remember my own name.

Cat   Ahhhhhhhhhh. What makes you think I can help?

He   I just assumed, since you're a Learned Cat.

Cat (*taps head*)   Very wise.

He   So can you help?

Cat   I don't know. It's your dream.

He   Wait. I thought I woke up in class! This is still a dream?

Cat   Ahhhhhhh. Now we're getting to it.

He   Getting to what?

Cat   The nitty-gritty.

He   Of . . .?

Cat

> Of the Wisdom of the Ancient City,
> The Meaning of the Cryyy-yyy-yyye in the Night, Bae-bae,
> The Cause of Fear and Pity,

The **Cat** *extends its hand.*

And I'll tell you more for Fi'ty.

He   Fi'ty what?

Cat   Cents. Unless you got gold.

He   So, for fifty cents, you'll give me an answer?

Cat   Is that what I said?

He   Is it?

Cat   That's for me to know and you . . .

He   . . . to find out.

He *gives the* **Cat** *fifty cents. The* **Cat** *goes to work.*

Cat   You say you don't know who you are—

He   Correct.

Cat   And you say you don't know who *I* am—

He   Also correct.

Cat   Don't you *see*?

He   See *what*?

Cat   Oh, my God, this man is in the dark!

He   Yessssss!

Cat

> Consider this, and ponder, Oh, My Broth-uh:
> How can you see *Thyself*,
> If you cannot see the *Oth-uh*?

The **Cat** *taps his head smugly and goes.*

He   What!?! That wasn't an answer! That was terrible! I want my money back!

Ms. Gummm *appears, floating over the plain.*

Ms. Gummm   The second Peeeeeeeeeewwwww-nic War was fought more than two hundred years after the Battle of Marathon, between the Rooooooman Republic and the Carthaginians . . . led by Hannnnnnnniballllll . . . From North Aaaaaafrricaaaaahhh haaa hhaaa hAAAHHH HAHHHH . . .

He   Oh, God, I'm missing hundreds of years of history class. (*Slaps himself.*) Wake up! Wake up!

The wind blows on the plain. **Hannibal** *appears, with his* **Elephants**—*the* **Classmates**, *who do not wear elephant suits.*

Hannibal   HEY YOU! SOLDIER! MAKE WAY THERE! CAN'T YOU SEE I'VE GOT ELEPHANTS COMING THROUGH?

He   I . . . don't think I'm part of your army.

Hannibal   NONSENSE! I'M HANNIBAL! EVERYONE I ROLL OVER BECOMES PART OF MY ARMY!

He   I think I'll stay behind. I got a feeling I'm a lover, not a fighter.

Hannibal   ARE YOU SOME KIND OF COWARD, FELLA?! FOLLOW ME!

He   Where are you going?

Hannibal   OVER THE ALPS! TO ROME! TO DIVIDE AND CONQUER!

He   Why?

Hannibal   What kind of question is that?

He   It's just the kind of thing I would need to know, you know, before I joined your army and followed you, and like . . . divided and conquered and killed people, not to mention elephants.

Hannibal   Look at me, son. I'm a leader. What else do you need to know?

He   What are you trying to *do*?

Hannibal   Make a name for myself. What else is there?

He   I'm . . . not sure.

Hannibal THEN STEP ASIDE, ZERO! YOU'RE EITHER SOMEBODY IN THIS WORLD, OR YOU'RE NOBODY! YOU HAVE A NAME, OR YOU DON'T! COME ON, ELEPHANTS! FOLLOW ME! OVER THE ALPS! THEY SAY IT CAN'T BE DONE! I'LL SHOW THEM! I'LL SHOW THEM AAAAAAAALLLLLLL! YAAAAA! YAAAAA!

Hannibal *exits, followed by the* **Elephants.**

He Hey, there, elephants! You know you're not going to make it! I mean, I'm no Oracle of Delphi, but from what I remember in Ms. Gummm's class, most of you fall off the mountain!

A puff of smoke; the **Oracle of Delphi** *appears, coughing. She looks a lot like* **Ms. Gummm**.

Oracle Holy smoke! There's gotta be a better way. My card. Oracle of Delphi, at your service.

He Are you okay?

Oracle I'd like a job in a smoke-free environment.

He What're you doing on my flat, windy plain?

Oracle A Learned Cat told me you had some questions.

He How do you know that phony cat?

Oracle (She/He/They) crossed my path on the way back to ancient Egypt.

He How much do *you* charge?

Oracle Please. I'm touched by the Goddess Herself. The ways of mortals, money, and shifty cats mean nothing to me. The Truth is all that matters.

He I like the sound of that.

Oracle So?

He So. I need some answers.

Oracle About?

He About *me*! About who I am?

Oracle Oh. That's easy. She told me this would be a tough one.

He She who?

Oracle *points skyward, then checks a clipboard. Note: The bracketed points in the following speeches should be filled in with the actor's own information.*

Oracle Okay. It says right here that you were born on [ ], you live in [ ]. You think of yourself as [eg., creative, spiritual, and open minded]. You're thrilled by being on stage and in front of crowds—oh, boy, you must be pretty thrilled right now—wave to the folks out there—

She points to the **Theatre Audience**. **He** *sees them. They both wave. Maybe the* **Theatre Audience** *waves back.*

He   Wow! Have they been there all along? I'm thrilled!

Oracle (*back to clipboard*)   —and a song lyric that expresses you is . . . (*flips page*) "[   ]."

He   What is that you're reading?

Oracle   It's the fact sheet that we gave to your playwright so he could write this play about you.

He   Wait. You're the Oracle of Delphi, like the Know-It-All of all time. You just read stuff off a fact sheet?

Oracle   Listen, munchkin, everyone thinks what I do is some sort of supernatural flubbadidubba, but the fact is I DO MY RESEARCH, which is what you're supposed to be doing right now. (**Ms. Gummm's** *voice.*) "Facts that stick!" remember? Maybe you better focus, Eddie-Puss. Phocus! "P-H-O-C-U-S!"

He   But what you read off that sheet . . . is that really the answer to who I am?

Oracle   I'm gonna tell you a big secret, sweetie-pie. You ready? Listen up: Your *questions* are your *answers*.

He   What?

Oracle   Your questions are your answers. Think about it, honey. I gotta get back to my class . . . I mean, to my cave.

He   Wait, wait, wait! Didn't I put my name there on that sheet?

Oracle (*looks at it*)   Cripes! You forgot to put your name on your paper.

She exits through the smoke, coughing loudly.

He

My questions are my answers.
Hmmmmmm. Okay:
What is the center of the Universe,
Who wrote the book of Love,
How much wood could a woodchuck chuck,
And is there God above?
Why am I on this windy plain,
Forgotten in a dream?
How in the world do I fit in
To Hist'ry's flowing stream?
I need a tag that blows my horn:
Did I have a name when I was born?

We hear a smack, then a baby cries. A circle of light becomes the "cradle." The voices of **Mother** *and* **Father** *sing a lullaby.*

Mother and Father

> Child of tomorrow
> Help us to see:
> What will you wonder,
> And who will you be?

Father He's been here for a month now. Don't you think we should name him *something*?

He Pop? (*Papi, Pappa, Dad, Daddy, etc. may be substituted.*)

Mother It's almost time.

He Ma? (*Mami, Mamma, Mom, etc. may be substituted.*)

Mother I can almost see who he's going to be.

He I remember this. Why do I remember this? *How* do I remember this?

Mother There! Do you see it! That expression on his face.

Father He looks so full of questions.

Mother He has an ancient soul. He should have an ancient name.

He An ancient name—

Mother and Father Homer! Like the poet . . .

He *Ho*mer?! Like the cartoon?

Mother . . . or . . . Socrates, the questioner.

He Wai' wai' wai', hold up . . . Ms. Gummm said that dude didn't end well, something about hemlock. I ain't been sleepin' *all* the time.

Father Hannibal, the—

He HELLLL n—

He *stops them.*

I got this. I got this. How 'bout . . .

He *walks into the cradle light.*

He "Dionysus."

Mother Ohh! I think I just heard him!

Father Did he say . . .?

Mother and Father "Dionysus!"

Mother "Spirit of all that grows."

He Spirit of all that *flows.*

Father   "Spirit of the revels."

Mother and Father   "Spirit of the Theatre."

He, Mother, and Father   "Dionysus!"

He   Why did that *take* so long?!

Mother   We were waiting to see who would arrive.

Father   Who you would be.

Mother   We wanted to make sure the name would stick.

He   "Dionysus." I'm feelin' it.

Mother   But we just ended up calling you "Dennis," for short.

Father   Yeah. It's just . . . easier for other people.

He   "Dennis." Hmmm.

Father   We had one other option that we liked.

He   What?

Mother   Meeeeeeww-ci-laaaaaggge.

Father   Meeeeeeew-ci-laaaaaaaage.

Mother and Father   Meeeeeeeeeeeeew-ci-laaaaaaaaaaaaaaaage.

Mother *and* **Father** *dissolve. The* **Classmates** *appear and blow* **He** *back to the classroom,* where **Ms. Gummm** *still floats in the air.*

Ms. Gummm   Eeeeeeeeeew must eeeeeeeewwwwws mewwwwwwww-ci-lage. If you want it to stick. Dionysus! Dionys! Dennis!

He *startles awake.* **Ms. Gummm** *is on the ground, The* **Classmates** *at their desks.*

Ms. Gummm   Dennis! Wake up!

He   I'm awake!

Ms. Gummm   Where have you been?

He   Uh—

Ms. Gummm   Who do you think you are, sleeping in my class?

He *is silent. The* **Classmates** *stare. They still look a little like frogs.*

Ms. Gummm   Answer! Just who do you think you are?

Dennis   Dionysus.

Ms. Gummm   What?

Dionysus (He)   That's who I am. My real name. I'm Dionysus.

The **Classmates** *giggle.*

Dionysus (He)   Go on and laugh, ya'll, but that's the real me: Dionysus.

The **Classmates** *laugh.*

Ms. Gummm   Class!

The **Classmates** *are silent.*

Ms. Gummm   I know that's your full name, young man. I see it every time I put a red "X" next to it for disrupting my class, which I will do ONCE AGAIN right after the bell rings. But what is your point and why are you now taking up my valuable lecture time after your little nap?

Pause. All wait.

Dionysus (He)   I have a question.

The **Classmates** *gasp.* **Ms Gummm** *rears back.*

Ms. Gummm   Aaaaaa quesssssstionnnnn?

Dionysus   Can't we ask questions?

Ms. Gummm   How could we get it through History if you all asked *questions*? There are simply too many *facts* to cover.

Dionysus (He)   But the Oracle of Delphi—

Ms. Gummm   The Oracle of Delphi?!

Dionysus (He)   Yeah . . . She was sort of like you . . .

Ms. Gummm (*pleased*)   Ohhhhh. Well?

Dionysus (He)   And she told me I should ask questions.

Ms. Gummm   In your dreams! Now, class, does anyone else have . . .

She drips with derision.

. . . a question?

She waits. Silence.

That's what I thought. Now, then . . .

Classmate #1 *slowly raises her hand. The lullaby melody is heard.*

Classmate #1   I do.

Ms. Gummm   And I'm sorry, who are you? You can't expect me to remem—

Classmate #1   [real name]

Classmate #2 (*raises hand, before* **Ms. Gummm** *can speak*)   [real name]

Classmate #3 (*hand up*)   [real name]

Classmate #4 (*hand up*)   [real name]

They all continue to raise their hands and say their names. **Ms. Gummm** *cowers, recedes, and disappears. When she is gone the lullaby is still heard, but with a hip-hop beat.* **Mother** *and* **Father** *appear and start to rap to their own a cappella beatbox. They are terrible, but it's kind of great, too.*

Mother and Father

> A-ptch, a-ptch, a-ptch-a-ptch-a-ptch-ahh
> Child of tomorrow
> How will you flame?
> Ask us your questions
> And teach us your name.
> Chuka-chuka-chuka
> Woot woot!
> Ask us your questions,
> Teach us your name.
> Ask us your questions,
> Teach us your name.

Classmates   And the rest . . . will be history.

Dionysus (He)   [actor says his real name] Let the revels begin!

Curtain call.

End of play.

Suggested Exercises for Educators and Teaching Artists for *Marathon and Mucilage: A Contemplation on an Appellation in Dream Time*

Before reading or seeing the play

- Homework Assignment:

  Ask each participant to find answers to the following questions: Why were you given your name? What is its meaning? Then ask each to write a paragraph explaining why they think the name does or does not suit them. Finally, ask the question: If you could change your name, would you? If no, why not? If yes, what name would you choose and why?

- Classroom Exercise:

  Research the following names and places from Ancient History: Achilles, Aeschylus, Aristotle, Battle of Marathon, Demosthenes, Dionysus . . . especially Dionysus, Euripides, Hannibal, Homer, the Oracle of Delphi, Socrates, Sophocles. Make a class collage of images of your research. Be sure to use mucilage!

  Bonus research: What was the significance of cats in ancient Egypt? Add images of Egyptian cats to your group collage.

After reading or seeing the play

- Classroom Exercise:

  Ask the group: What was the strangest dream you ever had? Get into small groups three to five. Share the dreams. Have each group plan and then improvise a group dream that combines elements of each person's dream. After each dream improvisation, ask the rest of the group what that dream was trying to tell us.

  Class discussion: How are dreams and plays similar?

- Additional Exercise:

  Play a game of questions. Split the group into two lines of equal participants facing one another. Start at one end of the line: the first two students facing each other must create a dialogue using only questions. There is no leader, but the first to speak starts with a "big" question, such as "Why are we here on earth?" The answer must be another question, of any scale, but should logically respond to the prior (i.e., "Will you change the way you live if you find out?" etc.) If someone doesn't respond with a question, or repeats a question, they're eliminated. You cannot make a comment, disguised as a question, like "I don't know, why don't you be quiet?" In other words, each person must respond with a genuine question that connects to the one before. Each time a questioner is eliminated the next person in the opposite facing line steps in to challenge the winning questioner. The eliminated party goes to the end of the opposite line (helping to ensure that pairs will keep getting mixed). Each new pair starts with a fresh question. Pass through the entire line at least twice if you can. Choose an MVQ at the end of the game: a "Most Valuable Questioner."

Discuss as a class or reflect in writing: what value is there to asking questions as a way of learning? [Note this is called the "Socratic Method."]

Hand out index cards and have students write: What one pressing question do you have and who in history or present day would you like to have answer it? Create another collage with the class responses. Be sure to use mucilage.

Figure 2 Dionysus Rodriguez as Dionysus and Demi Sparks as The Oracle of Delphi/Ms. Gummm in *Marathon and Mucilage* by Chris Ceraso. Produced at Drew University, 2015, photographed by Lynne Delade, photo courtesy of Lynne Delade.

Figure 3 C.J. Moten as Akili in *Homecoming Dance* by Evelyn Diaz Cruz. Produced at Drew University, 2015, photographed by Lynne Delade, photo courtesy of Lynne Delade.

Figure 4 Seven Richardson as Charisma in *Charisma at the Crossroads* by Nina Angela Mercer. Produced at Drew University, 2018, photographed by Lynne Delade, photo courtesy of Lynne Delade.

Figure 5 Alizé Martinez as the Judge in *Charisma at the Crossroads* by Nina Angela Mercer. Produced at Drew University, 2018, photographed by Lynne Delade, photo courtesy of Lynne Delade.

Figure 6 Zachery Halley as James and Antonella Sanchez as Krystle in *The Aftermath* by Paris Crayton III. Produced at Drew University, 2018, photographed by Lynne Delade, photo courtesy of Lynne Delade.

Figure 7 Ayanna Paquette as Kalima in *Southwestern High* by Cassandra Medley. Produced at Drew University, 2019, photographed by Lynne Delade, photo courtesy of Lynne Delade.

Figure 8 Alberto Noel Caceres as Jazz and Jasmin Casiano as Angel in *Stare and Compare* by Evelyn Diaz Cruz. Produced at Drew University, 2019, photographed by Lynne Delade, photo courtesy of Lynne Delade.

Homecoming Dance

A play in one act

Evelyn Diaz Cruz

Background and Insights into *Homecoming Dance*

from Evelyn Diaz Cruz

Notes on Casting

This play is Afro-Caribbean and Latino/a/x centric in flavor and casting. The roles of the Uber Driver and the Old Person on the porch are intentionally non-gender specific; pronouns should be adjusted accordingly.

Notes on Production

This play is set in the year 2020 and references an event from twenty years prior. If necessary, the time frame and use of slang may be modified to coincide with the dates you are working with. I am happy to help you with adjusting the time frame and references if need be. The staging is highly adaptable, ranging from minimalistic to elaborate.

The Inspiration for This Play

I was invited to write a play for the AdvantageArts program in partnership with the Marion A. Bolden Center in New Jersey. Every summer high school students work with Drew University Theatre students and faculty studying and creating theatre. As the commissioned playwright, I offered workshops and got to know the students in order to create a play that they could perform. During one such workshop, I was profoundly touched by the story of a young man who shared the pain of having just lost his grandmother, the beloved matriarch of his family. His grief was palpable and yet his strength of character at this early stage in his grieving process was remarkable, as was his sobering expression of regret that his grandmother had not been appreciated for all that she was for the family. Now that she had passed, he realized how much she had contributed. His sharing was a precious gift to all of us in the room. I knew I had to write this play as a reminder to honor our loved ones.

Major Themes

Ancestors, kindness, regret, guilt, bullying, crossroads, life's regrets, forgiving others and ourselves, being proud of and reclaiming one's heritage, pitfalls of ambition, spiritual connections, a sense of responsibility.

Food for Thought

My hope is that beyond the larger themes of being self-conscious of one's heritage and bullying, audiences question their notions of what leads to success. May this play also infuse a sense of responsibility to consider how ambition can cloud our values. I hope this play reinforces our sense of the largesse of sincere relationships and the ability to authentically forgive ourselves when we fall short.

Entrance into the Theatre

At twenty-one years old and a single mother of two children, I started a job as an executive assistant at San Diego State University's Chicana/o/x Studies Department. Having never been on a university campus before, the world opened up for me there, where I joined an all-women's Latina theatre troupe performing agit-prop style theatre. This theatre company included study groups on class inequity regarding issues on health, housing, and education. We used that information to inspire our original theatre performances at rallies, student conferences, etc. Using a satirical ragtag aesthetic, our focus was on education rather than aspirations of the professional stage. Creating theatre for social change ignited my consciousness. I was hooked! From that springboard I began studying theatre at the university in a more serious way.

Characters

Akili, *college-bound high school senior (eighteen years old)*
Anjanee, *sister to Akili (seventeen years old)*
Tony, *friend to Akili (eighteen-ish years old)*
Rafael, *friend to Akili (eighteen-ish years old)*
Mom, *mother to Akili and Anjanee (forty-ish years old)*
Taina, *girl at a dance, Caribbean-Latina (eighteen-ish years old, not skinny)*
Old Person, *parent to Taina (sixty-ish, but haggard from life's heartaches)*
Uber Driver, *immigrant male (gender can be adjusted)*
Possible Extras: *Dancers; Musicians; DJ (could be voice-over); Teacher; Street People; Double Dutch Jumpers; Vendors; Homeless Person*

Place: A vibrant city with lots of diversity and a Caribbean vibe.
Time: The present.

Scene One

Lights up. We see the inside of the modest but tasteful home of **Akili** *and* **Anjanee**.

Akili (*knocks on the bathroom door*)   Anjanee, let's go. I will not be late catching the bus on account of you.

Anjanee (*quickly opens the door*)   I am ready! I've been waiting on you, brother.

Akili (*yells*)   Bye, Mom. Mom?

Akili *goes to knock on another bedroom door.*

Anjanee   She's asleep. She did another overnight.

Akili   What's up with Banana Republic? Every week her schedule changes now. She didn't sign up for that.

Anjanee   I know right? It sucks.

Akili   That can't be legit! She's management!

Anjanee   She said the job has changed. I don't know . . . Something about algorithms.

Akili   What? Like in music?

Anjanee   No, for like scheduling hours. It's this whole new system they got now.

Akili   How so?

Anjanee   All I know is she is getting killed on this new system. Every week her hours change.

Akili (*puts his ear to the bedroom door*)   Mama, are you awake? We're leaving for school. (*Pause.*) Alright?

Hearing no response, **Akili** *turns and motions for* **Anjanee** *to get going. They start to exit.*

Akili (*to* **Mom**'s *door*)   . . . Don't forget we are going to be late getting home, because we are staying afterwards for the dance.

Mom   Hold on. What was that?

Akili (*almost out the door*)   There's a dance tonight after school.

Mom *opens the door. She is youthful looking, but a bit tired and disheveled.*

Mom   Whoa! Just a minute there, babies.

Akili   What's the matter?

Mom   Tonight? You can't go out tonight.

Akili   Why not?

Anjanee   Yeah, why? What's the matter?

Mom   Do you know what tonight is? (*Pause.*) It's Friday the 13th!

Akili   Whaaaaa . . .? Ohhh . . . Come on. Really?

Anjanee *is more subdued in her reaction.*

Mom   I had my cards read—

Akili   Ok . . . Here we go.

Mom   It is in the cards *and* the numbers. Twenty years ago, exactly! On the same lunar cycle as tonight, a girl was killed by a drunk driver. It was predicted on this night. Same moon. Same date. A dance. That's a fact. And they say she was also warned. And here you are, saying you are going to a dance tonight? No no no, baby! Not tonight you're not.

Akili   I am celebrating with my friends. It's my last dance before graduation. I have to be there.

Mom   Akili, you've seen what happens when kids go against their parents' wishes. The neighborhood is full of those examples.

Akili   Superstition, Mama. Plain and simple. (*Pauses and struggles to stand up to his mother.*)

In two weeks I will be gone. I'm eighteen already. You can't stop me.

Mom (*pauses thoughtfully*)   No, I can't stop you, Akili. Anjanee? What about you?

Anjanee (*struggles between the two*)   It is just one night. I don't have to go.

Akili (*to* **Anjanee**)   How in the . . .? You know what? Never mind. I give up.

Mom *is in his way.* **Akili** *walks around her to get to the door.*

Anjanee   Why are you so worried? We will be fine. (*Checks in with* **Akili** *and changes tone.*)

But hey, if it upsets you that much, I don't have to go.

Mom (*to* **Akili**)   At least wear this for protection. (*Takes her amulet off.*)

Akili   No thank you!

Mom   Wear it, Akili, or I swear you will not get out of this house.

Akili   I am not wearing *that*!

Mom   It will protect you. (*Tenderly.*) Do it for me? Do it for your grandmother then.

Akili   Why did you have to go there?

Mom   This belonged to her. It can't do you any harm to wear it. Can it? (*Pause for a standoff between the two.*) Maybe even bring you some good luck?

Akili   Ugh! Fine!

Mom *kisses* **Akili**'s *forehead and places the amulet around his neck.*

Akili   I'll hide it under my shirt.

Mom That's fine. Is that what you're wearing?

Akili I have clothes in my locker.

Mom Okay.

Akili (*irritably puts it on*) Fashion *faux pas*.

Anjanee *is enjoying* **Akili**'s *displeasure*.

Mom That's my baby! (*To* **Anjanee**.) Promise me you will come straight home from school?

Anjanee I will, Mama. Don't worry.

Akili (*to* **Anjanee**) You ready?

Mom *kisses both her children, makes a mark on their forehead as a blessing ritual.*

Scene Two

They exit to the street. Once outside the sounds of the street come alive. This could be achieved with actual people in place or sound cues or video projections.

The feel is festive, artsy, urban swag, and a bit gritty too. Not everything is pretty, but there is an art and a pulsating life vibe that is electrifying, genuine, and good. There is beautiful architecture and sometimes it is tagged up; sometimes the graffiti is beautiful. There is a sense of community.

The following suggestions should be acted out with a sense of fun energy and should make sense to the time/place being referenced:

- *Jazz from a record store.*
- *A Muslim man selling pies is saying things like "Smells goooood."*
- *Another person is selling loose cigarettes and says, "Got some loosies."*
- *A homeless person known in the community says "Hello," or some other familiar greeting.*
- *Girls are playing Double Dutch.*

If using real actors for Double Dutch, **Anjanee** *tries to jump in.* **Akili** *doesn't let her or takes her out if she makes it in.*

- *Another homeless person is sleeping in a doorway.*
- At the bus stop the **Man Who Dances** is performing for folks as they wait for the bus.

Akili, *still upset, takes his seat at the bus stop and is rude to someone who approaches him—could be a panhandler or the* **Man Who Dances**.

Anjanee That was rude.

Akili Whatever.

Anjanee   Why you so mad?

Akili   I just hate this place.

Anjanee   This here?

Akili   Yes, this here. Look at this. It's dirty. It's crowded. And folks are just plain stupid!

Anjanee   Hey, brother! That's harsh. That's your people you're talking about.

Akili   Yeah, don't I know it. I am going to be so glad to get out of here.

Akili (*seeing that he has hurt her feels a little bad*)   . . . Awww, come on. Don't be like that. You know what I mean.

Anjanee   Not really.

Akili   This is what adults do. It's called progress. They move away and make their own life.

Anjanee   Like *grandma* did when she left the *island*?

Akili   Exactly!

Anjanee   Except grandma came here with her family. What about Mama?

Akili   She will come too.

Anjanee   She will never do that. Her roots—*our* roots go too deep here.

Akili (*sarcastically and scary*)   Roots . . . Like spells and potions.

Anjanee   Don't be a jerk just cuz Mama's a little old-school superstitious.

Akili   A little? How ridiculous was that? How am I going to show up with this gross thing around my neck?

Anjanee (*sassy*)   So don't wear it.

Akili *looks away, purposefully ignoring her, but considering what she has just said. Slight pause before he answers her sarcastically, but doesn't take it off.*

Akili   Amulets! Save me now!

Anjanee   Well, I wouldn't have minded. A little protection don't hurt nobody. Besides, she does it cuz she cares.

A dark cloud has moved in.

Akili (*concerned*)   Hey, what's that behind you?

Anjanee   What? I don't know.

Akili   Don't move.

Anjanee (*scared*)   Okay.

Akili *makes the shush sign as a caution to be quiet.* **Anjanee** *freezes and follows* **Akili**'s *sign language.* **Akili** *moves towards her as if transfixed on an image, raises his hand, and then gooses his sister to scare her.*

Akili   It's an evil spirit!

Anjanee *screams.* **Akili** *is beside himself with laughter at her fright.*

Akili   I am sorry, sis. I couldn't resist.

Slowly **Anjanee** *starts to see the humor and has to laugh a little, but more out of relief.*

Anjanee   I hate you. (*Laughs.*)

Akili   Anjanee, listen to me. We come from a very backward people. And I, for one, am getting out. And you are welcome to come with me. There is nothing here for me, *for us.*

Anjanee   You saying you better than everyone?

Akili   NO! I'm saying—(*Changes his delivery method and starts joking.*) Look! I don't know what I am saying! But know this, when I leave for college this summer, I am on my way up! I am done with being unrepresented. I am done with lack of access to basic services here. I am done! Stick a fork in it! Done!

Anjanee   Well, maybe Mom is right. It might be bad luck to go out tonight. Especially if you're feeling so negative already. This is home!

Akili   Not negative. Positively done! Good riddance (*uses quote fingers*), "home!"

Anjanee (*mildly sarcastic*)   Good riddance, backward folks!

Akili (*emphatically*)   Hello! Home is where the heart is.

Anjanee   Goodbye generations of struggle here.

Akili   Thank you, Boo!

Anjanee   Goodbye family, ancestors, people.

Akili   Wait up now. I didn't say that! I just want better for all of us. Is that a crime?

Anjanee   Goodbye, baby sister.

Akili   Stop it. You know what I mean.

Anjanee   I *do.* (*Beat.*) Do you?

The bus has arrived. A **Homeless Person** *has approached them. It is obvious s/he needs a helping hand.*

Akili (*motions for his sister to get on first*)   Go ahead.

After getting **Anjanee** *on the bus,* **Akili** *gives the* **Homeless Person** *the few coins he has in his pocket.* **Homeless Person** *nods in appreciation.* **Akili** *and* **Anjanee** *board* *the bus. Lights fade. Sounds of a bus pulling out. Jazz music and urban sounds are heard coming up in contrast and in complement to the darkening clouds.*

Scene Three

Lights up. We see the school dance in full swing. Music can be from any current genre depending on the local flavor. **Akili** *is dressed to kill with the amulet under his shirt.* **Akili** *and* **Tony** *check it out, joking and laughing on the sidelines.*

Tony So then I took, and I said, "Hey, *Mamita* . . . I lost my teddy bear. Maybe can I sleep wit chu' tonight?"

Akili Oh no! Please.

Tony Seriously. She was all like—(*Makes a kissy face.*) And then I was all like—

Tony *really starts to show off his ridiculously exaggerated kissing skills.* **Akili** *is still cracking up laughing when* **Rafael** *comes up to them and interrupts.*

Rafael Hey, *Papa*! Congratulations, bruh! (*They shoulder bump handshake "Hello."*) I heard you won that college scholarship.

Akili Sure did! Thanks, man. Congratulations are in order.

Rafael Proud of you, bruh! Now don't go and get big-headed on us. Or we gon' have to keep it real for ya.

Akili Man, shut up!

Rafael Just sayin'. You that you gon' be hobnobbing with fancy chess players don't forget who taught you everything you know. Mr. College Man. I am proud of you, man!

Akili *and* **Rafael** *fist bump, grab hands, and bro hug.*

Rafael Ha ha! Now where's that fine sister of yours?

Akili (*emphasizes her name and a bit of a threat attached*)   Anjanee *(beat)* decided not to come.

Rafael Awww . . . That's too bad. We stuck with ugly you for the night?

Akili Don't make me hurt you. Don't even look at my sister.

Rafael Whaaa . . .? Come on now, I am a nice guy. (*To* **Tony**.) Ain't I a nice guy?

Tony (*jokingly*)   With honorable intentions!

Akili Now I'm glad she isn't here, because I *would* have to hurt you. Both of you.

Rafael WHAT I DO?! (*Referring to* **Akili**.) Yo! He ain't laughing no more.

Tony *and* **Rafael** *laugh harder at* **Akili**'s *expense.*

Rafael Just messin' with chu, bruh. Just messin'.

Tony   She does make you look good though.

Akili *half-pretends he is going to go in for a chest-thump to kick* **Tony**'*s butt.*

Tony   Just kidding, just kidding!

Rafael   Chillax, man! Oh, man, there are some hotties here tonight! Ewww . . . All these curves and me with no brakes. Boom!

Akili   Keep messing with me and I'm gonna make you have an accident.

Tony   Hey! What did the girl traffic light say to the car?

Akili   What?

Tony   Don't look! I am changing! Haaaaa.

Akili   Can we retire him?

Rafael (*referring to* **Tony**)   Why? I like him. That's mahomie!

Akili   I'm not referring to Tony. Our governor! That's the same tired joke he was saying about the traffic situation. He is awful!

Rafael   Oh him. Well, I like him too.

Akili   You have got to be out of your mind. With all the cuts to education he has made?

Rafael   We don't need school anymore. Haven't you heard. They did a whole thing on Fox News about how college is for dummies.

Tony   Oh snap! Akili he talking about chu.

Rafael   There ain't no jobs waiting for us? And besides, I know a thug when I see one. So personally, I think he will make a great president. Straight up. I like it real! If you be a thug, be a thug. So I know what I'm dealing with. Just sayin'.

Tony   Akili, you gonna let this fool talk like this?

Akili   Look I am here to have fun. Not talk political woes.

Rafael (*sees the girl*)   Well, *whoa* is me! Check it out. Check it out.

A couple of students are getting a little freaky on the dance floor, and a teacher comes by to break it up before it gets to be too fresh. **Akili**, **Rafael**, *and* **Tony** *all kind of groan and side snicker in disappointment.*

DJ (*offstage voice*)   We gonna mix it up in here and will be taking your requests in a minute. Behave yourselves out there.

From somewhere in the crowd a space is opened and a girl (**Taina**), *in an outdated outfit from approximately twenty years ago, appears in the crowd. [Note: The outfit shouldn't be too showy as being out of date, just enough to be obvious.]*

Rafael   Oh snap! I remember her from last year.

Tony   I think I remember her too. What's up with dat?

Rafael (*tapping his head*)   I think homegirl got some serious stuff going on!

Tony   She could stand to show a little booty! And she never talks to nobody! I definitely remember her. Oh snap she's coming over here! (*Teasing* **Akili**.) She looking at you.

Taina   Hi.

Akili   Hey. What's up, girl?

Taina   I just heard someone say that you got all these awards today. That's wicked cool!

Akili   Umm . . . yes . . . *cool.* (*Giggles at the outdated slang term "wicked cool."*) Thank you.

Tony (*teasing with more old-school slang*)   Yes! And bodacious.

Rafael   Hello, sweetheart. How you doing? May I introduce myself. My name is Rafael and if you would like to get a little freak on later, please know that I am your *Papi* for the night! A'ight?

Taina (*sincerely confused*)   Excuse me?

Rafael   Well, hello. How you doin'? (*Fake admiration of her body.*) You know they say milk does a body good, but DAMN girl did you have to drink the whole cow?

Taina (*confused and concerned*)   What? Why? Do I look milky?

Rafael *mischievously starts to say something inappropriate, but is cut off by* **Akili**.

Akili   Rafael, stop it. (*To* **Taina**.) Don't listen to him. He's crazy. We don't let him out much.

Tony   Where you from, girl? (*Checks out her outdated clothes*.) Or I should say, where you been? I love your dress. Can I just say, you are really wearing it!

Tony *and* **Rafael** *laugh and cut up.* **Akili** *is about to get annoyed.*

Akili   Okay, that's enough. Don't you got something to do? (*To* **Taina**.) I apologize for both of them.

Taina   That's okay. I remember my first drink. How obnoxious I was.

Tony   What she say?

Rafael   Yeah, she's talking to you!

DJ (*offstage voice*)   Get your old school dance on for this special request.

Taina (*ignoring* **Rafael** *and* **Tony**)   I love this song. You want to dance?

Tony *and* **Rafael** *insincerely encourage* **Akili** *to dance with* **Taina**.

Tony   Go ahead.

Rafael   Yeah. You should, bruh.

Tony (*more teasing and laughing with old-school talk*)   Yeah, go cut a rug.

Akili   I don't think so. Thank you though. You go ahead.

The song is a pop song approximately from twenty years earlier. **Taina** *falls in with the crowd and is an excellent dancer. Her vibe makes everyone want to dance.* (Note: *A song like Michael Jackson's "Thriller" works thematically but may be too controversial.*)

Akili *and* **Taina** *connect as if by magic and* **Akili** *can't help but get swayed into the choreography. They dance wonderfully together. Even* **Rafael** *and* **Tony** *join in after a few minutes.*

Music goes low, the dance continues softly to fade into the background. Lights on **Akili** *and* **Taina** *as the crowd fades away.*

Akili   Oh my God! Where *have* you been, girl? Have I met you before?

Taina   I don't think so.

Akili   So what brought you here?

Taina (*pauses*)   I love to dance.

Akili   Well, I don't. I mean not typically. I don't. In fact, I hate dancing and getting all sweaty, but this was crazy good. I don't even care that I am perspiring like—like I don't know what! (**Taina** *laughs.*) Girl, I am serious. You just don't know.

Taina   It's in your bones!

Akili   You brought it out in me.

Taina   Cool. Dancing is our higher power.

Akili (*tries to remember*)   My grandmother used to say something like that. She loved dancing. Said it was her church!

Taina   Ancestors live through us in the dance!

Akili   Don't take this wrong, but you kind of remind me of her.

Taina   Your grandmother?! (*Laughs.*)

Akili (*laughs*)   Yeah. I don't mean you look old or nothing. It's just that—Never mind! Sorry.

Taina (*laughs*)   Don't worry. It's perfectly fine.

Bachata music and dance has started on the dance floor.

Taina   Hey, do you bachata?

Akili   That's way too old school.

Taina   Just try it.

Akili   I don't think you'll take no for an answer.

Taina   Glad you know it.

Akili   After you . . . (*Follows her to the dance floor.*) You know, my mother told me not to come out tonight.

Taina   You should have listened.

She takes his hand and shows him how to bachata.

Taina   Okay, just follow me. To the right . . . One, two, three, and a little hop on the fourth. One, two, three, hop.

Akili *follows effortlessly and a bit mesmerized; by the time the dance finishes they have formed a good healthy bond with a higher power.*

Lights come up. The dance is ending. **Dancers** *if still on stage exit dreamlike magically, while* **Taina** *tries to say goodbye.* **Akili** *keeps her from exiting.*

Akili   Thanks for the dancing lessons.

Taina   I didn't teach you anything you didn't already have.

Akili   And I want to apologize for those clowns.

Taina   That's okay. Been there. Done that. Just glad that's behind me.

Akili   Being foolish? Or mean?

Taina   Both.

Akili   Really? I can't picture you putting someone down.

Taina   I didn't actually. It was more like I just didn't do anything while my best friend was put down for her weight and her cheap clothes.

Akili   Oh.

Taina   And thanks for standing up for me earlier. I wish I had done that for my friend.

Akili (*sees that she still feels bad about it*)   I am sorry. We all mess around. I am sure it wasn't that bad. What happened? If you don't mind me asking?

Taina   I had a friend. We did everything together. She was super-smart, and I was well . . . always kind of struggled. It was our senior year and I had already been accepted to college, and the way my parents were acting, you would have sworn I hit the Lotto. But I knew I wasn't going to graduate without this math class. She stayed up all night to help me study and I barely passed. To celebrate we went to this dance and I . . . well . . . The Queens of the school actually talked to me. For some reason they started making fun of my friend, and when they asked me if she was my friend, I said something like, "No, not really. I mean I know her but I don't like . . . *know her*, know her." And when a guy they liked started talking to her these girls went in for the kill. They said things like "Love your dress. Is that really a XXXL?" and "Be careful slow dancing. He has a heightened sense of smell." My friend looked at me, but I pretended as if someone was calling me. (*Pause.*) And even though we had come together, I took off with those girls in their car instead.

Akili   When did this happen?

Taina   It's been awhile, but it sure feels like it was yesterday. (*Pause.*) Pretty messed up huh? I will never forgive myself for that. I am determined to say I am sorry.

Akili   I think I know how you feel. My grandmother's dead and I wasn't always good to her either.

Taina   Oh?

Akili   Yeah. She loved me more than anything. And you know how I paid her back? By denying she was my grandmother when she came to this fancy scholarship dinner the school has every year. My mother couldn't make it. So my grandma came and walked in with her pretty simple dress and big smile. She didn't have the right image that I was trying to portray. Not all spiffy and fashionable like the other mothers. She walked in, and you could just feel the judgment from them and I was embarrassed, like a dumb-ass! I can't believe I actually felt ashamed of her. (*Pause.*) It was a huge affair with so many people, that I was able to dodge her. She lived with us, so when I got home that night, she was there, and I know she knew what I had done but worse is that I think she knew *why*. But she just gave me a big hug and said how proud she was of me and my accomplishments. That I was her dream come true and that she loved me. But I know she knew what I did.

Taina   I think I know how you feel.

Akili   You know I've never told anyone that story. No one.

Taina   Thanks for trusting me with it.

Akili   Thank you too.

Taina (*pause*)   Well. Good night. (*Almost makes it offstage.*)

Akili   Hey, do you have to go home right now?

Taina   Kind of.

Akili   Listen, I like you. I don't usually like everyone I meet. But I'm leaving for college soon and—Would it be crazy to ask you to come with me to this beautiful spot where you can see all of the city?

Taina   Sounds kind of far. Where is that?

Akili   A graveyard. (*Immediately* **Taina** *reacts with a big head shake no.*) But just trust me. You'll love it.

Taina   How will we get there? How will I get home?

Akili   I'll drop you off. I will get an Uber.

Taina (*confused by the word "Uber"*)   . . . An *Uber*? And you want to go there now? What for?

Akili   I want you to meet my grandmother.

Taina   What?!

Akili   You'll see, you'll see . . . there's nothing spooky. I promise. I just want to see her grave one last time before I leave and I want your company. I think you understand why I need to do this and I don't want to go alone. Please say yes. (*Pause.*) Please?

Taina (*pause*)   Okay.

Akili   Yeah? Really?

Taina   Yes. (*Beat of slight hesitation.*) Sure.

Akili (*teases* **Taina** *by mimicking her and using quotation fingers*)   ". . . Cool."

They exit laughing.

Scene Four

Lights up. We see the gravesite on a mountain top with a view of city lights in the distance. **Akili** *and* **Taina** *enter laughing, somewhat dancing, maybe singing the same song from the dance. Both are having a great time with each other. They reach the grave and compose themselves a bit.*

Akili   This is it. Just look at that view.

Taina   You weren't kidding. It's beautiful. Why did your family bury her so far away?

Akili   I guess it was affordable?

They are silent for a moment as they contemplate **Akili**'s *answer.*

I come here to think sometimes and just get away from everything. (*Addresses the grave.*) Grandma, I didn't properly introduce my *cool* friend—(*Realizes he doesn't know* **Taina**'s *name.*) By the way, what's your name?

Taina (*playfully mimicking the line from the Sherlock Holmes movie* The Hound of Baskervilles)   "Well I'd tell ya, but then I'd have to kill ya."

Akili (*laughing*)   With my grandmother right here! You won't get away with it. She was into spirits. So don't mess. I am protected.

Akili *dangles the amulet sticking out from under his shirt. They laugh.*

Taina   What's that?

Akili   This is what my mother made me wear tonight. For protection.

Taina   Looks amazing.

Akili   It's weird.

Taina   Why do you say that? It looks really old too.

Akili   It is actually. It belonged to my grandmother.

Taina   Is it for good luck?

Akili   Good luck. . . to ward away evil spirits . . . prevent tiger attacks while you bathe . . . You name it and my mother has a cure for it.

Pause as **Taina** *really looks at it.*

Taina   I think it is cool.

Akili (*laughs again at* **Taina's** *use of the word cool*)   Well, I've never been attacked by a tiger in my tub. So I guess it works. You hear that, Grandma? She thinks it's *cool*.

Taina   May I see it?

Akili *takes it off and hands it to her.* **Taina** *studies it long and hard. It has a message for her.*

Akili   Typically, you're supposed to take a cleansing bath with it too. But I think my mother knew she wasn't going to get the full commitment out of me tonight.

Taina   It's not too late.

Akili   Yeah, well maybe it'll rain. Dang it! I forgot the egg-shell powder.

Taina   Rain would be a beautiful cleansing. I'll bathe with you. (*Realizes what she just said.*) With clothes on of course!

Akili   Of course!

Taina   It *does* have an energy.

Akili   Girl, not you too.

Taina   Maybe you should return it to your grandmother. Maybe bury it here.

Akili   Maybe we should do a voodoo dance on her grave too. She'd love that.

Taina   Not a bad idea. Let's show her what you learned today. Come on.

Akili *teases by playing bachata music from his phone.*

Taina *is rather fascinated by the phone/music.*

Taina   Wow! That's amazing. Perfect magical accompaniment. Come on!

Akili *tries to resist, but gives in.*

Akili   Whatever.

Their dance has the feel of a higher power at work: a connection with **Akili's** *grandmother and the ancestors.* **Taina** *and* **Akili** *break the spell with good-natured laughter.*

Akili (*to the grave*)   Me dancing is pretty funny huh, Grandma? (*Sentimentally to* **Taina**.) Awww . . . I can hear her laughing.

Taina   Well, yeah . . . That's cause you dance funny. (*Jokingly to grave.*) He's still learning. Forgive him.

Akili (*laughing*)   Yes. (*Suddenly very sentimental.*) Forgive me.

Taina (*long pause*)   She has.

Akili   I would do anything to go back in time.

Taina   Me too.

Akili   You'll find your old friend.

Taina (*sighs*)   I don't know that. (*Frustrated.*) I feel so stuck. At least you have this place.

Akili   Yeah. But the worst part is that I never got to apologize.

Taina   Maybe all we can do is try to be better next time. Try to be kinder.

Akili   Not just in word either. But in *deed.*

Taina   Indeed!

Akili (*referring to* **Taina**'s *play on words*)   Nice.

Taina   Without that kind of commitment, we won't find peace. Take it from me. (*Intentionally trying to keep the mood light talks to the grave*) What's that? Sure thing. OK . . . I will let him know.

Akili   What she say?

Taina (*as if trying to decipher*)   Nunnn . . . yaaaa?

Akili   Nunya?

Taina   Nunya business!

Akili   Well played!

Taina (*refers to the amulet*)   I hear her saying you should bury this, take time out from the past and come back for it when you're ready.

Akili   Ready for what?

Taina   You'll just know.

Akili   Sounds kind of crazy but I'd love to bury it along with all the struggles I see, along with all the day-to-day grind and have everyone work less and enjoy life more.

Taina *has been burying the amulet as he speaks.* **Akili** *has been sitting down looking out at the view.* **Taina** *rejoins him and looks at the breathtaking view. It is the purest of innocence and love.*

Akili   I knew you were the right one to come here with.

The lights get warmer. Both look out at the view. **Akili** *takes* **Taina**'s *hand. There is a long pause before* **Taina** *speaks.*

Taina (*softly*)   Taina.

Akili (*couldn't hear*)   What's that?

Taina   Taina. My name, is Taina.

They sit side by side gazing out at the view, holding hands, as the lights fade. Sounds and lights of the city far away take over.

Scene Five

Lights up. We hear the sounds of the metro pulling into a train station. It is approximately five months later. **Akili** *is in his hometown on his first winter break from college. He looks around for his Uber taxi. Not seeing it. He pulls out his cell phone.*

Akili   Hey, sis. What's up? I saw you called. No don't bother Moms. I'll call her later. (*Pause.*) Because I can't. I have too much going on to come home this time. It's only my first semester. Give me a break. It's just not easy to come for visits. None of your business where I am. Next summer? Home for the whole break? I don't know. I can't promise. (*Exasperated.*) Because I might have a job next summer. Don't start on me. You starting to sound like you think you're my mother. Oh, girl, please. Of course I love my family. Look I am sorry. I just can't right now. I have so much on my plate, it's ridiculous. You know what? It's alright, you don't get it. Yeah, seriously. That's right. Whatever.

He sees the Uber.

Okay gotta go. Kiss Mom for me. Tell her, I love her. I'll call her back later. Bye!

Hi. Are you my ride? What's my name?

Driver   Yes I am. Hi, Akili.

Akili   Great. Thanks.

He gets in.

Driver   You here on winter break from school?

Akili   Yes.

Driver   I thought so. You coming to spend time with your family huh?

Akili   No, not this time.

Driver   Oh . . . . Okay, okay, no problem. You going to hang out with some friends. That's good too.

Akili   Actually I am going to see a girl.

Driver   Ohh I see. A special lady.

Akili   No. Well, actually yes. I guess. We met briefly before I left to school. But her number doesn't work and she hasn't kept in touch.

Driver (*jokingly*)   Women, ehh?

Akili (*laughs*)   Yeah, right? Everyone is busy, I get that. I just want to know what's up with her? That's all.

Driver   Do you think she will remember you?

Akili   I am sure of it. (*Beat.*) Well at least that's the plan.

Driver   Sounds like you really like her. Sometimes it is like that. You meet someone and POW! Can't get them out of your mind. (*Smiles and drifts at his memory.*)

Akili   Sir? The light has turned green.

Driver   Oh okay, no problem, no problem. (*Drives a bit.*) What you going to say when you see her?

Akili   I don't really know. This is just something I have to do.

They drive in silence. **Akili** *is looking for the house.*

Akili   Okay, I think that's it right there. Yes. Yes. Definitely. That's it. Right here, right here.

He gets out of the car and then thinks for a minute. He is nervous with anticipation.

Ok. Great! Thanks, man.

Driver   Thank you. And good luck.

Akili *goes to knock on the door and feels nervous for some reason and stops for a minute to check his hair, his teeth for food, straightens his clothes, etc. and then knocks. It takes a while for an older person with a heaviness of spirit to open the door.*

Old Person   Yes? How may I help you?

Akili   Hello. Forgive me for just dropping by like this, but is Taina home?

Old Person (*disturbed*)   What? Who are you?

Akili   I am a friend of hers. Well sort of. I met her this past summer at our high-school dance and afterwards I dropped her off here.

Old Person (*mounting anger*)   What are you talking about?

Akili   I am pretty sure it was this house.

Old Person   Go away!

Old Person *tries to close the door.* **Akili** *still tries to talk to engage.*

She was wearing a . . .

Akili *describes the outfit* **Taina** *had worn to the dance.*

Old Person   Who the hell are you?

Akili   My name is Akili. Look. I am sorry. I hope I didn't get her in any trouble or any—

Old Person How could you? Who do you think you are? Coming here and asking for my Taina?

Akili I don't mean any disrespect. I just thought that maybe—

Old Person Taina was my daughter! And she was wearing that outfit twenty years ago when she was killed in an auto accident coming back from her high-school dance.

Akili Wha. .? Nooo that's imposs—

Old Person Is this your idea of a cruel joke? Who sent you here?

Akili No! I swear, I—

Old Person Get off my porch before I hit you or call the cops!

Old Person *raises their cane as if to hit* **Akili** *and backs him off the porch. Infuriated, the* **Old Person** *slams the door.*

Stunned **Akili** *finally composes himself and takes out his cell phone. He wipes and holds back tears as he talks. The rain starts to fall.*

Akili (*trying to compose himself, wipes away a tear*) Hey, Mom? Yeah, it's me. I am here. Yeah. How about that? Surprise! (*Pause.*) I have no idea where this rain came from either. I miss you too. I've been doing a lot of thinking, Ma. We have a lot to catch up on. Oh yeah?

That's awesome! That sounds amazing. I can smell your good food from here. (*Long pause.*) Hey, Mom, can I ask you an important favor? Would you come with me to Grandma's grave? Tonight. Please? Yeah, it's important to me. I have something I need to retrieve. I'll explain later. (*Pause as he struggles with the next line trying not to cry.*) I need to apologize to you and to Grandma. Thanks, Ma. (*Pause.*) I love you. I love you. I'm coming home.

Lights fade as indigenous African-based Caribbean music or a fusion of some sort with drumming that connects **Akili** *to his roots comes up and holds the audience, builds to a crescendo. Tears come down* **Akili**'s *face as rain begins to fall. The rain is a cleansing.*

End of play.

Suggested Exercises for Educators and Teaching Artists for *Homecoming Dance*

Before reading or seeing the play

- Classroom Assignment:

  Create a "family heritage museum" with your class. Ask each student to bring in a family heirloom or cherished object that carries meaning from their family history and/or culture (if they can't bring in the actual object, they can bring in a photo or drawing of it). Ask the students to write a description (about one paragraph long) of the object and why it holds meaning for them and their family or cultural heritage. Some suggested prompts: Who did it belong to? Who owns it now? Who gave it to them? When do you use it/look at it? How does it make you feel to see or handle it?

  On the day this assignment is due, set up the room to resemble a museum. Each student should display their object and description. Divide the class in half. The first half stands next to their "exhibit." The second half visits the various exhibits. Invite them to ask questions of the student exhibitors. After an appropriate amount of time, switch and have the visitors to the museum become the exhibitors and vice versa.

- Classroom Exercise:

  Ask the students to write a monologue in which they speak to the object they presented in the "family heritage museum." The student should tell the object about a time when they felt that this object and/or the ritual surrounding it was no longer useful, and they wanted to distance themselves from the object, the ritual, or both. Where were they? What made them feel this way? What did they do as a result? How did they feel afterwards?

- Homework Assignment:

  Ask the students to create a response monologue from the perspective of the object from the museum. Ask the students to consider what the object might want from the student. What has the object seen or carried with it all these years? What might the object want to ensure is not forgotten? Consider sharing these monologues out loud, with one person reading the "student character" and one person reading the object. Ask the student which monologue they want to read.

After reading or seeing the play

- Classroom Exercise:

  Break the class into small groups. Have each group discuss the following: Who or what was Taina? Describe the character's history as you understand it. What was her purpose in the play? Have you ever met someone who helped you solve a problem or with whom you revealed a moment that you regret? After ten minutes, return to the full group. Have the small groups share their discussion points.

- Classroom Exercise:

As noted by the playwright, the play was inspired by a young man who wrote a poem of gratitude for his grandmother, who had passed away. Ask students to choose someone in their life (living or deceased) for whom they are grateful. The students should write a poem of gratitude for this person. It does not have to rhyme. Ask volunteers to share their poems.

Bonus round: Divide the class into pairs (a group of three is fine if you don't have even numbers). One person should read the poem, while another performs accompanying gestures. To create the gestures, have the pair decide on eight of the most vivid words in the poem. Then they should create a gesture for each of those words. Encourage them to explore abstract gestures, rather than try to enact the word (like the game charades).

Snap the Sun

Pia Wilson

Background and Insights into *Snap the Sun*

from Pia Wilson

Notes on Casting

The cast consists of two teen girls (Dawn and Lisa), one teen boy (Jason), and one teen of any gender (KC).

Notes on Production

There aren't any curse words. As to slang, before making any changes, please contact me. Snapchat and Instagram are bound to go out of style at some point. If the producers want to update the social media platforms in the play, please contact me.

The Inspiration for This Play

I was at a house by a beautiful lake, and the view was stunning. I wanted to take a picture and show people on Instagram this beautiful site. No picture I took matched what I saw with my eyes. And so, I decided to just be in the moment.

Major Themes

Being in the moment. How we view ourselves versus how people view us.

Food for Thought

I hope the play inspires people to take in and enjoy the environment around them, instead of trying to share the environment with people not there at that time.

Entrance into the World of Theatre

A friend of a friend needed a play, so I offered to write one. I became more interested in theatre once I became involved with it as a writer. I write plays as well as TV and film. I love plays because they are so character rich and can be much more experimental than TV or film is allowed to be. Language is important in plays, which I love. In TV/ film, the visual is considered more important. My favorite part of theatre though is how it changes from performance to performance and how you get to experience your work through the audience's eyes. It's ephemeral in nature, and I love that.

Characters

Lisa
Dawn
Jason
KC

Place: in the woods near camp.
Time: present.

Dawn *is staring out on the horizon. She holds her phone up to take a picture. She looks at the picture, and it isn't what she wants. She tries to take the picture again with the phone horizontal. Again, the picture isn't good. She tries standing on her tippy toes, crouching like a tiger. She doesn't know it, but her friends—*Jason, **Lisa**, *and* **KC**—*have snuck up on her. They start laughing.*

KC   What are you doing?

Lisa   Are you and your phone dating?

Jason   Yeah, is there something we should know about?

Dawn   Ha ha, real funny. I'm trying to take a picture of the sunrise.

Lisa   This is crazy. It is really too early for us to be up like this.

KC   Camp life. In the city, yeah, it's too early. Out here, it's different. I don't mind so much.

Jason   Nah, it's still too early. (*Taking* **Dawn's** *phone.*) Let me see.

Dawn   Give me back my phone, Jason.

Jason (*taking a picture and looking at it*)   Hmm. That is not good. (*Takes another picture from another angle.*) Huh. Weird.

Dawn   Give me my phone.

Jason *ignores her, holding the phone up in the air and trying to take the picture that way. Still not satisfactory.*

Jason   Your phone is broke.

Dawn   No, it is not. It's brand new.

KC (*to* **Jason**)   What did you think you could do that she couldn't?

Jason   I don't know; I'm taller.

Dawn *and* **KC** *look at each other and start laughing.*

Dawn and KC   What?

KC   Taller!

Dawn   So dumb.

Lisa *takes out her phone and tries to take the picture. Doesn't come out well for her either. She tries to take a selfie with the sunset, and it comes out even worse.*

Jason   Don't break the phone with your face.

Lisa   Only if I was taking a picture of you!

Dawn *and* **KC** *giggle. It's not clear whether they're laughing with* **Lisa** *or at her.*

Lisa *looks at the horizon.*

Lisa   It's like the phone can't see what I see.

KC   While you and your phone are really close, you're not the same. You are not one being.

Dawn   Her phone is Lisa's OTP.

KC   The human eye has a lot more pixels—

Jason   Nerd alert!

He starts to beep like a robot, saying "nerd alert" over and over in a robot voice.

Dawn (*talking about* **Jason**)   That is the nerdiest thing I've ever seen.

Lisa (*to* **Dawn**)   For real. (*To* **KC**.) KC, we don't need a lecture.

KC (*speaking louder*)   The human eye has a lot more pixels than any phone camera.

Jason   Yawn.

KC (*as if* **Jason** *has said nothing*)   About 130 million pixels. P.S. Everybody, we're all nerds. That's how we got to come on this trip in the first place.

Jason   Nope. My squad is cool.

Lisa   What squad? Your squad of one?

Dawn   We're your squad, Jason.

Jason   To be honest, no, you're not. My squad can hoop and play football and be smart. And they all have shoegame.

Lisa   Oh boy. Shoegame.

Jason   You know what's up.

KC   Amazing.

Jason   Yeah, you know what's up.

Dawn   Why is your head so big?

Jason *waves off the comment.*

Lisa   Roast him!

Jason   How are you going to tell somebody to roast me? Your skin is so crispy you look like you've been roasted since you were born.

Lisa   Rejected! I'm beautiful. I'm so pretty that the camera can't even capture it, like the nerd said.

KC   That's not exactly what I said. And again, we're all nerds here. This is a science camp.

Dawn   You just failed terribly, Jason.

Lisa   He tried though.

Jason (*insincere*)   You're bullying me.

KC   It's not our fault you can't roast and can't handle the fire.

Jason (*insincere again*)   That hurt my self-esteem.

Lisa   Excuses. Excuses.

The sky catches **Dawn***'s eye again.*

Dawn   Look, guys.

Lisa   It's so pretty. All the colors. I wonder why it doesn't look this way at home.

Jason   It does, dope.

Lisa   No, it doesn't. The sky is bigger here.

KC   Actually—

Everybody groans.

Fine. If you don't want to know . . .

Everyone continues to stare at the sky.

You really don't want to know?

Dawn   Go ahead and tell us before you die, KC.

Jason   It does look the same. We just never look at it.

Lisa   She said "KC," not "Jason." Somebody call a counselor: Jason's gone loopy.

Dawn and Jason   Loopy?

KC (*to* **Lisa**)   Are you a hundred years old or something?

Lisa   No, I just keep it a hundred.

Jason   Ha, Lisa's old. Hi, Granny.

Dawn and KC   Granny?

KC   Are you seven years old or something? Say Grandma.

Jason (*to* **KC**)   OK, Grandma.

KC   Nice. OK, that was a good one. I respect that.

Dawn *takes another picture of the sky.*

Lisa   It's never going to look the same.

Dawn   That's OK. I just want the picture.

KC   Yeah, it'll be good to help you remember how the sky looked up here when you get home.

Lisa   How big it is.

KC   It's not bigger. There's just less obstruction out here. No tall buildings to get in the way. Not so many people.

Jason   That's what I was going to say before I was so rudely interrupted. It's an optical illusion, like moon illusion.

KC   Told you: we're all nerds.

Jason   Nope. Knowing stuff doesn't make you a nerd.

Lisa   Jason's right, everybody, knowing stuff doesn't make you a nerd. Knowing about things like moon illusion does.

Dawn   What's moon illusion again?

KC   Jason? Want to explain?

Jason   I don't know. Let me Google it.

Lisa   You know what it is!

Dawn   And you know we don't get internet out here anyway.

Jason   It's killing me! You know how many Snaps I'm missing right now?

Lisa   I'm missing everybody's TikToks.

Jason   At least they will still be there when we get back to civilization. The Snaps will be gone!

KC   I'm pretty sure Mike and Derek will Snap their sneakers a billion more times when we get back.

Jason   I told you: they've got shoegame.

KC   I bet you know more about moon illusion than you do about sneakers.

Jason   No, I don't.

Dawn   It's just us up here, Jason. You don't have to pretend.

Lisa   Yeah, nobody's going to Snap you saying you don't know anything about sneakers.

KC   Or care about sneakers.

Jason   Oh, I care about sneakers.

Lisa *takes a picture of the sky.*

Lisa   For Insta, when we get back. I know it won't look the same, but . . .

Dawn   But at least everyone will still be jealous anyway.

KC   Will they be jealous?

Dawn   Wouldn't you be, if you weren't here?

Jason   They're jealous because you got to come up with me.

Everybody else groans.

Dawn It would be nice if you would just relax, Jason. It's just us. You don't have to keep up a front all the time.

Jason OK. I like talking about different stuff with you guys.

Lisa I'm not a guy, but carry on.

Jason I like sneakers and all. But that's all Mike and Derek want to talk about. I mean, OK, when you get new sneakers, snap them, yeah. But nobody gets new sneakers every week! It makes me tired, man.

Dawn It's OK, Jason, this is a safe space to nerd out. Anybody else?

Jason And to be even more honest, it's exhausting to have it all: good looks, smarts, and coolness. I'm the total package.

Dawn Like I said: Anybody else have something they want to say in this safe space?

Jason To be even more really really honest—

Dawn Anybody else? I'll take a squirrel at this point. Anybody but Jason.

Jason I'm still your fave.

Lisa Well, to be honest, I don't know what moon illusion is. I mean, I kind of know, but I'm not sure.

Dawn and KC Really?

Lisa I said I kind of know, guys! I just might have to look up one or two things.

KC We're not judging you, Lisa. We're just kind of surprised.

Dawn Yeah. You're the queen of selfies, but you're also the queen of astronomy.

Lisa It takes a star to know one.

Dawn (*rolls eyes*) I think I just sprained my eyes from rolling them. Oh my God, somebody, help.

Lisa *gives* **Dawn** *a playful tap.*

Jason Moon illusion is an optical illusion, Lisa. The moon seems bigger when it is close to the horizon than it does when it's higher in the sky. Sort of like a pimple that looks bigger on your nose than it does on your cheek. You know all about that, don't you, KC?

KC Ha ha, so funny I forgot to laugh.

Jason But laughter is the best medicine. Help you clear up that face.

Dawn Look, guys, the sun is almost up. Let's take a group selfie.

Lisa To go where?

Daw   Insta.

Lisa and Jason   No.

Dawn   Are you saying you don't want to be seen with me?

Jason   Not just you.

Lisa   Insta is forever.

Dawn   Fine. Snapchat.

Jason   Not my Snap.

Lisa   Mine either. And I need approval over who you send it to.

Dawn   Forget it then. I'll just Snap the sun.

KC   I think they just don't want me in the shot, Dawn. I am the biggest nerd in school, after all. You can't pretend to be cool, when you've got photographic evidence you've been hanging around me. You guys get together, and I'll take the picture.

Jason (*as he pulls* **KC** *into the picture to take the selfie*)   God! Come on, nerd!

Dawn *hands her camera to* **Jason**.

Dawn (*uses air quotes when she says "tall"*)   Since you're so tall, you have the longest arms.

They all do their own pose and when **Jason** *takes the picture, lights blackout.*

End of play.

Suggested Exercises for Educators and Teaching Artists for *Snap the Sun*

Before reading or seeing the play

- Classroom Exercise:

  Ask students to think of or imagine a place where they have no access to the internet or social media? Where are they? What time of day or night is it? What do they see? What sounds do they hear? What do they smell? What might they touch (what objects, surfaces)? How does it feel cold, hot, rough, soft?

  Who else is present? How does the lack of technology change your interactions with the other people?

  Notice how your body feels recalling this place and time. Do you notice any physical changes in your body, including your breath?

  After the meditation: Ask students either to draw a picture or write a poem that captures how this meditation made them feel. They do not need to write their names on their work. Display the drawings and poems on a wall, board, or dedicated part of the classroom, like a gallery. Allow students time to view the gallery.

- Classroom Exercise:

  Wall Poems (courtesy of Judy Tate, Asylum Productions):

  Create a second gallery opposite the one above by constructing a "word wall." On a large piece of butcher's paper or giant Post-It™ pads, write the following categories: Color, Item of Clothing, Vehicle, Kind of Music, Time of Day. Under each category divide the section into two subheadings, "The Real Me Is" and "The Virtual Me Is." Using Sharpies or colored markers, let students travel from section to section filling in words and short phrases under each category that characterize their two selves, real and virtual.

  After everyone has written words and phrases in each category, let students again study the entire board, each with their own piece of paper or notebook. Let them pull words and phrases, their own and others, from all categories to construct a poem which portrays a person (now a character) with elements of both selves. Note: the poems can be structured in any way the writer chooses so long as they contain the phrases "The Real Me" (is) and "The Virtual Me" (is) at least once each.

  Have each student read their character poem with the class if they are comfortable.

After reading or seeing the play

- Classroom Exercise:

Divide the class into groups of four (if you don't have even numbers you can have a group of three). Each person in the group should select a character from the play (they should each choose a different character, or you can randomly assign them characters). Have students create a face mask out of paper. On one side, ask them to write how they think this character wants to be perceived by others. On the other side, they should write what this character is really like. (They should use the play text for inspiration, but they can also use their imagination.) They should then individually explore how the person described on this side of the mask stands and moves. What might be a typical gesture of this character? Next, ask them to choose one line of dialogue from the play that fits this persona.

Ask each small group to present their characters wearing this side of the mask. Standing in a line, they should relay their individual line of dialogue and characteristic gesture; i.e., Person One says a line of dialogue and simultaneously does their gesture to Person Two, who then relays their own line and gesture to Person Three, and so on.

After each group has "performed" their relay, repeat the exercise, but using the flip side of the mask. As a class, discuss the differences students felt embodying these two sides of the characters: What did they notice about themselves and about how others interacted with them?

The Bottom Line

A one-act play

David Lee White

Background and Insights into *The Bottom Line*

from David Lee White

Notes on Casting

The character of Jordan can be played by an actor of any gender or ethnicity. Robin and Olivia should be Black/Female. Portis should be white/Male.

Notes on Production

Slang may be updated to language that is more current, provided the intent of the dialogue doesn't change.

The Inspiration for This Play

The play was inspired by the years I spent working in Trenton, New Jersey, writing plays for young actors based on situations in their own lives. I often collaborated on these plays with Rodney Gilbert, and his input was vital in shaping their points of view. For years, people living outside of Trenton were terrified to set foot in the city, primarily because of the local newspaper which capitalized on crime by publishing stories with shocking headlines. In talking with the paper's editor, I was struck by the way he felt it was important to distance himself from any story and only present "the facts." He seemed blissfully unaware of his own biases. During one performance of my play If I Could, in My Hood, I Would ... *he took questions from the audience and was confronted (for the first time?) by city residents who took him to task for not understanding the racial dynamics at work in Trenton. It was fascinating to watch these issues slowly dawn on him, but I'll never know if it really changed the way he viewed his journalistic responsibility or not. He left the paper shortly after that and moved on to another city.*

Major Themes

Media vs. reality. Understanding the social and cultural context that accompanies every crime story.

Food for Thought

I hope it inspires the audience to look a little deeper into the stories behind the public story. Communities can never completely separate themselves from their historical context, and it's impossible to fully understand a story that appears in the news without also understanding the dynamics of the community in which the story takes place.

Entrance into the World of Theatre

I've been doing theatre since the fifth grade, which was the first time I was ever given the chance to do it. I performed throughout high school and college and received an M.F.A. in acting. After pursuing an acting career in Chicago, I relocated to New Jersey where I spent fourteen seasons as the Associate Artistic Director of Passage Theatre in Trenton. Passage specialized in producing new plays and that, combined with the work I was doing with young people in the area, encouraged me to write new plays specifically for them. In many of my plays, there are roles for adult actors as well so that student actors can work side by side with professionals. Rodney Gilbert was one of the professionals I hired several times and he, in turn, hired me to work with him in Newark. I think theatre is unique in that anyone can do it. You don't need to be an expert in any kind of specialized technology. You can learn to do it in your basement, backyard, or classroom. All you need to start is a group of people that want to tell a story to an audience. It's the entertainment medium from which all others grow. If you want to do a play bad enough, nothing can stop you.

Characters

Newspaper staff:
Portis, *male, white, newspaper editor, middle-aged*
Jordan, *male or female, any ethnicity, intern, early twenties*

Jack Holland's family:
Olivia, *female, Black, seventeen*
Robin, *female, Black, Olivia's mother, thirties*
AJ, *male, Black, Olivia's cousin, twelve (or slightly younger)*

Place: A home in the city.
Time: The present.

We're in the living room of the Holland house. **AJ** *is arranging various food dishes on the table.*

Robin (*from offstage*)   AJ? (*Pause.*) AJ you hear me?

AJ   Yes, ma'am.

Robin   Come in the kitchen and help me with the potato salad.

AJ   I want to make sure everyone is sitting in the right place.

Robin *enters.*

Robin   Your cousin can set the table. Where is she?

AJ *shrugs.*

Robin   You want to use your talking voice? Can't hear a shrug.

AJ   I don't know where she is.

Robin   Okay. Finish setting the table, then come to the kitchen. I need you to cut the potatoes. (*Pause.*) You hear me?

AJ   Yes.

Robin   Yes, what?

AJ   Yes, ma'am.

Robin *exits.* **AJ** *continues to set the table. After a moment, there's a knock on the door.* **AJ** *answers it. It is* **Portis** *and* **Jordan**.

Portis   Hello, sir.

AJ *stares at them in silence.*

Portis   Is your mom or dad home?

AJ   No.

Portis   Is anyone at home?

AJ   My Aunt Robin.

Portis   Can I talk to her?

AJ   We're about to have dinner.

Portis   Mmm. I can smell it.

AJ   My aunt cooks good.

Portis   Can we talk to her? Can we talk to your aunt?

AJ *considers for a moment, then—*

AJ   Hang on.

AJ *exits.*

Jordan   Can we just walk into someone's house like this?

Portis   Kid let us in.

Jordan   Maybe they don't want to be bothered.

Portis   We're not bothering them.

Jordan   But—

Portis   Maybe instead of saying all your questions out loud, you could just jot them down. Then when we get back to the office you can ask them all at once.

Jordan *takes out a notebook.*

Jordan   I forgot my pen.

Portis *digs in his jacket and takes out a pen.*

Portis   Here. But bring your own stuff from now on.

Jordan *clicks the pen. A light comes on.*

Jordan   It has a light on it.

Portis   It's so you can write in the dark.

Jordan   Cool.

Jordan *clicks the pen off and on. This annoys* **Portis**.

Portis   Stop.

Jordan   Sorry. Am I allowed to talk to them?

Portis   No. You are an intern. Watch, listen, and take notes.

Olivia *enters through the front door, surprising* **Portis** *and* **Jordan**.

Olivia   Who are you?

Portis   Oh! Geez. Hi.

Olivia   Who are you?

Portis   Ed Portis. I'm from the *Daily Standard*. This is –

Olivia   MOM!

Portis   It's a newspaper.

Olivia   I know it's a newspaper. MOM!

Robin *and* **AJ** *enter.*

Robin   What's going on?

Portis   Ma'am. Hi. Ed Portis. I'm with the *Daily Standard*.

Jordan   It's a newspaper.

Olivia   We know.

Robin   Who's that?

Portis   This is Jordan. My intern.

AJ   Wants to talk about Jackie, I bet.

Robin   AJ!

AJ   Wants to write about Jackie.

Robin   AJ, go to the kitchen and cut potatoes.

AJ   Don't mess up the table.

Portis   I won't.

AJ   Everybody's gotta sit where they belong.

AJ *exits into the kitchen.*

Robin   Getting ready to eat.

Portis   I can see that. Smells good.

Robin   All AJ's favorite foods. The kid is picky. Make him what he wants or he won't eat at all.

Portis   I was the same way. My mom must have made hot dogs three times a week just to get me to eat. Look, your son is right. I work at the paper. I'm a writer.

Robin   I know. I read your column.

Portis   Really?

Olivia   You write all that stuff about what the city was like in the old days.

Portis   Yeah. That's me.

Olivia   This ain't the old days.

Robin   Mind yourself, Olivia. (*To* **Portis**.) You wrote that story about the apartments over on Stuyvesant.

Portis   Glad they're fixing them up, but if they price out the current tenants—

Robin   They're not gonna be able to afford to the live there.

Portis   It's gonna be a problem.

Robin   A big problem.

Portis   You remember how nice those places used to be?

Robin   Oh, yeah. I grew up on Randolph.

Portis   I grew up on Sullivan. My mom made Sunday dinner for the whole neighborhood sometimes. Potluck. Bring what you can.

Robin   Mine did too. Fried chicken, macaroni salad, burgers on the grill . . .

Portis   We'd still be in the back yard until the sun went done.

Robin   We weren't allowed to go to the other side of the park. Never really saw Sullivan.

Portis   I never really saw Randolph.

Jordan   And I'm not from around here.

Portis *shoots a look at* **Jordan.**

Robin   We still try to have dinner at the same time every Sunday. Just the four of us. (*Pause.*) The three of us.

Portis   We're sorry for your loss, ma'am. Sorry about your son.

Olivia   You writing about him?

Portis   I don't want to interrupt your dinner, I really don't. But if I could have just five minutes—

Olivia   No.

Portis   I don't mean any harm at all.

Olivia   This is our first dinner at home since –

Jordan   We want to write about the real Jackie.

Portis *glares at* **Jordan**.

Robin   The real Jackie, huh?

Jordan   Yes. Not the shooting, not the robbery, that's already out there. We just want to know who your son was.

Robin   Why don't you sit down and stay?

Olivia   Mom!

Robin   Give me a minute. I have to make sure AJ isn't burning the place down.

Portis   We don't want to intrude.

Olivia   Already did that.

Robin   Take a seat. Olivia will be happy to talk to you.

Olivia   No I won't.

Robin   Olivia's a bit upset about this whole thing.

Portis   Understandably.

Robin   I'm trying to teach her that not everyone is out to drag us through the mud.

Olivia   Mom!

Portis   No one is dragging anyone through any mud.

Olivia   We'll see.

Robin   We have guests, Olivia. Mind yourself.

Olivia   Okay.

Robin *starts to exit to the kitchen, then turns around.*

Robin   You think anybody's gonna listen to you about those apartments on Stuyvesant? You think what you wrote can change anything?

Portis   Maybe it can. I don't know. I hope so.

Robin *exits.* **Olivia** *goes to sit down at the table.* **Jordan** *is clearly afraid of having spoken out of turn, but* **Portis** *gives her a supportive squeeze on the arm.* **Portis** *and* **Jordan** *sit down.*

Portis   So. What school do you go to?

Olivia   The only one.

Portis   No, there are a few charter schools that—

Olivia   —That are all gonna close in a couple of years. Who needs the hassle?

Portis   Almost prom season. You going?

Olivia   Oh, my God. What are you doing?

Portis   I'm just . . . small talk, you know?

Olivia   Let's not do that.

Portis   I'm sorry.

Olivia   I mean do I look like someone excited for prom?

Portis   No, I was . . . I'm sorry. You're right.

Olivia   You want to talk about Jackie, let's talk about Jackie.

Portis   Okay. He was your brother, right?

Olivia   Yes.

Portis   Both parents?

Olivia   What do you mean?

Portis   You both have the same mom and the same dad?

Olivia   Funny question.

Portis   I only ask because around here –

Olivia   "Around here?"

Portis   In the city. I meet a lot of people and they're siblings, but they have a different set of parents, that's all.

Olivia   Would that make me any less of a sister?

Portis   Of course not.

Olivia   Then just write that I was his sister.

Portis   Okay. Is there anything that you'd like people to know about Jackie? Something that might help our readers to understand who he was?

Olivia   Yes. Write this down.

Jordan *sits poised, ready to write.*

Olivia   At an early age, Jack Holland abandoned a promising future and descended into a maelstrom of bad decisions and reckless behavior.

Portis   Hold on.

Olivia   By seventeen, he had dropped out of school and was living on the streets. He made his living getting suburban kids high and eventually ran afoul of some bad dudes who jumped him one night at the corner of Sullivan and King. Jack Holland drew his gun and fired, but the bullet went wild, striking a five-year-old girl who was sitting on her porch minding her own business. Put the little girl in the hospital with a bullet in her jaw.

Jordan (*writing*)   Let me just catch up.

Olivia   Might have ended there but that little girl had cousins, you see, and they didn't like the fact that Jack Holland shot up that adorable little girl. So those cousins jumped him the next week and didn't leave anything to chance. Put two bullets in his bandit head. Bam! Bam! Too bad Jackie made some bad choices. Another thug down. Best if they all just keep killing their own.

Portis   Okay. Um . . .

Jordan *pulls out his phone.*

Portis   What are you doing?

Jordan   Looking up "maelstrom."

AJ *enters with two chairs.*

AJ   Aunt Robin wants to know if you all eat baked beans.

Portis   Oh, we're not staying.

AJ   She's afraid 'cause the beans might be cold but I think they taste best that way.

Portis   No, no. That's okay.

Jordan   I'll have some beans.

Portis *glares at* **Jordan**.

Jordan   I'm starving.

AJ   Good. Everybody gonna sit at the table and eat.

AJ *spoons beans on plates and puts them in front of* **Portis** *and* **Jordan**.

Jordan   Thank you.

Portis   Yes. Thanks.

AJ   Hot dogs on the way.

AJ *exits.*

Portis   So your brother got involved in a gang and was killed in retaliation for shooting that girl.

Olivia   You're cutting to the chase, huh?

Portis   That's what people are saying. Is that not true?

Olivia   Sure it's true. Or maybe it was more like this. (*To* **Jordan**.) Ahem . . .

Jordan *prepares to write.*

Olivia   Jack Holland was a promising young kid. Just look at this cute picture from his third-grade yearbook. He made all A's and his teachers say he was the brightest kid in his class. But the culture, my friends! Oh, my! The culture just wouldn't leave Jack Holland alone! The culture is sick, you see. It turns promising young boys into degenerate young men. And the world just lets it happen—poverty, poor education—we're all in the hands of the bankers, my friends! Wall Street had Jack Holland tied up with his hands behind his back until he couldn't take it anymore and he just lashed out!

Portis   Okay. Listen—

Olivia   Personality disorder. That's what he had. Gotta be a pill for that. How come he didn't have it? Where are all the doctors? What about healthcare?

Jordan   Wait. Stop! What are you talking about?

AJ *and* **Robin** *enter.* **Robin** *is carrying a bowl.*

Robin   Potato salad. Hope you like it.

Jordan   Thanks!

Portis   We're not staying.

Robin   Hot dogs will be done in a few minutes.

Portis   Sorry, ma'am. That's not why we're here.

Robin   Something wrong with the beans?

Portis   I'm sure the beans are delicious.

Jordan   Taste them.

Portis   Jordan—

Robin   I add a little more brown sugar than what's in the can. AJ likes them that way.

They all stare at **Portis** *while he tries the beans.*

Portis   They're very good.

Robin   Come on, AJ. Help me out. You okay, Olivia?

Olivia   I'm perfect.

AJ *and* **Robin** *exit.*

Portis (*to* **Jordan**)   Let's go.

Jordan   We're leaving?

Portis (*to* **Olivia**)   I'm sorry, young lady. I really am. We interrupted you at a very private time. My fault.

Olivia   So you don't want to hear about Jack?

Portis   Maybe another time.

Olivia   So that's the only shot I get, huh? One chance to set the record straight and if you don't like the sound of it, you just walk away and print whatever you want?

Portis   Look, I get it. Newspapers stink. Blogs stink. Social media stinks. We have to write stories without taking in the big picture. It's all true. But I don't have room to write a cultural analysis. To write this story, I need some basic facts about Jack. He was the fiftieth homicide this year and we haven't had a murder rate this high for eleven years, so . . .

Olivia   Yeah! My brother the record-breaker! He get a medal for this?

Portis   I understand you're upset.

Olivia   My brother was shot and killed. Damn straight, I'm upset.

Portis   Maybe I'll come back when you're feeling better.

Olivia   Maybe I'll never feel better.

Pause, while the three stare at one another.

Jordan   Tell us about Jack. We want to know about Jack.

Olivia   Okay. Sorry. Just the facts?

Portis   Just the facts. What happened first?

Olivia   First, there was slavery.

Portis   Ooookay . . .

Olivia   We got rid of it eventually, but not before we fought a huge war over it because a lot of people really, really didn't want to give it up. Heaven forbid a bunch of landowners should pick their own cotton.

Portis (*to* **Jordan**)   You don't need to write that.

Olivia   The thing is, see, even after all that death, people were still pissed about giving up slaves. Especially because now there were all these free slaves running around annoying everyone. Sure, there was this brief moment when Black people got the right to vote about seventy years later, but then white people started hanging Black people so Black people got pissed and started marching.

Portis   And ...

Olivia   And what?

Portis   And we came together. As a country. Because that's what we do.

Olivia   Sure. That's what we do.

Portis   And we can still do that. We can.

AJ *and* **Robin** *enter.*

Robin   Everything okay out here?

Olivia   Everything's fine.

Robin   I have this funny feeling that Olivia is holding you all hostage with facts from her AP History class.

Portis   She's smart.

Robin   Oh, I know she is. So here's what's gonna happen. We're all gonna sit here and we're all gonna talk.

AJ   And eat all at the same table.

Robin   And we're gonna talk civilly because there are young ears here.

AJ   Oh, man!

Robin   Some people here have heard enough horrible things in two days to last a lifetime. Some people need to hear that we can talk without fighting.

Portis   No worries. Olivia wasn't talking about the present. She was talking about the past.

Robin   She does that. She bring up Dr. King yet?

Portis   I have a feeling that's where she was headed.

Olivia   Black people started marching. Scared the hell out of everyone. So they shot Dr. King.

AJ   Don't say "hell."

Robin   "They" didn't shoot Dr. King. One crazy man shot Dr. King. One crazy, evil man.

Olivia   One crazy, evil man representing the desires of a lot of other crazy, evil men.

Portis   And that act of violence brought us all together because we realized just how futile racism was.

Olivia   Actually, it just made everybody mad. Black people were mad at being second-class citizens and white people were mad that Black people were still whining. And that's where Jack comes in.

Robin   Olivia. You cannot blame your brother's actions on the legacy of slavery and racism. That is not how justice works.

Olivia   Should be how it works.

Robin   Pardon my daughter, Mr. Portis. She's still young and doesn't realize what a waste of breath it is to hate everyone equally.

Portis   I get it. My family is Irish.

Robin   What do you mean?

Portis   Me, my brothers, and sister . . . we're second-generation Americans. But I don't run around shooting people because my grandfather couldn't get a dishwashing job when he sailed over from Dublin.

Robin (*to* **Portis**)   That's not exactly what I'm saying, Mr. Portis.

Portis   Sorry. That was a little . . . I'm just saying that other ethnicities have their own cultural oppression to deal with.

Olivia   See what I mean?

Robin   Be polite, Olivia.

Olivia   Politeness doesn't get anyone anywhere.

Portis   Your mother's right, Olivia.

Robin   Mr. Portis. I will tell my own child when she's right and when she's wrong.

Portis   I just meant –

Olivia   Telling Jack to be polite didn't do much good did it?

Robin   Your cousin is in the room, Olivia.

Olivia   Said his prayers, said "Yes, ma'am" and "Yes, sir." For all the good it did him.

AJ   That little girl got a bullet from Jack's gun. Messed her face all up. She's gonna have to have an operation.

Robin   AJ! (*To* **Olivia**.) Where did he hear that?

Olivia   They were talking about it at the funeral. (*Looks at* **Portis**.) Someone had a newspaper.

Robin   He shouldn't be hearing that.

Olivia   It's in the air, Mom. All the horrible details. Can't go anywhere without hearing them.

Jordan   This is why we want to write about Jack. Just about Jack.

Portis   Not Jack's friends, not the history of African-American culture. Just Jack.

Olivia   You can't write about Jack without knowing about his friends. And you can't write about his friends without knowing about his community. And you can't write about his community without writing about this city.

Portis   But what's the bottom line? I'm a reporter. I have to get to the bottom line.

Olivia   No one wants to read the bottom line. They just want to read the parts that scare them. "The winds of liberty blow and black folk find themselves at the center of the storm."

Portis   Wait. Say that again.

Olivia   Say what again?

Portis   "The winds of liberty blow . . ."

Robin   It's just an expression.

Portis   Righteous Saahir.

Olivia   What about him?

Portis   You got that phrase from Righteous Saahir.

Robin   We are not gonna talk about Saahir.

AJ   He was a friend of Jackie's.

Robin   AJ!

Portis   Let me tell you something, Olivia. I am all for justice and racial equality. I always have been. But Saahir is a troublemaker.

Olivia   That's not true.

Robin   Some of Saahir's friends were trouble, Olivia.

Jordan   Who are we talking about?

Portis   Saahir is an activist. But he's no Dr. King. That's for sure. Dr. King didn't blame every societal ill on white people.

Olivia   You white washing Dr. King?

Robin   Olivia!

Olivia   Besides, Saahir does not blame every little thing on white people.

Portis   The hell he doesn't.

Robin   The things Saahir said weren't the issue. It was the company he kept. Some of those boys were bad influences on Jackie. You know this, Olivia.

Portis   Then why didn't you keep Jack away from him? Why did you let him keep coming around?

AJ   He fixed our windows.

Portis   Huh?

Robin   Windows on this house were old. Last winter, the cold creeped in. Saahir spent all day in the freezing weather putting insulation in. Cut my heating bill in half.

AJ   I got new notebooks for school. Didn't have to write on the back pages of Jackie's old notebooks.

Olivia   Saahir is a friend of the family.

Robin   Some days, I'd rather have the cold back.

Portis (*to* **Olivia**)   If Saahir was such a good friend to your family, how come he didn't stop Jack from selling dope to college kids?

Olivia   I don't know. Why don't the college kids grow their own dope instead of driving here to get it?

Portis   Because they can!

Olivia   So people can break the law just because they can? Funny. Jack used to say the same thing.

Portis   That's not what I meant.

Robin   So what did you mean?

Portis   Do you know what it's like watching the city you grew up in, the city you love, turn into this demoralized, criminalized ghetto? I've spent my whole life here and every year I think "It has to get better. We can still turn this around." But it never does. Sometimes I start to feel a little more at peace, and then a little girl gets shot through the jaw while playing with a dollhouse on her front porch.

Olivia   I'm sorry the lives of black people have been an inconvenience to you.

Portis   Black people . . .

He stops himself.

Olivia   Black people what?

Portis   Ms. Holland . . .

Robin   Black people what, Mr. Portis?

Portis   I didn't . . . I wasn't saying . . .

AJ   I'm gonna get the hot dogs. Can't just eat beans and potato salad. I mean it's really good and everything but it's not a full meal. We all need to sit down and have a full meal.

AJ exits.

Portis (*to* **Robin**)   But you grew up here. You know what I'm talking about. You know what I mean.

Robin   I think I know exactly what you mean.

Portis   We should go.

Robin   Yes, you should.

Jordan and Olivia   No!

Robin   Don't "no" me.

Portis (*to* **Jordan**)   Are you kidding me?

Olivia   Mom!

Jordan   We don't have the story yet.

Portis   You are on thin ice, young (lady/man).

Robin   Do not talk to me like that –

Jordan   We can't just leave –

Olivia   But Mom –

Portis   I will say when we leave.

Everyone begins arguing with one another. Eventually **AJ** *enters from the kitchen carrying a tray of hot dogs. The door slams behind him and everyone jumps, then immediately goes silent. They don't want to argue in front of the kid.* **AJ** *carries the hot-dog tray to the picnic table and sets it down.*

AJ   Nobody eat anything until I come back with mustard.

AJ *exits back into the kitchen.*

Portis   Ms. Holland. This is my fault. I'm sorry. You're trying to have a family dinner. I'm sorry. We'll go.

Olivia   I want to tell you one thing about Jack.

Robin   Olivia—

Olivia   Just one thing. You can print it or not print it. I don't care.

Portis   Okay.

Olivia   The day before I started high school, I was really scared. All my school stuff, my notebooks and everything, looked like stuff a little girl would have. So Jack took me shopping. I got all these really sharp looking folders and a backpack and everything. I got some new sweatshirts and jeans – adult looking, you know? I wasn't a kid anymore. I walked into the first day of ninth grade feeling like a new person. Then I came home and sat on the couch and just cried like a baby. No idea why. Jack came home and saw me there, just bawling my eyes out. So he takes the dining-room chairs and a few blankets and makes a fort. He tells me to get in and he gives me a flashlight. He brings me some of my old books to read and puts some of my old stuffed animals in there to keep me company. You see, he knew that what I needed was to just be a little girl for one more night. So, I sat there in my cave, reading my books, surrounded by my stuffed bunnies. The next morning, I got up, put on my new clothes, and went back to school.

Portis   That's a nice story, Olivia. But I can't print that.

Olivia   Why not?

Portis   Because I have four inches to fill with facts about his death and the story doesn't have anything to do with that.

Olivia   That story is the only thing I have to say about Jack. It means everything.

Portis   I'm sorry.

Olivia   That's Jack whether you like it or not. Whether it sells newspapers or not. That's the brother I love. That's the brother I miss. That's the bottom line.

They all look over at **AJ** *because he has begun crying.*

Robin   You all should go.

Portis   Of course. Let's go, Jordan.

Jordan   Wait.

Jordan *walks over to* **AJ** *and hands him his/her pen. She clicks it a couple of times to show him how it lights up. He finds it interesting and he calms down a bit.*

AJ   Thank you.

Portis   Come on, Jordan.

Jordan *walks back to* **Portis** *and they prepare to leave.*

Robin   Hold up. AJ, come here.

AJ *walks to* **Robin** *and she speaks to him in a low voice. We don't hear what she's saying but she's clearly telling him to be strong. He stops crying. She continues talking, pointing to the picnic table, then pointing to* **Jordan** *and* **Portis**. **AJ** *nods his head, then goes to the table, takes two paper plates, puts hot dogs and potato salad on them and carries them halfway to* **Portis** *and* **Jordan**.

AJ   Would you like to stay and have some hot dogs?

Portis   Very kind of you. But we have to get back. We have a deadline.

Jordan   I'll stay.

Portis   You can't stay.

Jordan   I'm staying here.

Portis   You have to come back to the office.

Jordan   No.

Portis   You realize that if you bail on me, I can't let you continue to intern with me. You know that, right?

Jordan   You weren't paying me anyway.

Portis   Good day, everyone.

Portis *exits.* **Jordan** *sits at the picnic table.*

Robin   AJ, would you like to say grace?

AJ   Bless everybody here. Bless hot dogs. Bless Jack. Bless everybody at this table and everybody not at this table. In Jesus' name we pray.

All   Amen.

Olivia (*to* **Jordan**)   You want something to drink?

Jordan   Sure. Whatever you're having is fine.

Olivia *pours* **Jordan** *a drink.*

Olivia   You just lose your job?

Jordan   I didn't lose anything. I would still love to ask you some questions, though.

Olivia   What for?

Jordan   I don't know. Maybe I'll write something on my own.

Olivia   Okay.

Jordan   Tell me about Jack.

Olivia   What do you want to know about him?

Jordan   Everything. Start at the beginning. It's all important. I want to hear the whole story.

End of play.

Suggested Exercises for Educators and Teaching Artists
for *The Bottom Line*

Before reading or seeing the play

- Classroom Exercise:

  Hand out paper and writing utensils to students. Ask them to spend five minutes in a freewrite. Encourage them to continuously write, even if they stray off topic. They should address the following prompt: Write about a specific issue that divides people in your family or community.

  Next, break the class into small groups of four, and have each student share the freewrite with the rest of the group (if writers are comfortable doing so). Each group should then choose an "issue" to take forward into the following improvisation:

  An unexpected guest arrives at a private family gathering, with the need to address or learn more about the divisive issue. Decide why the family has gathered. Assign the following characteristics to the family members:

  - the one who wants to welcome the guest,
  - the one who wants to challenge the guest,
  - the one who wants to keep the peace and move on.

  Each group should practice and perform the improvisation (it does not need to be scripted). Once all of the groups have performed, the class as a whole should discuss: what makes a community trust or mistrust an outsider?

After reading or seeing the play

- Homework Assignment:

  Ask each student to find a brief news story that depicts a controversial person or event in their community. What are the larger social issues at play in this event? How was the person or community depicted? What parts of the new story are objective, and which are subjective? Does the writer reveal any possible bias?

- Bonus Assignment:

  Ask students to research: What is "Newspaper Theatre," and who was Augusto Boal?

- Classroom Assignment:

  Try out any of these suggested techniques drawn from Boal's work. Complementary reading:

Ask the students to create and perform a scene in which the news item is read, but add information generally omitted to give a more "complete" version. This additional information can be sourced from other news, research, or the knowledge possessed in the group. After each performance, discuss what is left out of the initial newspaper story.

- Parallel action:

  Have the students create and perform a scene in which the news item is read "while parallel actions are mimed to show either the context in which the reported event really occurred, or to complement the spoken story."

- Interrogation or field interview:

  Have the students report the news as if characters are being interviewed, like the football players might be interviewed at the half time of a game. This allows for a "hot-seating"/ dynamic investigation with the audience of the performance.

Work cited: Meir, Uri Noy. "The Twelve Techniques of Newspaper Theatre." imaginaction.org. nd. accessed May 21, 2020.

The Aftermath

A one-act play

Paris Crayton III

Background and Insights into *The Aftermath*

from Paris Crayton III

Notes on Casting

The character of William must be African-American. Everyone one else can be any race.

Notes on Production

Language can be modified if needed to match the times. Everything else is up to the director.

The Inspiration for This Play

Working with the wonderful students of Newark through the AdvantageArts afterschool program offered by Drew University! And because I've always wanted to see a food fight in real life.

Major Themes

The truth will eventually come to light.

Food for Thought

The essential question of who started the food fight.

Entrance into the World of Theatre

I became interested in theatre at my kindergarten graduation, and it hasn't let me go since. I write plays to share in the experience with the actors as well as the audience. Theatre, for me, is the most powerful art form there is.

Characters

Krystle, *a student. Thinks her boyfriend, James, is cheating.*
James, *a student. Fed up with his girlfriend, Krystle.*
Jennifer, *a student. Is upset about her new dress being ruined.*
Tony, *a student. Desperately needs help on a quiz. Or does he?*
Amanda, *a student. Not too great at keeping secrets.*
William, *a student. A brainiac who loves words.*
Val, *a student. Has a crush on James that she is trying to hide.*
Danielle, *a student. Carefree. Can see the bright side of things.*
Jessie, *a student. Nervous about the upcoming test and has suspicions about the teachers.*
Shay, *a student. Owns a camcorder.*
Principal Mayor, *a man at the end of his rope. Trying to keep calm.*
Ms. Waters, *a teacher, fairly new to the school. Has a secret.*
Mr. Johnson, *a teacher, knows how to handle the students. Also has a secret.*

Place: A school cafeteria.
Time: Lunchtime.

(/) Indicates an overlap in dialogue.
(—) Indicates someone being cut off.
(. . .) Indicates a brief pause to think.

Lights rise on the aftermath of a food fight. Everyone is seated in a circle as **Principal Mayor**, **Ms. Waters**, *and* **Mr. Johnson** *stand in the middle of the carnage trying to get to the bottom of things. The tension is still extremely high and the students are still on level one hundred.*

James   and once again I am to blame for all of this, huh? / You can never take any responsibility. It's always my fault. Because . . . because you went through my messages.

Krystle   Of course you're to blame . . . why should I take respons . . . If you weren't going behind my back / I wouldn't have to check your messages.

Tony   all I was doing was eating chicken nuggets when William hurled / his Sprite in my face . . . You did! Then why am I soaking wet? Oh accident my bottom.

William   I didn't hurl . . . you hear him saying I hurled something? Amanda bumped / into me and I accidentally spilled . . . whatever, man.

Amanda   I was dodging the jello that was coming straight at me. / Just got my hair done yesterday. Now look at it. Full of spaghetti sauce.

Daniella   Accident my bottom? Why don't you just say ass? Always got to be / so proper . . . ass isn't a curse word. ass is just ass. Say ass, Tony!

Tony   Because I don't curse. I have an extensive vocabulary. / I will not succumb to peer pressure.

Val   Mr. Mayor, I'm missing geometry. I shouldn't have to miss class just because some of these children have no / home training. It's not fair to us who actually want to learn. Oh, James, please, you could never be on my level.

James   You hear her talking 'bout children? You're a child too, Val . . . / Nobody's trying to be on . . . Krystle, could you get off my back?

Krystle   Don't worry about what she's saying. Who are these other girls you've been texting? / No . . . you don't tell me to get off your back. I WANT ANSWERS!

Jessie   Yeah so . . . I'm still hungry. / Are we going to discuss us actually getting to eat lunch as opposed to wearing it?

Jennifer   Jessie you're always hungry. I want to know who's going to pay for this dress. Does the school have money to reimburse me?

There is silence. Finally. **Principal Mayor** *glances around at the students.*

Principal Mayor   Now that you've gotten that all out of your system . . . who wants to tell me what happened?

All of the students begin to talk simultaneously.

Principal Mayor   One at a time please!

Val   I'll go first.

James   What makes you think you can go first?

Val   I'm not sure if your mom taught you this, but ladies are always supposed to go first.

James   I'm a feminist, so we're on equal playing ground.

Principal Mayor   Okay, so James and Val won't go first. Anyone else?

Mr. Johnson   How about you, Tony?

Tony   Gladly. So I was—

William   Of course the teacher's pet gets to go first.

Tony   William, for the last time, I am not the teacher's pet!

William   Yeah right. You should wear a collar.

Mr. Johnson   That's enough! Tony, please continue. And please be as elaborate as possible.

The lights shift as a lunch table is rolled onto the stage. **Tony** *goes to sit at it. As he calls the names of his tablemates, they go and sit. We play with time here. At times we are in the present, at other times, in the past.*

Tony   I was sitting at the table with William, Val, and Amanda. Enjoying the delicious chicken nuggets prepared by the immaculate kitchen staff. Val and William were in the middle of a conversation.

Val   I'm not letting you cheat off of my quiz.

William   Come on, Val! How much do you want?

Val   I'm not taking your—

William   Ten dollars? . . . How about twenty? Twenty-five is my final offer.

Amanda   Why didn't you just study?

William   And when exactly would I have time to do that when the new *Call of Duty* and Lil Uzi Vert's album dropped this week?

Tony   Seems like you need to get your priorities straight.

William   No one was talking to you.

Val   But he does have a point.

William   Do you all think just because you make straight A's that you're better than me?

Val   Your words, not mine.

Tony   I don't think that I'm–

William   Shut up, Tony.

Val   Don't tell him to shut up!

William   Oh, so what? You're protecting your man now?

Val   He is not my man.

Amanda   You know she has a crush on James.

Val   Amanda!

William   Krystle's boyfriend, James?

Amanda   I'm sorry. It slipped.

Val   I can't tell you anything.

William   Let me cheat off your quiz and I won't tell.

Tony   You shouldn't do that. That's blackmail.

William   Fitting, seeing that I am a Black male.

Val   William please don't say anything.

William   Then I better get an A.

Tony   As an upstanding citizen, and a valued student at this school, I can't let you do that.

William   And who's gonna stop me? You?

Time shift.

Tony   And that's when he threw his drink in my face.

William   That's bullshit!

Teachers   Language!

William   Oh, but Danielle can say ass? That's favoritism!

Danielle   Why are you bringing me in it?

William   You're in here, aren't you?

Principal Mayor   And there are no favorites here.

Students   Bullshit!

James   We're not stupid.

Ms. Waters   We know you aren't stupid. Would you like to tell your side of the story, James?

William   I don't get a chance to defend myself?

Ms. Waters   I'm sorry, sure, Alonzo.

William   I'm William.

Ms. Water   That's what I meant.

William   Yeah yeah . . . well this is how it really went down.

Tony, **Val**, *and* **Amanda** *return to the table.*

William   I was just sitting at the table, looking good like usual. When . . .

Val   I'll let you cheat off of my quiz if you let me touch your man muscles.

Everyone breaks out into laughter.

William   Hey! I'm speaking right now. You all will get your turn to speak. So, like I was saying, she's all like . . . can I touch your man muscles. And I tell her . . . You can touch them, but I don't need to cheat. I spent all last week studying.

Amanda   You? Studying?

William   Yeah. Is that so hard to believe?

Amanda   Yes it is actually. You never study.

William   Well, let's make a bet. I'll bet each of you ten dollars that I'll pass this quiz with an A. No, make it twenty dollars. Twenty-five!

Val   I'm not betting you.

William   Why not? Afraid you may lose? And guess what. The new *Call of Duty* and Lil Uzi's album dropped this week and I put them aside to make sure I could past this quiz.

Tony   Seems like you got your priorities straight.

William   No one was talking to you.

Val   But he does have a point.

William   I don't care. You think just because you make straight A's you're better than me?

Tony   I don't think that I'm—

William   Shut up, Tony!

Val   Don't tell him to shut up.

William   Oh so what? You're protecting your man now?

Val   He is not my man.

Amanda   You know she has a crush on James.

Val   Amanda!

William   Krystle's boyfriend, James?

Amanda   I'm sorry. It slipped.

Val   I can't tell you anything.

Val *throws her Jello™ at* **Amanda** *but* **Amanda** *dodges bumping into* **William** *who spills his drink on* **Tony**. *Time shift.*

William   And that's how it happened.

Principal Mayor   I hope you can understand why I have a difficult time believing that?

William   I'm telling the truth!

Principal Mayor   Amanda, did Val throw Jello at you?

Amanda   I plead the fifth.

Principal Mayor   What? You can't plead the fifth.

Ms. Waters   Val, did you throw Jello at Amanda?

Val   I sure did. She can't keep her big mouth close.

Amanda   That's not true. I just kept it closed.

Krystle   So is Val the one you've been texting?

James   Krystle, please.

Krystle   Don't tell me please. I got your please. Val, I'm gonna need you to get to stepping.

Val   Nobody wants James, Krystle.

Krystle   I want James, Val!

James   Awww . . . that's so—

Krystle   Shut your mouth. I haven't even started in on you yet.

Principal Mayor   Everyone will get their chance to speak. So, Val, you are the cause of all of this? I'm shocked.

William   Because she's a favorite.

Val   Wait . . . I didn't say I was the cause of anything. I threw that Jello after the food fight had already started.

Principal Mayor   So you didn't start the fight?

Val   Isn't that what I just said.

Principal Mayor   Then who did?

Val   I don't know. But I would like to go to my geometry class now if you don't mind.

Principal Mayor   You may not. But you can go to detention after school today.

Val   For throwing Jello? Who can get hurt with Jello?

Principal Mayor   Room 305, after the final bell.

Val   This is so screwed up.

Principal Mayor   Would you like for me to make it a week?

Val   No, sir.

Principal Mayor   Alright then. Is someone else ready to confess their truths?

The students are silent.

Mr. Johnson   Come on, guys, this will go much faster if we all cooperate.

Ms. Waters *is smiling from ear to ear.*

Jessie   Ms. Waters, why are you smiling like that?

Ms. Waters   Huh? Like what?

Jessie   You just gonna pretend that I didn't see you smiling like the grinch who stole Christmas?

Mr. Johnson   We are here to get confessions from you. Not Ms. Waters.

James   Confessions? What are we? Suspects?

Principal Mayor   Yes you are. Until we get to the bottom of this. You're all suspects. So I suggest you come clean.

Jennifer   Pretty hard to come clean when your six-hundred-dollar dress is covered in cafeteria food. I'm still wondering who's going to pay for this.

Principal Mayor   We will make sure to get it to the cleaners.

Jennifer   Cleaners? Did you hear the price of this dress?

Amanda   And what about my hair?

Jessie   Will everyone's clothes be going to the cleaners? Or just the favorites'?

All the students start to talk at once.

Principal Mayor   There are no fav . . . Hold it! Hold it! I think we're getting off topic here. The only thing I care about right now is finding out who started this ruckus. Or I can just give you all suspensions.

All the students talk at once again.

Principal Mayor   I said hold it! You all are giving me a headache and I'm fresh out of my medicine.

William   I'm sure there is a liquor store somewhere close.

Principal Mayor   DETENTION!

William   This is a moment for telling the truth, right? Your truth is off limits?

Principal Mayor   My truth has nothing to do with you.

Krystle   Woah, Principal Mayor, calm down. You're getting all red.

Principal Mayor   Can one of you

Ms. Waters   Yes, Mr. Mayor . . . okay . . . umm. . So who wants to . . . umm . . . confess?

James   Where did they get this teacher from?

The students laugh.

Ms. Waters   I'll have you to know that I graduated top of my class.

Mr. Johnson   Don't let them get to you. Avoid the sunken place.

Ms. Waters   You're right. Thanks, Brad.

Jessie   Oh . . . Brad? We're on a first-name basis now I see.

Ms. Waters   We are the teachers! We can be on—

Mr. Johnson   Don't let them get you. Once they do, they won't let you go. Be strong.

Jennifer (*mocking* **Ms. Waters**)   I will, Brad. Just hold on to me.

The students laugh again.

Mr. Johnson   That is highly inappropriate! That is a detention for you, Jennifer.

Jennifer   That's fine. I like detention. Just an extra hour to do homework at school. I got this thing all figured out. You can't break me.

Mr. Johnson   How about a suspension?

Jennifer   Nice try, but I know you can't suspend me because I didn't do anything. I'm the victim here. I got hit in the head with an apple core.

Ms. Waters   And who threw this alleged apple core?

Jennifer   It's not alleged. It's right here.

She picks up the apple core.

Mr. Johnson   Who threw it?

Jennifer   I don't know who threw it.

Jessie   Maybe it was one of you.

Tony   I'm sorry, but does anyone care that we are missing class for this tomfoolery?

Danielle   Tomfoolery? Tony, do you ever just use regular words?

Tony   And what constitutes as a regular word, Danielle?

Danielle   One that people use.

Tony   I just used it didn't I?

Principal Mayor   Look, I have tons of work to do and I don't want to be held hostage in this cafeteria all day. Can we please get on with this little charade? Jennifer, would you like to tell me your version of the story.

Jennifer   I sure would. Me, Danielle, and Jessie at the table. Everything was fine until Ms. Waters walked by breaking the sacred laws of the lunchroom.

Danielle   With all due respect, Ms. Waters, lunchtime is for lunch. I'm sure not one of us is thinking about a quiz.

Jessie   Speak for yourself.

Ms. Waters   No need to be scared. I'm sure you'll do great. Sorry to disturb you.

Danielle   It's fine. Here, Jennifer, take my peas.

Jennifer *shakes her head no.*

Danielle   Come on. I don't want them, and you know I hate throwing food away.

Jennifer   What makes you think that I want them?

Danielle   Jessie?

Jessie   I can't eat anything. I'm too nervous about this quiz.

Danielle   What's up with all this quiz talk in the lunchroom? Enjoy the food. Enjoy the people.

Jennifer   Enjoy the peas.

Ms. Waters   Oh, I almost forgot—

Danielle   If this is any more talk about quizzes, I swear . . .

Ms. Waters   It's not. I was just going to say that I love your dress, Jennifer.

Jennifer   Why thank you, Ms. Waters? It was six hundred dollars?

Ms. Waters   Wow . . . six hundred dollars! Give me an application to wherever you work.

She leaves the table.

Jessie   There is something strange about Ms. Waters. I just can't put my finger on it.

Jennifer   I think she's cool.

Jessie   No . . . something's up with her. It may have something to do with Mr. Johnson.

Jennifer   Shut up, Jessie.

Jessie   No I'm serious. Do you think that maybe they like each other?

Jennifer   That's none of my business. and it's none of yours either.

*An apple core is thrown at **Jennifer**'s head.*

Jennifer   Ouch! Who's throwing—

Danielle   Yes! I've always wanted to say this. Fo—

Jessie   FOOD FIGHT!

Danielle   Damn it, Jessie!

*She tosses his peas at **Jessie** who also throws food at him. Time shift.*

Jennifer   . . . and all the while I'm screaming, NOT THE DRESS! NOT THE DRESS! But you see how far that got me.

Principal Mayor   Jessie, you screamed food fight?

Jessie   Wouldn't you? That happens once in a lifetime.

Danielle   Which is why I wanted to say it!

Principal Mayor   That's a detention for the both of you.

Danielle   It was worth it.   **Jesse**   It was worth it.

Principal Mayor (*to* **Krystle** *and* **James**)   So that means one of you started this whole thing.

James   I didn't start nothing.

Principal Mayor   Okay . . . Krystle would you like to tell me what happened?

Krystle   James is a lying, cheating, sack of cow's crap is what happened.

James   See, why you gotta go there. /   **Krystle**   Because that's what you are.
No matter what I do you're going to   I don't want to hear it. / No I'm not. Talk
find . . . you gonna let me . . . you gonna   to whoever you've been texting.
let me talk?

Principal Mayor   Krystle just tell me . . . James don't . . . Please just. QUIET! . . . Krystle the floor is yours.

Another lunch table is rolled onto the stage.

Krystle   James and I were sitting at our normal table. Just the two of us. The way it's supposed to be.

Krystle *and* **James** *sit at the table.*

Krystle   Are you cheating on me?

James   Come on, don't start with this.

Krystle   Are you too scared to just tell me the truth?

James   So where is this coming from all of a sudden?

Krystle   I went through your messages . . . so many messages that weren't from me.

James   First off, why are you going through my phone? Secondly, I can text other people if I want to.

Krystle   Not other girls.

James   Krystle—

Krystle   No! answer my question.

James   What question?

Krystle   Have you been cheating on me?

James   Lower your voice.

Krystle   Don't tell me to lower my voice. I haven't even begun to get loud!

James   You're embarrassing me.

Krystle   And how do you think I feel being cheated on? I'm embarrassed too!

James   No one is cheating on you.

Krystle   I always knew there was something strange going on, I just couldn't put my finger on it.

James   Once again you are jumping to conclusions when you—

Krystle   Shut up, James. I'm sick of your lies.

James   Don't tell me to shut up, Krystle?

Krystle   Tell me who it is.

James   Krystle!

Krystle   TELL ME! Is it that new student from France?

James   What are you—

Krystle   Just like a man. Gonna keep on lying even though you've been caught red handed. Red just like this apple.

She tosses the apple.

James   You don't have any proof.

Krystle   Here's your proof.

She tosses milk in his face. Time shift.

Krystle   So as you can see, he deserved it! And you better be thankful that that's all you got.

James   Why do I even put up with you?

Krystle   I've been asking myself the same question.

Principal Mayor   So Krystle, you started the food fight by throwing the apple?

Krystle   It was out of anger. What would you do if the love of your life was as low down as he?

Principal Mayor   You've caused quite the disturbance today and I'm afraid that I have no choice but to suspend you.

Krystle   Just me? What about this cheater?

Principal Mayor   Your relationship is none of my concern. Okay, students, you may all return to your classes now that we've gotten to the bottom of—

A student approaches who has yet to be seen until now. He/she is holding an old-school camcorder.

Shay   Um . . . Principal Mayor?

Principal Mayor   Yes?

Shay   Krystle didn't start the food fight.

Principal Mayor   She didn't?

Shay   No, sir.

Principal Mayor   Well, who did?

Shay   I don't want to say.

Principal Mayor   That doesn't help me now does it?

Shay   I can show you. I recorded the whole thing.

Principal Mayor   There's video?

Shay   Yes sir.

Principal Mayor   Okay . . . well?

Shay   Before I show you this, I need you to promise that you will protect me if anyone tries to retaliate.

Principal Mayor   Okay.

Shay   Promise me.

Principal Mayor   I promise.

Shay   And I also ask that we, the students, get another day to study for this quiz in light of recent events.

Principal Mayor   That seems fair enough.

Shay   Okay. You ready?

Principal Mayor   I'm ready.

Shay   Here goes.

As **Shay** *shows* **Principal Mayor** *the camcorder recording the other students go back in time to the beginning of the lunch period. This scene should be smoothly paced so all the conversations flow naturally.*

Val   I'm not letting you cheat / off my quiz.

Krystle   Are you cheating on me?

James   Come on, / don't start with this.

Ms. Waters   No need to be scared. / I'm sure you'll do just fine.

Danielle   . . . Jennifer, take my peas.

Val   I'm / not taking your—

Krystle   Are you scared? I went through your messages / . . . so many messages that weren't from me.

William   Twenty-five is my / final offer.

James   First off . . .

Jessie   . . . I'm too nervous about this quiz.

Amanda   Why didn't you just study?

James   Krystle—

Krystle   No! answer my question

Danielle   What's up with all the quiz talk in the lunchroom . . .

Tony   Seems like you need to get your priorities straight.

Jennifer   Enjoy the peas.

William   No one was talking to you.

James   Lower your voice.

Ms. Waters   . . . I love your dress, Jennifer.

Krystle   I always knew there was something strange going on. I just couldn't put my finger on it.

Jessie   There is something strange about Ms. Waters. I just can't put my finger on it.

Tony   I don't think I'm—

William   Shut up, Tony.

Jennifer   Shut up, Jessie.

Krystle   Shut up, James.

Val   Don't tell him to shut up.

James   Don't tell me to shut up, Krystle.

Ms. Waters   And how are you doing over here, Mr. Johnson?

William   . . . You're protecting your man now?

Mr. Johnson   I'm doing just fine, Mrs. Johnson.

Ms. Waters   Not yet I'm not.

Amanda   You know she had a crush on . . .

Jennifer   That's none of my business

Mr. Johnson   I want to kiss you so bad right now.

Krystle   TELL ME!

Ms. Waters   Not in front of the students.

Mr. Johnson   I don't care anymore. I need you now.

He approaches **Ms. Waters**.

Tony   . . . I can't let you do that.

Ms. Waters   No stop.

William   And who's gonna stop me?

Mr. Johnson   Get over here.

Jennifer   Just like a man . . .   **Jesse**   Just like a man.

Mr. Johnson *and* **Ms. Waters** *are secretly playing a lovers' game when she accidentally pushes him a bit too hard, sending his food flying in the air.*

Krystle   . . . just like this apple.

She throws the apple.

Val   I can't tell you anything.

She throws her jello.

Danielle   Yes! I've always wanted to say this. Fo—

Jessie   FOOD FIGHT!

Food is thrown everywhere. No one is innocent. Everyone is throwing something at each other. Including the teachers. **Shay** *pauses the video, and everyone freezes.*

Shay   So as you can see, Mr. Johnson and Ms. Waters were actually the first ones to toss food.

Principal Mayor   Yes . . . Yes I do see. Can I speak with the both of you in my office?

They slowly unfreeze and the three off them exit.

Shay   So what do you want me to do with the video?

Shay *gets no response.*

Students   Oh . . . what the hell!

Shay *presses play and the chaos continues. The audience is invited to join in on the fake food fight. This goes on for a while until . . .*

Blackout.

End of play.

Suggested Exercises for Educators and Teaching Artists for *The Aftermath*

Before reading or seeing the play

- Classroom Exercise:

  Divide the class into groups of four; each group will create a scene with the following characters:

  - a school authority figure;
  - three students.

  Have each group improvise a scene: A transgression of school rules has occurred that resulted in a significant disruption of the school day. Groups of students (three at a time) are being interviewed by the authority figure to get to the bottom of it. Let the group choose who will play the authority figure and who will play the students.

  Each "student" receives a number drawn at random: one through five, which indicates that student's status in the group, including in relationship to one another as well as to the school authority. Note: you may also use a deck of cards to assign status according to the hierarchy of the deck; UNO™ cards are also playful and effective. Important: all participants must accept their status *as given*, in character, and not as they see themselves.

  In this first round, the authority figure should assume their own high status at level "one."

  Should you choose to repeat the exercise to vary the game or to include more students:

  - On rounds two or more, the authority may take a "two" or a "four" position, to make the game more challenging.
  - Further advanced play: All participants receive their "status number" in secret, which they wear on their forehead (attached by a headband or double-stick tape). Each must treat the others according to their number and must behave in the manner in which they are being treated.
  - Top-level play: a truth is revealed that changes the status of at least one of the characters by the time the improvisation ends.

- Classroom Exercise:

  Ask students to form a "continuum line," which spans the longest distance in the room. First, explain to the students that one end of the line indicates "complete agreement," while the other end indicates "complete disagreement." Next, ask students to take a position in the continuum line in response to a series of questions:

- Food fights are fun.
- I feel confident that I can trust my peers to be honest with me.
- I feel confident that I can trust the authority figures in my life.
- Video or other forms of surveillance protect people's rights.

Ask one volunteer from each end of the continuum, as well as one from the center, to share why they took this position. If you do this for each question, try to encourage new volunteers to speak up. Let these answers lead to class discussion.

After reading or seeing the play

- Classroom Exercise:

  Repeat the continuum line exercise described above. Discuss as a class: How did people's positions shift since seeing the play, and why?

- Classroom Exercise:

  Have students research the film *Rashomon* (Content warning: film involves a rape.) by Akira Kurosawa. Next, divide the class into small groups. Ask each group to imagine an incident in which a person or group is being blamed for something they may or may not have done. There should be as many characters in the scenario as there are people in the small group. Then, each group should create three different tableaux that show the incident from different perspectives of each character and reveal a different truth. Have each group show their "*Rashomon* images" to the class. After each group's showing, ask how the story shifted, depending on whose perspective was shown. How was that shifting perspective used in the play *The Aftermath*?

  End with a class discussion: How do we know what's true? What makes a source trustworthy?

Charisma at the Crossroads

An interactive stage play with music and dance

Nina Angela Mercer

Background and Insights into *Charisma at the Crossroads*

from Nina Angela Mercer

Notes on Casting

- *There is flexibility with gender for all casting possibilities in this play, except for the character Charisma.*
- *Opportunities for double or triple casting are indicated in the "Characters" descriptions. However, note that the actors playing Jahwan and Shakeemah can play the Prosecutor Banker and the Psychologist/Teacher respectively as well.*

Notes on Production

All slang can be updated or modified to reflect the regional vernacular specific to where the play is being produced. Such updates or modifications must not alter meaning or tone.

The Inspiration for This Play

I was inspired to write this play after spending time with the youth who were participating in the Advantage Arts program in Newark, New Jersey. I was able to visit their afterschool sessions twice. During that time, we engaged in conversation about issues that resonated for them. We also experimented with improvisation related to various prompts. Once I was able to reflect on what I learned from them, I began to shape the story. I was very impacted by the idea that there is a break down in communication between adults and young people, one that can have dire consequences if the voices of the youth are not valued and amplified. So, I was inspired to write a play about the importance of speaking truth to power. Ultimately, this play illuminates and celebrates the power that all younger generations have in relation to society's futurity.

Major Themes

- *Friendship*
- *Confidence/determination*
- *Community responsibility*
- *Consumer culture*
- *The criminalization of youth*

Food for Thought

I feel that adults often try to hide truths from young people while simultaneously judging them for choices adults struggle with as well. I hope that this play can inspire intergenerational communication about our fears and our dreams. The play is interactive for that reason. I hope that the play also challenges youth to become critical readers of popular culture and history such that they feel confident grappling with the political satire in the play.

Entrance into the World of Theatre

I had an intensely rigorous relationship to live performance throughout my upbringing through dance classes, youth theatre camp, and public performances. My first jobs were in the performing arts. Though I did not study theatre in undergraduate school, the love for live performance never left me. The primacy of connection with the audience in theatre and the ephemeral urgency of live performance changed my understanding of what the written word could do when used for the stage. In my adult life, when I encountered a profoundly life-changing experience connected to a social justice issue that impacts many in our society, I reached for my pen to respond and discovered a calling. I have a deep appreciation for the emphasis on collaboration in theatre. I love that I can take an idea, shape it into a story, embellish it with language, enliven it with characters, stylize it with aesthetic choices. But it is only through sharing that world with a director, dramaturg, actors, and designers that it can be fully realized. And, still, it will be different each time it is performed for an audience. The audience will add to the show with its laughter, its rapt attention, and its collective lean forward in suspense. Yet the story told will have a different meaning for all who experience it. And, still, all involved will have shared in its creation. There's magic in that. In this era, when technology and speed seem to be the priorities for communication, I still find live performance to be especially powerful in ways that can be transformative. We need that in the world.

Characters

Genesis/Court Reporter and **Referee, Town Crier/MC** and **Magician**, *seventeen years old; Brooklyn born. They moved to this new city with their mom when they were eleven years old, after their parents divorced. They are a writer, MC, and Magician, the Griot of this tale.*

Jahwan/Defendants/Ancestors' Wildest Dreams, *seventeen years old; a gifted coder who is a huge anime and manga fan. He also has a talent for choreography and dance. He is Shakeemah's older brother. He walks his talk. He is courageous in his thinking, but he listens first. He is action/movement. He has a sense of humor, but he knows when to get serious.*

Shakeemah/Defendants/Ancestors' Wildest Dreams, *fifteen–sixteen years old; an avid reader with a distinct sense of fashion. She creates dance choreography with her brother, Jahwan. This is something they've been doing since they were little kids. Their parents used to make them dance at all the family events. She is outspoken, sassy, smart, and kind at her core. She is fiercely independent, but she is also fiercely loyal to those she loves.*

Charisma/Defendants and Counsel by Consensus, or Something Like That/ Ancestors' Wildest Dreams, *eighteen years old; she became a mother six months ago. She brings her son to daycare at school. She aspires to get a business degree from Drew University, and then she hopes to get a fashion degree from Parsons. She wants to own her own clothing line. She has her family's support. She has been sketching fashion designs since she was in elementary school.*

CEO of Fuego Designs/Judge/Ancestors' Wildest Dreams, *woman.*

Jury (Television Heads)/Ancestors' Wildest Dreams, *ensemble; as the Jury, they appear wearing Television Head masks.*

Prosecutor Banker/Ancestors' Wildest Dreams, *all genders possible.*

Psychologist/Teacher/Ancestors' Wildest Dreams, *all genders possible.*

Djembe/All Percussion, *musicians.*

Director/Teacher, *facilitates audience discussion.*

Member of the Stage Management Team, *to move set items or deliver props.*

All adults in the play should be played by the youth/children.

Any city. Day time. A park bench. **Jahwan** *and* **Shakeemah** *are in tableaux near the bench.* **Genesis** *slides onto the stage from anywhere, wearing a top hat, and making a grand entrance. They wear a whistle around their neck.*

Genesis, MC   Here ye, Here ye! We welcome all and everyone to our version of one kind of right side up and another kind of upside down. We are the Poet, the Town Crier, and Griot, the Ones who exist both outside the plays on this stage and inside them. There will be three plays, you see, or rather two inside one! Let's see—There is this one, here, where we talk to you all directly, occasionally asking for your commentary. Do you understand us? (*Brief pause to check in with audience.*) Ok, good. In the other one, we are a poet and friend of our dear Charisma, who is embarking upon an important moment in her life at the crossroads. And, then, in yet another one, well – that's the upside down at its most real. It is yet another crossroad. And there, we are the Court Reporter. But don't trust us. Or yourselves. We are all up for questioning. And, now, we offer you the current scene as evidence . . . Here we are . . .

Genesis *motions toward* **Jahwan** *and* **Shakeemah** *with their arm, as if displaying furniture at a store.*

Genesis   The setting: afternoon, after school. A downtown park bench just across the street from our local high school, which sits right at the place where the crossroads meet. And, Genesis—that would be *moi* and also *moi*—we are standing on the park bench while Shakeemah, our girl, sits on the other end of the same bench staring at her cell phone as usual! Jahwahn, Shakeemah's brother, is nearby, trying to remember dance choreography.

Genesis *blows their whistle and takes off their top hat. They hold it out for a* **Member of the Stage Management Team**, *who enters the stage just as* **Genesis** *takes off their top hat.* **Jahwan** *begins to dance as* **Shakeemah** *watches while checking her cell phone from time to time.*

Shakeemah   You really think Legacy 7 is gonna hire you for that music video, Jahwan? It's not like they put a call out for choreography or dancers. I saw the post on IG, and it only said extras.

Jahwan   They only know what they know, until I show up. Well, I mean, until *we* show up.

Shakeemah   We? Genesis, do y'all hear him, sliding me into his plan!?

Genesis *is preoccupied with other thoughts, looking back toward the school.*

Genesis   We hope Charisma is doing alright in there.

Jahwan   Don't worry about Charisma. She's been preparing for this one moment since elementary school. Come on, Shakeemah. I only ask you for one favor a year, and this one could mean us both getting the bag. You know you want that bag, Shakeemah! You know you want that Red Lobster money. Believe in the Law of Attraction, and come help me remember these moves so we can take Grandma to Hawaii, or wherever she wants to go.

Shakeemah Yo. You are hilarious. You know Grandma Daisey ain't getting on no plane! But you definitely have a way of persuading me.

Genesis Why are we always so nervous for other people? It's so funny how we can read our poetry in front of an audience of strangers and not even trip off of it, like even if we are nervous before we start, once we're up there it's like we have to get everything out, and we don't feel anything blocking us. But when it's Charisma, it's different. She's been through a lot. We don't want to see her disappointed. We got her back through whatever but . . .

Jahwan *puts a finger in the air and pop locks.*

Jahwan Ain't no "but." We got her back through whatever. We got each other's backs. Therefore, we win. Case in point: Shakeemah, while we wait for Charisma, entertain us with your memory of the tightest choreography known to human-kind all throughout this city.

Shakeemah Alright, alright . . . I won't make ya'll wait any longer.

She walks over to her brother with confident flair. She starts showing him how she remembers the choreography. They repeat the combination a couple of times. **Genesis** *paces on the park bench.*

Just then, **Charisma** *storms toward the bench. She is clearly upset.*

Charisma I am so tired. And I am too young to be this tired. But I am! I am so freaking tired of trying.

Genesis What happened? We were worried. We could feel something was wrong. See?

Jahwan Sit down and take a breath for a minute.

Genesis What's wrong, boo?

Charisma *just shakes her head.*

Jahwan Did you meet with the designer?

Charisma *just shakes her head more.*

Genesis Did you leave your sketches home?

Charisma *shakes her head even more.*

Jahwan Come on. Talk to us.

Charisma I hate this place!

Shakeemah That's a start.

Charisma The guidance counselor pulled me into her office before I could go to the gym for the mentor circle meet and greet thing.

Genesis What for?

Jahwan   That lady stays on me. After my SAT scores came in, she was all over me about the silent protest we planned. She's all—you have too much at stake to get caught up in all of this "resistance business." Yo. What good are high SAT scores, if we can't LIVE!

Charisma   It seems like living has to look a certain way for her, because I didn't do anything. At least not anything recent, except be a mom. Yeah. That's it. And I guess that's too much for her. All that judgment clouds her vision.

Genesis   What does lil' man have to do with it?

Charisma   She asked me what my plans were for the meet and greet, who I wanted to be my mentor, stuff like that. And I told her I wanted to talk to the woman from Fuego Designs. I even pulled out my sketches. I was so excited. I was telling her how Donte and his family share custody with me and my family. I told her how we're all committed to being a solid foundation, and my college plans are part of that.

Shakeemah   That's so dope.

Jahwan   Yeah, that's what's up.

Charisma   And, then, I tell her how I want to intern at Fuego in the summer, every summer if I can, and then go to Parsons once I have my undergraduate business degree. And she's like—Charisma, you're a bright girl, but I don't want you to get disappointed. She's like—You need to think about a more practical plan, maybe start with a community college, don't worry about the fashion degree. She says, because I am a young mother, I may need to modify my plans . . . She's telling me all this now?! Right before I go in to talk to Fuego?! I been going to this school for a whole four years and any time I was in her office, she barely seemed like she remembered me from the last time! And, now, she got an opinion. Messed me all up.

Shakeemah   It's nothing wrong with community college. I want to work for a while. Save some money, and travel. Maybe take some classes at the community college. But, that's me . . . that's what I want.

Jahwan   How is she going to tell you the opposite of what you and Donte and both of your families already decided? Does she not notice that you bring lil' man to the in-school day care *and* get your work done?

Genesis   Is this why you're not at the meet and greet?

Charisma   When I walked out of her office, I just went in the bathroom and looked at my sketches, and everything just looked dumb. I started thinking, you know, maybe she's right. Like, who am I to think I can just walk into the gym with these dumb sketches and be down with Fuego.

Jahwan   You can't listen to her. You can't listen to anybody telling you that kind of stuff. It's poison. You gotta dance through it.

He busts out a complicated dance move.

My pops always tells me that you can't just believe everything adults tell you, because some of them need deprogramming. It's good ones, and it's ones that just don't see right. You can see the evidence of that in so much happening around us, from the local to the national. Look at this country right now. Look who's running it. Scared old people who don't look anything like us. And they definitely ain't living like us. How can they make decisions for us?

Genesis What time is it, Shakeemah?

Shakeemah *checks the cell phone that never leaves her hand.*

Shakeemah 3:30.

Genesis You still have time. Stand up.

Genesis *offers* **Charisma** *a hand to help her get up.*

Genesis Where's your sketchbook?

Charisma It's in my bag.

Genesis Ok. Good. Listen, you remember when we first moved here from Brooklyn with our mom, and we came into the classroom for the first time?

Charisma Sixth grade. Miss Cannon's class.

Genesis Yeah, and we started crying because people kept looking at us and laughing. We were too sensitive for our own good. Already a poet . . .

Shakeemah It was probably just because y'all looked cute. Y'all still cute, Genesis.

Genesis Thank you. But we felt ugly. We didn't feel cute. And, Charisma, the teacher had you take us to the bathroom, and you told us that it was just the stupid boys, and they probably said something dumb, but that didn't have anything to do with us. And, then, at recess, you introduced us to Jahwan, and you were like . . .

Jahwan He's the coolest.

Genesis Yeah, whatever . . .

Charisma And we made a deal.

Genesis Right. We promised that when people—ANYBODY—tried to make us feel small, we would remind each other, that it's just not our problem. We gotta keep it moving. We got dreams. We got wild dreams to make real. Our own lives mean something.

Charisma I gotta go do this, don't I?

Genesis How are you gonna tell lil' man to follow his dreams if you won't follow yours?

Charisma Ok.

She looks at **Genesis** *and* **Jahwan** *and they nod at each other.* **Jahwan** *puts* **Charisma**'*s bag on her shoulder.* **Genesis** *gives her a hug.* **Shakeemah** *gives* **Charisma** *a fist bump.*

Charisma *begins walking back toward the school.*

Genesis   We'll be out here waiting for you.

Charisma   Thanks, fam.

She exits.

Shakeemah   Ok, Jahwan. Let's get it.

She turns on her cell phone. She and **Jahwan** *perfect their dance routine as* **Genesis** *hypes them up. Then,* **Shakeemah** *and* **Jahwan** *freeze in tableaux.*

A **Member of the Stage Management Team** *brings* **Genesis** *their referee hat. They put it on, stand on the bench, and assume a gestural position invoking the role of* **MC** *and* **Magician**. **Jahwan** *and* **Shakeemah** *exit the stage.*

Charisma *under spotlight. She is in the gym, waiting for her turn to talk to the* **CEO of Fuego Designs**, *who stands with her back to the audience off at a distance. The* **CEO of Fuego Designs** *stands on an elevated platform, making her appear larger than life.* **Charisma** *holds her sketch book close to her chest. Finally, her turn comes up. She stands, facing the audience.*

Charisma   Hi, it's good to meet you. My name is Charisma Freeman. Yes, ma'am. Ok. Ms. Mitchell. Yes, I'm a senior this year. And, I really admire what you've been able to build with Fuego Designs. You inspire me. I have watched you grow your brand with a strong online presence. I've been studying your designs since I was twelve, because I was always up under my older sister when I was small. I wanted to *be* her, dress like her, do everything like her. That's why I started sketching my own designs. Eventually, I wanted to be flier than her. (*Laughing a little.*) So, you and my sister inspired me. I think it's so amazing that you have built your sales online so strong and can now open a boutique! And you're selling your own original designs! And you grew up in my 'hood! Yes. Yes, ma'am, I mean, Ms. Mitchell, I brought these sketches of mine to show you . . .

She takes a deep breath and holds her sketch book out to the **Audience/CEO of Fuego Designs**.

Charisma   I want to work toward my dreams.

Lights fade down with **Charisma** *and the* **CEO of Fuego Designs** *in tableaux.*

Genesis *jumps down from the bench still wearing their referee hat.*

Genesis, Court Reporter   Ladies and gentlemen, good people, and those who make our eyebrows go up, we must interject, because there's another side of life. We know that judgment twitters like birds too loud in the morning before another school day. Good people, we, therefore, also offer you as evidence, another version of Charisma's journey back inside the schoolhouse, one she shares with many. But, for this perspective shift to work, we need you to tune yourselves to the television screen that lives inside your brain. We must break it, dear jurors. Fight the power!

Genesis, Court Reporter *gestures toward the* **Jurors as Television Heads**, *who file into the courtroom. Then* **Genesis, Court Reporter**, *points to* **Charisma** *who marches to join other* **Student-Defendants** *in front of the* **Judge**.

Genesis, Court Reporter   We offer you Charisma! She is on her way into the lethally dangerous courtroom of adult opinion, also known as—These Disjointed States of Reality versus Our Children of Tender Age and Well-Seasoned.

And we duly name ourselves Genesis, Who Was the Poet Before, But Now Shall Be the Court Reporter, and Town Crier, in this case of utter disrepair and flagrant inhumanity.

No justice! No peace!

Charisma, Jahwan, Shakeemah, *and other* **Student-Defendants** *march around the stage in various configurations, followed by the* **Teacher-Psychologist** *and the* **Prosecutor Banker.**

Genesis, Court Reporter   All stop! All sit! All rise!

All   Here comes the Judge! Here comes the Judge! Here comes the Judge! Here comes the Judge!

The **Ceo of Fuego Designs** *turns to face the audience on the elevated platform, becoming the* **Judge.** *A* **Member of the Stage Management** *brings a table, chair, napkin, and plate of food for the* **Judge.** *The* **Judge** *sits down, puts a napkin on her neck, and speaks between bites of food.*

Judge   I would like to call the court to order as we consider the plight of this case. The People vs. The Guilty, also known as The Children, Tender and Well-Seasoned. Does the Prosecution have an opening statement?

Prosecutor Banker   Your Honor, I come before the court today to argue in defense of this land, and our most wealthy people. We will try, Your Honor, to present the facts of the case most fairly.

Judge   Prosecutor Banker, the lunch your spouse made for me today was excellent. The caviar . . . delightful.

Prosecutor Banker   Why, thank you, Your Honor. I will be sure to relay your high compliments to the little spouse upon my return home. The cost, of course, will be absorbed by the people.

Judge   My people.

Prosecutor Banker   Our people. Their debts exceed the rights of man, and yet their efforts continually amaze me. In such a nearing collapse of this country as we know it, they celebrate us by buying everything we sell. We are a country built on credit card debt, and soon—we will eat them all!

Judge   To the point, Prosecutor Banker. You're boring me, unless there's more food, freshly seasoned . . .

Prosecutor Banker   The children's offenses are many. Too many to name in full. And yet, for the record, we must attempt to detail exactly what they have done.

Judge   May the jury turn on their television sets for full comprehension.

Lights flicker around the **Television Head Jurors** *on the screen.*

Prosecutor Banker   The children's offenses are almost unspeakable. Yet, I will name them at your most greedy request. You have no honor.

The **Judge** *smiles with ridiculous pride and continues eating in a sloppy way, despite the napkin. The* **Prosecutor Banker** *reads from a scroll.*

Prosecutor Banker   The children of these disjointed states of reality are hereby judged guilty before and without trial. But, still, the judge would have us tell you the charges against them. And, so, I shall! One! The children remind us of freedom, of what is possible when we live without fear. We hate that. Two! The children push us to think and live in new ways, but we are frightened of our own mortality. We are afraid to admit we cannot live forever. And three! The children demand we grow beyond our fears and keep pushing for better lives for everyone, without a need for borders, with or without government support. The children know the land belongs to all the people who need shelter here. They can afford kindness, because they have not become weak and greedy with fear. Oh no!

Judge   A shame. A sinful blasphemy against the fabric of this nation, a blight, increasing the national debt for which the children must pay. It sickens me! Is there anyone here to speak on behalf of these criminally minded children?

Charisma   I will, Your Honor.

Judge   And who are you?

Charisma   My name is Charisma, Your Honor. And I will speak on behalf of the convicted, if the court will not allow them to speak for themselves. I'm young. But I'm also a mother. My perspective is important, I think.

Judge   They cannot speak, because they have not learned their lessons. And I'm not sure if you have either. Clearly. But I'll let you speak for them so we can move this on along! I'm ready for dessert! Where is my cake?!

Charisma   Well, Your Honor, I will do my best.

A **Member of the Stage Management Team** *brings cake for the* **Judge***.*

Judge   Do.

Charisma   First of all, Your Honor, we would like to have Prosecutor Banker removed from this case as s/he has conflicting interests.

Judge   I told you . . . do not run tricks on me, young lady. If you do not get to the point, you will be held in contempt. Already, I do not like you much.

Charisma   Your Honor, we would also like to reject the jury's presence here. They are not a jury of the convicted's peers. They wear television sets on their heads!

Judge   How else will they understand?!

Prosecutor Banker   I would like to interject.

Judge   Yes, my friend?

Prosecutor Banker   I want to ask that the court forgo Miss Charisma's tantrums. We have witnesses who will prove the truth of our claims. I would like to call the Teacher who is also the Psychologist before the bench.

Judge   Come forward.

The **Teacher-Psychologist** *approaches the bench.*

Judge   I will begin with the Teacher. Teacher, please tell the court exactly what you have experienced in your dealings with the convicted, Tender, and Well-Seasoned Children?

Teacher   Your Honor, the convicted frighten me! When they come to school, their scowls prevent me from thinking straight! They snicker when I try to teach. They cannot be taught. They make fun of my efforts. I have nightmares whenever I try to sleep. I must confess we should eat them. It's the only solution.

Prosecutor Banker   Are there any of your colleagues who have a better time with the convicted?

Teacher   There are a few. But these are the experimental ones.

Judge   Shameful!

Prosecutor Banker   That's enough, Teacher. (*Giving her a tissue.*) You did just fine. We have duly noted your cooperation and will allow you to keep your job as long as you stay out of that nonsensical union. Now, Psychologist, can you please provide your professional analysis of the situation.

The **Teacher** *puts on the* **Psychologist's** *that delivered by a* **Member of the Stage Management Team**.

Psychologist   Your Honor, I, too, have tested the Convicted. These are our future rebels, Your Honor. If they are not forced to take strange medication and large doses of social media to silence their ideas, they will most certainly plague our future with rebellious acts of freedom. I recommend that the court act with swift justice for the sake of our national security! Eat them.

Judge   Well said, well said. Jury, I ask that you consider what you have heard here. And deliver your recommendation post haste.

Everyone looks at the **Jury of Television Heads** *on the screen, but they cannot respond, since they are only drawings of television heads. The* **Judge** *and the* **Prosecutor Banker** *look at each other, hunch their shoulders up in an "oh well" kind of way, and chant quietly and then loudly.*

Judge and Prosecutor Banke   Guilty! Guilty! Guilty!

Charisma   Wait! You can't do that! The jury can't even talk! There's no verdict! Throw it out! It don't count!

She encourages the audience to join the chant: "Throw it out! It don't count!"

Student-Defendants   Throw it out! It don't count! Throw it out! It don't count!

Judge ORDER! ORDER!

Genesis, Court Reporter *blows their whistle until all becomes still on stage. All other characters are now in tableaux.* **Genesis, Court Reporter** *takes off their top hat and walks toward the audience as* **Genesis, Griot** *and* **MC**.

Genesis So, my good people, it is inside chaos that we ask for your contribution. We've shared two stories—Charisma and her hopes and dreams with Fuego Designs, and Charisma in the upside down—where a far larger trial is being waged against our very own future in its totality. So, please, take off any evidence of a television head you may be wearing, and consider our plight. How do we manifest the dreams of our ancestors? What can we do as a community to ensure that Charisma and her son, and all of us, thrive? What role do you have to play in this unfolding saga known as our future?

Here, the play stops for a facilitated conversation with the audience led by the **Director/Teacher**.

The **Director/Teacher** *repeats the questions* **Genesis** *asked: 1. How do we manifest the dreams of our ancestors? 2. What can we do as a community to ensure that Charisma and her son, and all of us, thrive? And 3. What role do you have to play in this unfolding saga known as our future?*

Once this conversation with the audience has expired, the **Director/Teacher** *exits and* **Genesis** *speaks.*

Genesis We call on the names of our ancestors to guide us and pave the way for us, because they've already walked a long way. But, first, the drum . . .

Djembe Drummers *and other* **Percussion Musicians** *enter the stage. The* **Cast** *begins calling out the names of ancestors as they dance to the drum, becoming our* **Ancestors' Wildest Dreams** *as they dance and chant this litany of names.*

Once the short, rousing dance and ancestral praise ends, **Genesis** *leads the* **Cast** *and audience in a chanting.*

Genesis and Ancestors' Wildest Dreams Everything ain't what it seems. We are our ancestors' wildest dreams.

The chant should be repeated as long as it is felt.

End of play.

Suggested Exercises for Educators and Teaching Artists for *Charisma at the Crossroads*

Before reading or seeing the play

- Classroom Exercise:

  The character of Charisma says in the opening of the play, "There will be two plays, you see, or rather—one inside another." The first is a "realistic" conversation between four friends, but the play then changes to a non-realistic style where characters personify institutions or social systems that are in conflict with the human characters we have met.

  Have the students create character masks to personify each of these institutions: Banking/Finance; Justice; Education. Add additional institutions if you choose. The masks can be as extensive or as simple as you decide. Have the students move about the room wearing these masks. Ask them to notice what part of the body this character leads with as they move; encourage them to exaggerate that movement. Next, ask them to add a line of dialogue that this character might say. The line should be something quintessential or emblematic (perhaps offer an example). After a few minutes, invite volunteers to come up in front of the class and introduce themselves with a gesture and their line of dialogue. Ask the other students what they notice about the character's body. How does the actor need to move differently when wearing a mask (e.g., face the audience, exaggerate movement, move slower)? Discuss: What is the difference between an abstract character and a realistic character? What purpose does an abstract character serve? How does the mask help establish the abstract character for the audience?

- Classroom Exercise:

  Have your students create vision boards. Ask students the questions: "What are your hopes and dreams for the future? Where do you see yourself in ten years?" Have the class post drawings, photos, images, or poems on the board to depict these personal dreams (consider providing materials like magazines or allow them to print appropriate images from the internet). Encourage them to focus on how they want to feel, not just on things that they want.

  Discuss with the class: Who or what do you need to support you to achieve these dreams? What stands in your way of achieving these dreams?

After reading or seeing the play

- Classroom Exercise:

  Identify the specific hopes and dreams of each character in the play. Research the manner in which the following institutions (for which the class made their masks before see the play) enhance or inhibit the opportunities for young people to pursue and fulfill their dreams: Banking/Finance; Justice; Education.

Have a classroom debate about the above question, each side presenting the "pro" or "con" of the issue. Create a courtroom atmosphere, and let the class serve as the jury charged with deciding whether the institutions are guilty or innocent of thwarting or blocking opportunities for young people.

Afterwards, discuss the systematic changes that need to occur to support the hopes and dreams the class identified earlier.

- Classroom Exercise:

Have the class research the *griot*. How does the concept differ from that of a narrator? Who fulfills that role in your community? Divide the class into groups of three (if you need to have a group of four, you can have two *griots*). Have each group improvise a scene in which a young person is interacting with one of the masked figures described above. The young person is requesting something from the figure they need to fulfill their dream. The scene ends when they either are granted or denied that request. Add a *griot* at the beginning and end of the scene who interacts with the audience. In the first scene, they are preparing the audience for what they will see. In the final scene, they are commenting on what the audience just saw, or possibly facilitating a discussion. Discuss: How does the role of the *griot* change the play?

Southwestern High

Cassandra Medley

Background and Insights into *Southwestern High*

from Cassandra Medley

Notes on Casting

A Chorus of actors represent ages fourteen–eighteen, and should be multi racial, multi ethnic, male and female, and non-gender specific. They form a wall of people.

Notes on Production

Staging is intended to be totally flexible with as few props as possible. The Chorus Voices can provide atmospheric sounds.

All language references—curse words, lingo/slang/references to current events—can be adjusted, updated, modified. Technical devices should be updated whenever necessary.

The Inspiration for This Play

I have a vivid memory of being bullied in junior high school and high school. I also have memories of being part of a crowd witnessing other boys and girls who happened to be singled out and targeted for verbal and physical abuse. My own teen years were sometime before the digital age, so it is fascinating to see how the new technology has been adapted to the age-old human impulse to shame, humiliate, and abuse a chosen scapegoat. In fact, the new digital technology has allowed for even more vicious attacks toward targeted individuals. What does this mean for all of us at this present moment in history?

Major Themes

First, I am always fascinated with the universal attraction to violence, whether in one individual or with groups striking out at one another. In the case of mob violence, often when individuals are separated out, the mob will tend to dissipate—what causes this to happen?

Second, in what way might victims of bullying recover and perhaps heal?

Food for Thought

I hope my play will inspire discussions concerning the very themes I am trying to impart: bullying, possible reasons why bullies need to deflect attention from themselves, or suffer from hidden abuse, and personal anxieties. Ways in which targeted victims might recover.

Entrance into the World of Theatre

I was interested in the theatre from early childhood and was constantly making up, and acting out, stories. As a teenager, I joined a teen theatre repertory company and toured my hometown of Detroit, Michigan. I have written for television and film as well as theatre.

The thrill of writing for the theatre is that one is present at a live performance of actual actors performing to live audiences. One is part of a dynamic public exchange of energy, and each live audience an unpredictable challenge to the actors on stage; I find it really thrilling.

Characters

Kalima, *sixteen years old*
Chorus *(collective), a mixture of high school students*
Chorus Member *(individuals), will include:* **Young Lorraine**, *Lorraine's sister*
Denise, **Teen Boy**, **Teacher**
Lorraine, *forty years old*
Teacher

Place: Detroit, Michigan.
Time: June 2019.

Lights up on a **Chorus** *of actors. They form a semicircle with their backs to the audience. They represent ages fourteen – eighteen and should be multi racial, multi ethnic, male and female, and non- gender-specific. They form a wall of people.*

Kalima *and* **Lorraine** *stand with their backs turned as part of the Chorus, then turn to face the audience, and walk forward, smiling at each other, and referring to the building in front of them— which is to say, into the audience.*

Lorraine *gazes intently up at the building which should seem to be at least three stories high and huge.*

Kalima   Aunt Lorraine . . . why you wanna see this ole beat-up building?

Lorraine   Just to see for myself.

Kalima   See what?

Lorraine   Wow. My old Southwestern Highschool, now a wreck.

She points in the distance.

Girl, I envy you, having that brand new, shiny high school up the road there. You lucky so-and-so, you!

Kalima (*bitter*)   Ugh. Never have to walk inside that place again after tomorrow.

Lorraine   Woah. (*Bewildered.*) You don't seem . . .

Kalima   What?

Lorraine   I don't know. (*Beat.*) Everything okay?

Kalima   Just wanna get out of this town, and get on the college. Just like you did.

The **Chorus** *all pull out their cell phones—they make a collective "bling"—cell-phone text sound.*

Kalima *checks her cell phone.* **Chorus Member** *calls out the text as* **Kalima** *reads it.*

Chorus Member   Hey, "Monkey-Girl", what you up to? Stuffing down bananas?

Chorus *snickers and laughs, type on their cell phones for a few seconds.* **Second Chorus Member** *calls out the text as* **Kalima** *reads it.*

Second Chorus Member   Who's gotta sit next to "Monkey-Girl" at Commencement tomorrow? Better bring some air freshener with you!

Chorus *cackles, then pocket their cell phones. A brief, stressed look crosses* **Kalima**'s *face.*

Lorraine   What's wrong?

Kalima (*quickly*)   Nothing. (*Beat.*) Ok, next stop, Motown Museum. C'mon.

Lorraine   Hold up, take a picture . . . me in front of my old high school . . .

Kalima   You wanna stand in front of this wreck, and take a picture? Why?

Lorraine Stuff about . . . the past.

Kalima (*amused*) Auntie, you are so wac.

As they exchange smiles **Lorraine** *hands* **Kalima** *her own cell phone, poses, and* **Kalima** *snaps photo.*

Lorraine Well, tomorrow, you'll be taking all your selfies in front of your school, and with all your friends, "Ms. Graduating Senior."

Kalima (*firm and serious*) No, I *won't.*

Again, **Lorraine** *pauses, studying* **Kalima**.

Kalima What? You got away, right? College, then traveling the world.

Lorraine True. I couldn't get away fast enough.

Kalima And like Mom's always saying, I'm just like you.

The **Chorus** *all pull out their cell phones—they make a collective "bling"—cellphone text sound.*

Kalima *checks her cell phone,* **Chorus Member**, *calls out the text as* **Kalima** *reads it.*

Chorus Member (*calls out*) Hey, "Monkey-Girl"! Don't you be stinking up our graduation!

Hooting laughter from **Chorus**. **Kalima** *is clearly upset.*

Lorraine Kalima, whatsamatter?

Kalima Nothing. (*Quickly.*) Okay. Next stop, Motown Museum.

Lorrain Kalima?

Kalima Whaa? (*Obviously pretending, false cheer.*) Hurry up. Let's go.

Kalima *pulls out her car keys,* **Lorraine** *grabs hold of the keys, and studies the African beaded keychain.*

Lorraine (*re the keychain*) Kali, I sent you this all the way from Lagos . . .

Kalima (*much too quickly, obviously lying*) I know—I know I—see, what happened was, was that, it got ummm—the beads on it got tangled up with uh . . . this uh . . . with my gym locker and I tried to be careful, but it was all tangled up, and I hated that 'cause it's your last year Christmas present and I tried to—to get it untangled but then the—the—

Lorraine *puts a hand on* **Kalima**'s *shoulder.*

Lorraine What's going on with you, darlin'?

Chorus Members *make a regular cell-phone ringtone.* **Lorraine** *checks her phone. She doesn't answer it, annoyed.*

Lorraine Your Principal McGrath.

Kalima   You gonna speak? Or no?

Lorraine   Hold up. Still have an hour to—to think on it.

Kalima   Auntie Lorraine, you're a big deal to everybody around here.

Lorraine (*rather tense*)   Honey. I'm back here just to see *you*, and your mom, and to celebrate your graduation. With your dad joining us, too. Want us all to just enjoy all being together as a family.

Kalima   Mom and the whole neighborhood always brags about "Lorraine, our big-time doctor curing diseases all over Africa."

Lorraine   It's a little bit more complicated than that. Sometimes we cure, but a lotta times we fail. (*Beat.*) Honey, a commencement speech is no small thing to put together.

Kalima   Principal McGrath does the main speech, you just be the added attraction. That's all.

Lorraine (*gently*)   "That's all"? I just got here last night from Zambia; I've got a paper to present at a conference in Zurich day after tomorrow.

Kalima   Wow. Doctors from all over the world, huh?

Lorraine   "A Global Response to possible infectious Diseases."

Kalima (*trying to appear accepting*)   Right. Speaking for tomorrow's no big deal, compared to that.

Lorraine   Now wait a minute, nobody saying that. All I'm saying is that, is that, if only somebody had contacted me ahead of time . . . given me time to prepare.

Kalima   But, we kept trying and trying . . .

Lorraine   I know . . . it's hard to track me down from refugee camps out in the middle of nowhere. (*Beat.*) Tell you a secret? (*Beat.*) Public speaking scares me unless I'm really prepared.

Kalima is obviously disappointed, but remains polite.

Kalima   Okay. No big deal.

Lorraine   I'm still thinking it over. (*Beat.*) You know that if I was prepared, wasn't rushing all over the place, I would say "yes" right away. Right?

Kalima   Anyways, after tomorrow, I—I don't have to ever, ever think of that place.

The **Chorus** all pull out their cell phones—they make a collective "bling"—cell-phone text sound.

Kalima checks her cell phone.

Chorus Member   "Monkey-Girl" so black, black, tomorrow you ain't gonna be able to tell her face from her shiny black shoes.

Chorus Member "Monkey-Girl" gonna scratch her way all the way up to the stage and start chewing on her diploma!

They all snicker and laugh, type on their cell phones for a few seconds . . .

Chorus Member Here's a brand new "monkey face" for Instagram, y'all!

They snicker and howl with laughter, then pocket the cell phones. A stressed look on **Kalima***'s face as she pockets her cell phone.*

Lorraine Kalima, what is going on? Who keeps texting you?

Kalima *shrugs.*

Kalima Nothing that I can't handle.

Lorraine Kalima—

Kalima (*interrupting*) You always say for me to stay strong, so I'm staying strong.

Lorraine *reaches for* **Kalima***, as* **Kalima** *turns away from her, trying to smile.*

Kalima I'm great, no problem. We better get to the museum before the crowds.

Kalima *starts off,* **Lorraine** *stops her.*

Lorraine Staying strong about what?

Kalima C'mon. Gotta beat the traffic. I'll show you my favorite room when we get there.

Lorraine *holds* **Kalima** *back, staring into her face, studying* **Kalima***'s expression.*

Lorraine (*realizing something*) Oh, gawd.

Kalima (*gesturing at the building*) Auntie, let's go. They ought to tear this building down.

Again **Kalima** *attempts to move, but* **Lorraine** *holds her in place.*

Lorraine Kali. I see it in your face.

Kalima What's up? Wha?

Lorraine Show me your keychain. C'mon, please. Let me see it.

Embarrassed, **Kalima** *slowly pulls out her car keychain, handing it to* **Lorraine***.*

Kalima Like I said, it got tangled up in my locker at school, and then the thread just split . . . and uh—uh.

Lorraine *holds up the keychain.*

Lorraine Somebody else tore this up, didn't they?

Kalima *is too upset to even answer.*

Lorraine (*realizing*) This past September, when I was in Cape Town, and you called me . . .

Kalima   That was nothing, I got through it just like you said I would.

Lorraine   And then, you called me in October.

Kalima   You said I'd get through it, and I did, and I have.

Lorraine   All this time . . . I'm thinking you're talking about your *grades*. I'm telling you to "stay tough" because I'm thinking we're talking about your grade point average; which we all know is excellent . . . (*Realizing.*) . . . and your mom emailing me all the time about how worried she is about you.

Kalima   Y'all worry too much.

Lorraine   NO. Apparently, we haven't been worried *enough*!

The **Chorus** *all pull out their cell phones—they make a collective "bling"—cell-phone text sound.*

Lorraine *holds* **Kalima***'s hand.*

Lorraine   Don't read that.

Long pause.

You're being bullied, aren't you?

Kalima   Not really.

Lorraine   You calling me to say things were so tough in school. What you meant was, you were being bullied.

Kalima   I can handle it.

Lorraine   You've been bullied over these past few months, I bet the whole semester, maybe even the whole school year?

Kalima   Tomorrow it's over. I don't ever have to think about it.

Lorraine   Gawd, I'm so busy with my patients . . . meanwhile, my beloved niece is going through all this.

Kalima (*very distressed*)   It's no big deal. I've been handling it, I can handle it.

Lorraine   That's exactly what I would say to myself.

Lorraine *considers a moment, and then impulsively grabs* **Kalima***'s hand, pulling her forward.*

Lorraine   You know what? Let's go inside.

Kalima   Whaaa? Why?

Lorraine *gestures towards the building.*

Lorraine   C'mon, please? Come with me. It may be a "wreck," but I know these hallways. This time, let *me* be the tour guide. (*Beat.*) Okay?

Kalima *hesitates.* **Lorraine** *gestures for her to follow.*

The **Chorus**, *with their backs to the audience, form a doorway that opens up.* **Lorraine** *and* **Kalima** *walk through. They look around.*

Lorraine   Oh, yes, yes, here come the memories. The worst times were between the classes.

School bell sounds.

I see myself so clearly . . . the way I was back then.

Lorraine *gestures,* **the Chorus** *turns to face us, and* **Young Lorraine** *steps forward.*

Present-day **Lorraine** *and* **Kalima** *stand to the side, watching.*

Chorus Member *calls out to* **Young Lorraine,** *who freezes in place.*

Chorus   Uggggleee!

The entire **Chorus** *turns to face the audience, jeering at* **Lorraine**.

Chorus Member   She Black Barbie . . . .

Chorus Member   She "Nappy hair, Blackie" Barbie, that's who she is!

Young Lorraine *freezes in place. Present-day* **Lorraine** *turns to* **Kalima**.

Lorraine   And then, your mom would come by on the way to her own classes . . .

Lorraine's *sister,* **Denise,** *steps through the* **Chorus**. *Obviously frightened by the* **Chorus,** **Denise** *whispers to* **Young Lorraine**.

Denise   Just ignore them . . .

Teen Boy *calls out to* **Denise**.

Teen Boy   Yo! Denise! You be half-way good looking. You ain't no Beyoncé, or nothing, but you ain't half bad. How come you gotta have a Blackie freak-looking little sister?!

The **Chorus** *cackles. Both* **Denise** *and* **Young Lorraine** *freeze.*

Denise (*whispers to* **Young Lorraine**)   Just pretend they not there . . . c'mon . . . .

Young Lorraine (*calling out to* **Denise**)   Denise!

Denise *proceeds to walk past the* **Chorus** *and disappears into the shadows, leaving* **Young Lorraine** *frozen.*

Teen Girl   Where's ya sista, now? Not here to protect ya!

Teen Girl Two   Yeah, ya Blackie Barbie bitch!

Teen Boy *steps out from the* **Chorus,** *brandishing a handwritten note. He waves it in* **Young Lorraine's** *face.*

Teen Boy   HEY! Who the hell told you I was "in love with you?!"

The **Chorus** *cackles in unison.*

Young Lorraine (*to* **Teen Boy**) I—I—that's not my handwriting . . .

Boy *barks straight into* **Young Lorraine***'s face, as the* **Chorus** *cackles.*

Teen Boy HUH?! Who the hell told you I was "in love with you?!" YOU TOO UGLY FOR ANYBODY TO BE IN LOVE WITH YOU!

Young Lorraine (*to* **Teen Boy**) I—I—that's not my . . .

Teen Boy *barks straight into* **Young Lorraine***'s face.*

Teen Boy DON'T YOU BE WRITING ME NO MORE, YOU—

Teen Boy *mouths the words, as present-day* **Lorraine** *turns to* **Kalima**.

Lorraine . . . and he used the "N" word, plus lots of other ugly, ugly words. Then, they shoved me into the Girls' Bathroom . . .

Teen Boy *shoves* **Young Lorraine** *into one designated spot on the stage.* **Two Teen Girls** *follow behind, then enter the bathroom with* **Young Lorraine**.

Stage slide flashes a girls' bathroom mirror with the word "Black Nigger Lorraine" scrawled across the glass.

Lorraine (*to* **Kalima**) Those girls had marked up the bathroom mirror . . .

Young Lorraine *mimes scrubbing off the graffiti with her bare hands, as the* **Teen Girls** *laugh and taunt her. Suddenly the* **Teacher** *steps out from the* **Chorus**, *crossing into the girls' bathroom.*

Teacher (*with the usual authority*) What's going on in here, young ladies??

The **Chorus** *is quickly subdued and submissive. The* **Chorus** *moves off in various directions, then forms back as a wall of people with their backs to the audience.*

Teacher Miss Prentis? What was all that about?

Young Lorraine Nothing. It's . . . *nothing* . . .

The **Teacher** *returns to the* **Chorus** *with their backs to the audience.*

Kalima *now faces* **Lorraine** *in the present day.*

Kalima Nobody caught those kids?

Lorraine *shakes her head, "no."*

Lorraine I never told who they were.

Kalima (*beat*) Ma didn't stand up for you, as her little sister, or protect you?

Lorraine She was just a kid, like me . . . too scared. I realize that, now. Just like you've been too scared. (*Beat.*) Am I right?

Kalima They . . . They call me all kinds of stuff. Put it all over Instagram. Kids who I'll never know . . . laughing at me.

Lorraine People always find new ways to be cruel.

Kalima   But I've been being strong about it.

Lorraine   Nonsense.

Kalima   You were strong.

Lorraine   That's a lie, honey. My hiding it from myself was *not* being strong. My never talking about it to anybody was *not* being strong.

Pause.

Been giving you the wrong message, sweetness. I'm so sorry.

They hold each other.

Kalima   Being "Black" is supposed to be something that's "beautiful."

Lorraine   Being Black *is* beautiful.

Kalima   Not with the kids that keep coming after me.

Lorraine   Those kids are using you to attack what they hate about themselves. "Black is beautiful," only if you learn that it's true.

Pause.

Sad. Because their self-hate'll take a toll on their lives. I see this happen everywhere I travel in the wide world.

Pause.

But understanding why it happens does not excuse directing their self-hate at you.

Kalima   Rappers use the "N-word" all the time.

Lorraine   Sorry, I don't buy it. There's no way to rescue that word. The purpose and meaning of that word is the same as it ever, ever was. To hurt and shame our people. And for me, when we use it toward our own, we're just turning that hate back on ourselves.

Lorraine *and* **Kalima** *walk through the "doorway" formed by the* **Chorus***, and are once more outside.*

Lorraine   You ever thought of just blocking their messages?

Kalima   I know it was stupid, but I—

Lorraine   Nunno, wait, hold up . . . you're not stupid, Kali.

Kalima   I thought I could protect myself more, if I knew what they were saying.

Lorraine   Honey. Listen. Look at me. (*Beat.*) Victims all over the world believe that they should "be strong enough" to put up with whatever abuse they're suffering. I see this all the time. It's a lie.

Kalima *holds up her cell phone, presses buttons.*

Kalima   Done.

Lorraine *gives a mock wave.*

Lorraine   Thank you, Southwestern High.

Kalima (*bewildered*)   "Thank you?"

Lorraine *pulls out her cell phone, presses in a number.* **Kalima** *waits, curious.*

Lorraine (*into her phone*)   Principal McGrath, please, Dr. Prentis calling . . .

The voice answers on the other line.

And "Good afternoon" to you, too . . . Oh, I'm great, I have the title for my speech tomorrow . . .

Kalima   Speech tomorrow?

Surprised and delighted, she locks eyes with **Lorraine***.*

Lorraine (*into her phone*)   "Meeting up with Old Ghosts." (*Pause.*) That's right. I'm definitely on board. (*Pause.*) Making notes now . . . Yes, indeed . . . I am very much looking forward to it . . . Just email me the program and I'll be ready. See you tomorrow.

She clicks off her cell phone.

Kalima   Wait . . . thought it's so hard for you to give speeches in public. If you're not prepared.

Lorraine   Oh, I'm prepared. Never been so prepared in my whole life.

Kalima (*amazed*)   You're going to tell all of them what happened to you?

Lorraine   You bet I am.

Pause.

What happened to me has happened to so many people who'll be sitting there tomorrow. Some were bullied, some watched it being done to others, some did it to somebody else.

Pause.

It'll be my own story of what I went through, and how I survived, found my real friends . . . And how I'm *now* living the dream that I worked so hard to make real.

Lorraine *and* **Kalima** *freeze as the* **Chorus** *turns to face the audience.*

Chorus Member (*to audience*)   It'll be my story of what I went through, and how I survived, found my real friends . . .

Chorus Member (*to audience*)   It'll be my story of how I'm now living the dream that I worked so hard to make real.

Lorraine *holds out her fist to* **Kalima***. They bump fists together.*

Lorraine   Darlin', with me I decided to work in some very, very tough places, under some very rough conditions. That was my choice. Days when I have a victory over some illness, or realize a solution to a problem, those days are so absolutely satisfying, so wonderful.

Pause.

But there are also always very, very tough days, and there always will be those days, because that's what life is.

Pause.

So, I have to keep building on my self-love to help get me through. It's a lifetime job.

Pause.

You've got a whole new life waiting. You're gonna make so many amazing discoveries up ahead, and change in ways that you can't begin to imagine.

Lorraine *and* **Kalima** *freeze in place.*

Chorus Member (*to audience*)   You've got a whole new life waiting.

Chorus Member (*to audience*)   You're gonna make so many amazing discoveries up ahead . . .

Chorus Member (*to audience*)   . . . and change in ways that you can't begin to imagine.

Lorraine *and* **Kalima** *resume interaction.*

Lorraine   Kalima? Your Aunt Lorraine will always be cheering you on.

Lorraine *and* **Kalima** *hug, as . . .*

Lights go down.

End of play.

Suggested Exercises for Educators and Teaching Artists for *Southwestern High*

Before reading or seeing the play

- Classroom Exercise:

  Ask each student to do a freewrite based on the prompt "Bullying is . . ." They will need paper and a writing instrument. Encourage them to write without censoring themselves. Let them know that the papers will not be collected.

  After five minutes, ask the students to pause (it is alright if they are not finished). Ask the students to look at the whole paper and select eight words about which they feel strongly (they do not need to justify this choice). The students should next create a four-line poem based on their circled words.

  Break the class into small groups of four students. If you do not have even numbers, you can create a group of three or five. Have each student share the poem within the group. The group should then create a new, group poem, taking two lines from each individual poem to create an eight- to ten-line poem, depending on the number of participants in each group. Next, each group should create a group sculpture depicting bullying. Note: Rather than create realistic scenes, encourage to create abstract images that focus on how bullying feels.

  One participant in the group should read the group's poem aloud as the rest of the class observes the frozen image.

After reading or seeing the play

- Classroom Exercise:

  Have students play Augusto Boal's "Columbian Hypnosis."

  [See Boal, Augusto (2002) *Games for Actors and Non-Actors,* 2nd ed. Adrian Jackson, trans. London: Routledge: 51–55.]

  Next, position the students so that they are audience members viewing a playing space. In the playing space, ask a pair to repeat the Hypnosis exercise, but this time freeze them after ten seconds. Have one student hold up their other hand. Invite someone from the "audience" to position themselves so their face is six inches from this hand. Repeat, until there are at least four players. Freeze the image. Ask the class to imagine that this frozen image is titled "bullying." Ask them to imagine who the characters are and what might be leading to their behavior. Encourage them to notice the character(s) who are both leading and following a hand (i.e., both being bullied and bullying someone else). Discuss what leads to bullying and how might we prevent it?

- Class Discussion:

  In the play, Kalima is bullied on social media, while Lorraine was bullied as a high school student in person by other students. How are their experiences the same? How are they different? How does social media enable bullying? Do you think Lorraine's action of calling out bullying in her graduation speech an effective approach? Why or why not? How does Lorrainne's action of helping Kalima help her heal from her own past?

- Bonus Round:

  Divide the students into small groups. Have each group design a social media campaign against bullying at your school. Ask students to consider who might be an ally in this campaign. Have each group pitch their campaign to the class. Consider choosing a campaign or merging ideas and actually putting these ideas into practice.

Stare and Compare

A play in one act

Evelyn Diaz Cruz

Background and Insights into *Stare and Compare*

from Evelyn Diaz Cruz

Notes on Casting

The roles of Jazz and Alex are intentionally written as non-gender specific. In this version Jazz's pronouns are "she/her/hers" and Alex's are "he/him/his;" however, pronouns can be adjusted accordingly.

Notes on Production

An understanding of references to the Orishas and how that (they) informs our sense of self.

Link to New Jersey Institute for Social Justice, which may be useful as part of a lobby display pre/post-show. https://www.youtube.com/watch?v=eHXO1Pl-AJ4&t=1s

The Inspiration for This Play

On a recent trip to Puerto Rico, after Hurricane Maria devastated the island, I was reconnected with magnificent long-lost family and the soul-stirring spirit of my ancestors. The emotional reunion was heightened by the community organizing happening on the island. The shaved tops of the palms and felled trees laid bare both the determination and joyful spirit that is emblematic of the people. Coincidentally, I also had a commission to write a play for youth. I had taken note that youth these days are fascinated with selfies and their online profiles; not surprisingly perhaps, makeup has made a huge comeback. While some may call this the "Stare and Compare Generation," truth be told, I also love playing with makeup and styling my hair! I still love playing dress-up! It's theatre! I heartily embrace this generation's artistic expression and hope to offer a chance to them to consider how they may creatively contribute to worthy causes by using their unique gifts.

Major Themes

Awakening your authentic self and higher power through art, music, and dance; using your gifts to give back; pursuing social justice authentically; connecting with and thereby honoring one's family and heritage; listening to the Orisha that guides you.

Food for Thought

I hope this play inspires youth to think about giving back in a broader creative sense. Anything that a young person is passionate about may be used for a greater common good. Anything! It has been my experience that young people overwhelmingly want a way to give back, but too often there is a narrow array and perception of options articulated for them (e.g., tutoring, volunteerism at food banks, etc.). Undeniably, all forms of giving back are valuable and commendable, but if one is fortunate enough to be able to use their natural gifts in this regard it can also be magical.

Entrance into the Theatre

At twenty-one years old and a single mother of two children, I started a job as an executive assistant at San Diego State University's Chicana/o/x Studies Department. Having never been on a university campus before, the world opened up for me there, where I joined an all-women's Latina theatre troupe performing agit-prop- style theatre. This theatre company included study groups on class inequity regarding issues on health, housing, and education. We used that information to inspire our original theatre performances at rallies, student conferences, etc. Using a satirical ragtag aesthetic, our focus was on education rather than aspirations of the professional stage. Creating theatre for social change ignited my consciousness. I was hooked! From that springboard I began studying theatre at the university in a more serious way.

Characters

Serena
Angel
Dre
Jazz
Victor, Jazz's Brother
Alex
Crew Members and Friends

Place: New Jersey and Puerto Rico.
Time: Anytime shortly after Hurricane Maria hit in September 2017.

Scene One

Lights up. We see **Serena** *at her vanity shooting a self-video. She is already a flamboyant feminine personality and dresses that part.*

Serena Hollllaaaa . . . Short for Halleuuuujah! This is Serena the Queen-ahh checking in with you. Today I am showing you how to light up your face in a way that's guaranteed to keep you always camera ready and getting the most attention from that special person you are targeting. Someone posted on this feed that even though they never leave the house without full-on makeup—it is still *nada*! Okay, gurrrl . . . I am going to have to be blunt. I saw your pic. You got the makeup all wrong. So, my demonstration today, is for you, cuz let's *face* it, well . . . you could use some help. This is also for anyone else who thinks makeup won't *make up* for that starting line. It does! But you gotta learn how to package your stuff right, if you want to catch a bae. Helloooo! You want to celebrate your assets. Like, for real, those *bembes* (*smacks her lips for the camera*) if you have them, BOOM! Seriously. But even if you don't have them, we can just make it up. And I am going to show you how right now: Because let's face it we should always be camera ready. Right? Look at your friends on Instagram. Just like those other *mamitas* you see running around? You better know they stare and compare. So be ready with—

Angel, *a complete stylistic opposite to* **Serena**, *barges in.* **Angel***'s style is a natural look, wilder hair, inner-city urban hip and definitely a statement of pride in being Afro-PR, cowry shell jewelry, etc.*

Serena What the hell are you doing here?! I know you had to have seen the "Do Not Disturb" sign!

Angel No, I didn't.

Serena You are such a liar. You knew I was working!

Angel (*suppressing a chuckle while looking for musical instruments*)   —working. (*Sarcastically.*) Sorry.

Serena I'm gonna have to do this whole video over again. I could have been taping live!

Angel Look, I am just getting my *she'* and my books. Okay? Like . . . Umm . . . for reading?

Serena I hate you.

Angel I hate you too.

Serena (*pronounced as if saying "Bitch"*)   Witch!

Angel (*proudly reclaims the word*)   So I've been told.

Serena I am almost up to 1000 followers! And you just jacked m—

Angel Cry me a river. I had to get my stuff! (*Sarcastically.*) 1000 followers. For what? Ewww all the money you're gonna make?

Serena   At least I got a plan. What you got?!

Angel   I got community.

Serena   Oh yeah . . . Saving the world: One worthy cause at a time. How is that working for you?

Angel   Great! I got mad love for our community.

Serena (*false sincerity, sarcastic*)   Good for you! Every cause in the universe can count on you to help. I got news for you, sis: All that stress? Is showing on your face. You are only a year older than me, but you look at least five. Your forehead already has premature wrinkles. In fact, you should let me help you with that.

Angel   What the—? Man, forget chu'! Where's my *shekere*?

Serena   How should I know?

Angel   I left it right here on the bed with my fliers.

Serena   Another one of your event fliers? Yeah, that narrows it.

Angel'*s phone rings.*

Angel (*frustrated*)   Yeah hello! Sorry, man. I can't do it tonight. We're already booked. Of course, I care. I am insulted you even said that! Look (*pauses and struggles*) I don't even know these people. Who are they? Yeah. Ah ha. (*Pause.*) Is that right? Well I can probably pull some folks to go by afterwards. Yes. Alright already. I am down! I gotta go. Holla back. (*To* **Serena**.) Where is it?!

Serena   I said I don't know.

Angel   You're lying—

Serena *and* **Angel** *continue yelling at each other with shouts of accusations and denials until* **Mother** *bangs on the door for them to stop!*

Mother (*offstage*)   Hey, you two! Keep it down to a roar!

Angel *grabs her maracas and fliers and storms out. On the way out, enter* **Serena**'*s boyfriend,* **Dre**. **Angel** *and* **Dre** *almost crash into each other.* **Angel** *keeps going unapologetically, visibly irritated.*

Dre (*comically calling after* **Angel**)   Hey! Nice seeing you too. I am good! Thanks. YO! Catchu' later, Ma'. (*Staring after* **Angel**, *says comically and convincingly.*) Dang, your sister just loooves me.

Serena (*still irritated and fights laughing*)   Ya think?

Dre (*overly confident type*)   Yeah, look out for that one, cuz, she wants some of dis. (*Checks himself in the mirror.*) You ready?

Serena   I had a little technical difficulty. But yeah, for the most part . . . I guess so.

Dre   Gon' be lit! Perfect backdrop for this video. I am a genius. Did I tell you I am a genius?

Serena   Yeeesssss . . . but I would love to hear it again. (*Bats her eyelashes.*)

Dre   Did you get those last changes I sent you?

Serena   Yeah, but I didn't get to finish it. My sister sabotaged me.

Dre   Oh really? Hey look, no worries. We can always come back to that video. Where we are headed, this backdrop won't be available later. So, let's make like a hat and tip. You got any props?

Serena   Yes. Right here. (*Grabs a shekere from under her vanity.*)

Dre (*admires it*)   That's a sick *shekere*! We good to go. (*Holds the door out dramatically for her.*) My queen.

Serena *walks out like royalty.*

Serena (*pauses at the door dramatically*)   I. Love. You.

Dre (*teasing her, but obvious he loves her too*)   You a'ight.

Serena *hits him playfully.*

Dre   Let's go pimp some culture. (*Pause.*) Let's bounce.

Both exit excited.

Scene Two

A rec. center in New Jersey. Bomba music and dance workshop in progress. Banner indicates that this is a fundraiser for Hurricane Maria. The PR flag and "Puerto Rico se Levanta" slogans, murals, etc. are hung.

Angel *is in the musicians' group with her maracas or plays the congas or the box. Simple dance moves with an instructor/MC demonstrating, explaining, and inviting youth to participate. Enter* **Bomba Dancers** *to present a choreographed show. The costumes can be as simple as a skirt and headwrap or full bomba outfits.*

The dancers demonstrate how they control the drumming.

After the Bombaso show, the **MC** *opens up the floor to the audience and* **Bomberos** *and* **MC** *invite their onstage audience to participate.*

One of the coaxed dancers approaches the drummers with a simple but magnetic Bomba dance style. **Angel** *falls in love during the give and take of their music/dance exchange. (Note: The exchange is sensual but not sexual. The sense is that of connecting with a higher power as well as each other.) Everyone senses the energy and is having a blast! The feel is that of community getting real with all kinds of levels of dance expertise participating and a celebration of each other's efforts. Freedom.*

Serena *enters with her crew and is not interested in the music. She is surrounded by her groupies and one of them is filming her while she talks to the phone's video camera. The band fades into the background.*

Serena (*walking and talking*)   And this face (*gestures to indicate the whole face*) is what I like to call the hanging out at the rec. center, but not looking like you worked it too hard to be this beautiful (*winks*). Remember "stare and compare." But mos' def not trying to look all sweaty and ratched either. No, no, no, no, *chicas.* You want to have that fresh look of like "I ain't even trying to be this gorgeous" type of look.

Trying to signal the **Camera Person** *without disrupting her flow, she indicates to the* **Camera Person** *to hold up the lens angle for her best profile. During the following* **Angel** *comes up in back of* **Serena** *and is photobombing her shoot. Slowly, through her next lines* **Serena** *begins to realize something is up behind her.*

Serena   You got the Bomba in your bones and the sway in your hips. And for that unique Afro-Latinx vibe, you might want to carry an instrument of your choice and shake it baby. (*Shakes the shekere.*) I digress, but it is part of the whole package. Now the lips!

Don't go all greasy *bembe* during the day. Uggh . . . I like to use the Walmart Brand "Pinky," I know what you're thinking . . . Walmart?

Finally realizes that **Angel** *has been photobombing her. Turns to confront her.* **Serena's Crew** *and* **Angel** *laugh.* **Serena** *is furious. When the friends realize how mad she is they find it even harder to suppress their laughter, as they are definitely intimidated by* **Serena***. Throughout the sisters' following exchange the crew makes funny comments like "Oh snap," or "Daaaang," etc. to edge them on.*

Serena   —What the hell are you doing? How could you?

Angel   Me? How could YOU? Busting in here like this?!

Serena   You should be grateful.

Angel   For what? The disrespect?! You can't just come in here and—

Serena   —It's still a free country last time I checked.

Angel   You're not even interested in this music.

Serena   Is that what you call it?

Angel (*trying to control herself*)   You're ridiculous. You need to go. We're working.

Serena   So am I.

Angel   HA! That's a joke!

Serena   So is your face!

Angel *and* **Serena** *have started to get their faces up close practically yelling at each other.*

Crew Members *are now working to separate them in case it gets too heavy between the sisters, but still trying not to laugh at them.*

Angel (*to* **Dre** *who is holding the shekere*)   What are you laughing at?

The **Camera Person** *has started filming.* **Angel** *puts her hand to cover the camera.*

Angel   Gimme that before you make me do something I'll regret! Don't look or you gon' find it!

Serena   We're leaving, but don't flatter yourself why. (*To her* **Crew**.) Let's go. Nothing but a bunch of hicks here anyway.

Being spiteful, she flaps her arms like a chicken in a bad imitation of a Bomba move to make her **Crew** *laugh.*

The **Crew** *follows* **Serena** *who takes her time leaving and messing around just to spite or try to provoke her sister, and leaves like royalty.*

Serena   Serena the Queen-ahhh of New Jersey . . . is leaving. (*Dramatic exit.*)

The dancer-love-interest **Jazz** *has been watching.* **Jazz** *approaches* **Angel** *and catches her off guard.*

Jazz   Hey. You okay?

Angel (*surprised*)   What? Oh. Yeah. Of course. I'm fine.

Jazz   That was intense. Who's the witch?

Angel   My sister.

Jazz   Oh. I am sorry. My bad.

Angel (*suppresses a laugh*)   It's alright. No worries.

Jazz (*embarrassed and then jokingly*)   So . . . You got some serious sibling rivalry going on?

Angel (*laughs*)   Yeah . . . Something like that. (*Awkward pause for love connection.*)

Both try to talk at once, over each other.

Angel	**Jazz**
You are the best dancer!	You play so dope!
I could really feel it with you	No kidding? Me too! Like damn! You know?
Oh hell yeah! It was beautiful	I felt it too . . .
The spirit energy	The ancestors! *Ashe' Ashe' Ashe'*!

Another awkward pause for love connection.

Angel   Yeah, I felt it too . . . (*Beautifully awkward pause, excitement, connection*).

Hey, would you like to help me with another fundraiser after this?

Jazz   For what?

Angel   I promised to show up for an event for the New Jersey Institute for Social Justice to support their work for "150 years is enough!"

Jazz   Sounds cool.

Angel   It's one of their causes for fighting juvenile incarceration.

Jazz   I will have to bring my kid brother. I am kind of babysitting him. My moms doesn't like to leave him alone at night if she has to work. (*Motions.*) Yo, Victor! Come here.

Victor (*has been waiting his turn to play a simple instrument with the band; a clave, or maracas*)   Hold on a minute. They're gonna let me play!

Jazz   It will just take a minute. (**Victor** *obeys reluctantly but is a good kid.*)

Victor   Yeah? Wassup?

Jazz   Just an FYI, we gonna head out to another event right after this one, so stay where I can see you.

Victor   Ok. Who's we?

Jazz   Just a few of the musicians, you, me and—(*Awkward moment.*)

Angel (*quickly jumps in, offers a handshake*)   Hey, Vic, nice to meet you. I am Angel. I got asked to help at another event. And your sibling—(*Looks at Jazz for help.*)

Jazz   —Jazz.

Angel   —yes, Jazz, is gonna help me with it. You like playing music, *papa*?

Victor   Yeah. But, I am just learning.

Jazz   Want to play your first gig tonight? For an excellent cause?

Victor   I can't really play yet. I just started.

Angel   That's alright. You got rhythm?

Victor   Yeah.

Angel   I will show you how to keep time on the cowbell. You'll be fine. You down?

Victor (*excited*)   Hell yeah! Thanks.

Angel *and* **Victor** *fist bump.*

Angel   Thanks! Really appreciated.

Victor   I'm-a go practice then, ok, Jazz? (*He is already running back to the band.*)

Jazz (*yelling after him*)   Stay close by. Don't make me come looking for you!

Victor (*yelling back over his shoulder*)   I won't. I promise.

Angel   I like him.

Jazz   Thanks. He's good too. He likes hanging out with me. Go figure.

Angel   Sounds like we got a plan then.

Jazz (*excited*)   DOPE!

Angel (*happy*)   SICK! *Vamanos.*

Laughing at the spectacle, both go back to the music, maybe trying to dance, or play instruments, trying to catch paper towels, fun heightened, etc.

Music is starting up again. Paper towels are thrown out to the audience on stage, maybe into the actual audience in the house.

Blackout.

Scene Three

Stage reflects nighttime. **Angel** *comes into her bedroom. She is exhausted but happy with obvious rhythms still resonating in her body.* **Serena** *on the bed sniffling, has obviously been crying.*

Angel *tries to ignore her and gets ready for bed, settles in and checks her phone, obviously happy texting with her love interest* **Jazz**. *Finally, she has to acknowledge* **Serena** *who has been trying to get her attention through her tears and* **Angel**'s *texting. It takes a minute of silent communication each trying to achieve their objective.*

Angel (*finally frustrated enough to give up trying to ignore her*)   What's up with you already?

Serena   Nothing.

Angel   Good. (*Goes back to texting.*)

Serena *blows her nose, sighs, etc.*

Angel   Dang it, Sissy! If you want to apologize just do it already!

Serena (*sits up*)   You're wrong.

Angel   Good. Okay.

Serena   It's Mami.

Angel (*still texting but looks up and speaks to her as if talking to a child for sarcasm effect*)   Okaaaay . . . Use your words. (*Goes back to texting, under her breath.*) Drama Queen.

Serena (*sits up*)   Listen to me!

Angel (*alerts herself*)   What?!

Serena (*takes a deep breath*)   They're moving to Puerto Rico.

Angel (*still distracted and not interested*)   Who?

Serena   Our parents.

Angel (*stops texting*)   What? When? Why?

Serena   As soon as school lets out. For a whole year!

Angel (*confused*)   With us?

Serena   No. With the Statue of Liberty! Of course, with us!

Angel (*takes in the magnitude of it*)   But, but, w . . . w . . . why? I don't understand.

Serena   Oh, you don't? (*Laughs sarcastically.*) I thought you would be thrilled. Miss *Bomba* New Jersey!

Angel   Why would you think that?

Serena   Because (*uses quotation fingers*) "It's a chance to help Hurricane Maria victims."

Angel   Well . . . Oookay . . . But . . .

Serena   NO! Not okay. I am finally graduating high school, and I am getting ready to blow up this summer. I have plans . . . (*Fights crying again.*)

Angel   Mami's been wanting to go back for a long time, and now she has a damn good reason. A chance to do some—

Serena   Oh yeah, sure . . . What can she really do anyway? What will change?! Nothing! And you and all the saints can just exhaust yourselves to death for all I care!

Angel   I ain't no saint! But at least I am trying to understand it.

Serena   You know the best way to help those people? Send them money! Okay? Dineroooo . . . Chavoooos. Work here with opportunities that are *here*. Send *there*. And not get in the way.

Angel *is not entirely convinced she wants to go either. She struggles to find an argument.*

Angel   Look, it's not forever. And we have roots there. Even some family still there.

Serena   We don't know that family! Have they ever come here to help us when we were struggling? Hell no! They didn't! They think they're some kind of white Spanish blood. They look at us like we are beneath them. I am surprised you even *want* to know them.

Angel   It's not just about them.

Serena   We are American with over 100 years of mixed-blood Puerto Rican descent. They practically disowned Papi when he married Mami. Don't you remember those awkward "family" get-togethers when we were little, and they would come visit from PR? Well, I do! I want to see you dance *Bomba* in front of those "relatives." And we barely even speak Spanish.

Angel   Who cares what they think of us. Most Puerto Ricans know what's up and where we come from. Like that old saying: *¿Y tu abuela, adonde está?* [And your grandmother, where is she?]

Serena   HA! *¡La tenemos en el closet, bien amarrá!* [We have her in the closet, tightly tied up.]

Angel   Sounding pretty bilingual to me.

Serena   Knowing a few words does *not* make us bilingual. I can't leave now. What about all my connections, all my hard work? And what about college? I want to learn how to market my brand. I can do a lot of good in this world with money!   .

Angel   A year is not that long.

Serena   And I don't see you signing up for school yet.

Angel   Don't worry about me. I am taking a gap year.

Serena   Oh really? Since when?

Angel   I just want to be sure about what I want to study. But I am going.

Serena   When? By the time we get back here, you will have had a two-year gap!

Angel   I will figure it out. I know you will too. You can make money happen wherever you go.

Serena (*pause*)   I am not going.

Angel (*laughs*)   I want a front seat when you tell Mami.

Serena   This is my life.

Angel   You think you have a choice? How you going to pull that off?

Serena   I don't care how, but I am not going. You'll have to drag me by my *greñas* and even then, I will find a way to get back here to Newark. By any means necessary!

Angel (*feeling a little sorry for her*)   Look, Sissy, I know it's a big mov—

Serena   —Mistake! It's a big *mistake*. And it's cruel. I have a boyfriend. Dre loves me. *Really!* Loves me.

Angel (*lamely*)   If he really loves you, he will . . .

Angel *goes to sit down next to her, wants to comfort her but decides not to try to hug her or touch her.* **Serena** *after a pause breaks down and cries on her shoulder.* **Angel***'s phone pings and lights up; she wants to answer it but resists, struggles then firmly decides to choose to ignore it and turns it off.*

Slow fade-out to pitch black, during which we hear sounds of airplanes taking off, and landing in Puerto Rico.

Scene Four

Lights: up about 30–60. We see a bedroom in Puerto Rico.

Sounds: el Coqui and the Ocean

Sounds of the ocean take over and are heard in the background throughout this next scene. It's a new day. **Angel** *enters with jibaro hats, flyer for an event, mosquito repellent, etc.*

Angel   Hey. Good morning. Or should I say *"Buenos Dias."*

Serena (*tickles herself sarcastically*)   Ha ha ha! Ha ha!

Angel   Ready to reclaim our motherland?

Serena *purposefully doesn't answer and stares out the window. Slaps a mosquito.* **Angel** *offers the repellent.* **Serena** *uses it. It is pungent, smells like poison; she hates it but uses it.*

Angel   How did you sleep?

Serena *still doesn't answer, barely acknowledges* **Angel** *talking.*

Angel   Yo! Sis! Hello!

Serena (*snaps back into reality*)   What?

Angel   I said, how did you—oh never mind.

Serena (*looking out the window*)   I slept just great. Okay?

Angel   What's on your mind?

Serena   Thoughts.

Angel   Planning your escape?

Serena   Maybe. Why? Want in?

Angel   I don't think so. But keep me in the loop. Okay?

Serena   Sure. (*Pause for a sister moment.*) So what's the plan for today?

Angel   I heard there's a street festival today. I want to check that out.

Serena (*rolls eyes*)   Of course you do.

Angel   Be open minded. Okay?

Serena   I am trying. (*Swats at mosquito.*)

Angel   There's going to be a lot of art, graffiti, street theatre. Let's go.

Serena   I will pass.

Angel   Come on.

Serena   Nope.

Angel   . . . Or you know Mami will find something for you to do here.

Serena   OMG. For real. I'm in!

Angel   Nice! And Sissy . . .

Serena   Yeah.

Angel   Can you try to tone down the—(*Struggles to point out her style of clothing which is elegant but rather exaggerated.*) You know? (*Sees she has hurt* **Serena's** *feelings.*)—I mean just a little bit? We're not in New Jersey anymore.

Both **Angel** *and* **Serena** (*referencing the musical* Hamilton *and sharing a laugh*)   "Everything is legal in New Jersey."

Scene Five

Lights fade. Both **Angel** *and* **Serena** *get ready in the fade while the stagehands set up for the street fair amidst a burst of energy and music of island culture, street arts scene, and social consciousness raising reflected in the banners and maybe some street artists protesting in costumes, etc. Could also be some street salsa dancing, or conga playing, etc.*

Note on dancers: The dancers should be a good mix of all types dancing—women with women, elders with children, etc. for the fun of it. No showing off or Hollywood styles should be in this mix. Rather, it is a sincere genuine style that is reflective of the island culture of warm and welcoming.

Angel *and* **Serena** *stroll through the festivities.* **Serena** *is not as excited as* **Angel** *who is checking out some of the murals, banners, political messages like "Pa'l Carajo con Monsanto," etc. In front of the Anti-Monsanto sign is* **Alex** *who has a visible but interesting scar on his face. The scar is not ghastly; in fact it is rather attractive because of his attitude towards it. He has a certain swag of confidence.*

Alex (*can see that* **Angel** *and* **Serena** *are not locals so speaks in English with barely a trace or perhaps no accent*)   Hello. Welcome. Can I offer you some literature on sustainability efforts here in Puerto Rico?

Angel   Hey, *que pasa*?

Alex   You speak Spanish?

Angel   *Un poquito. ¿Cómo te llamas?*

Alex   Alex. And you can speak to me in English.

Serena   Oh, thank God.

Alex   You from New York?

Serena and Angel   No. New Jersey.

Alex   Okay. That's cool too.

Serena   Oooh thanks. (*Turns to* **Angel** *and rolls her eyes, then takes out her phone looking for interesting photos.*)

Angel   Excuse my sister. She's kind of distracted today.

Alex   I see that. Is she a photographer?

Angel   She's a makeup artist and always "working it." You know . . . looking for inspiration for her brand.

Alex   Really? That's cool. That's so cool. (*To* **Serena** *jokingly.*) Can you do something to hide this? (*Indicates his scar proudly.*)

Angel   Dang, how did you get that? Can I ask?

Alex   My souvenir from Maria.

Angel   NO SHIT?

Serena *feigns disinterest.*

Alex   Yeah (*half joking*) I am lucky though. My scars are only on the surface.

Angel   I feel you. But if you want her to, and I hate to admit it but my sister does voodoo with makeup. Sissy, show him what you can do with that.

Serena   What do I look like? Your trained monkey?

Angel (to **Alex**)   Ignore the 'tude, she works magic with her stuff. Got a YouTube following already.

Alex   You ain't putting no makeup on me!

Serena   Good! Because I am not in the business of offering free consultations.

Alex (*laughs in true sympathy to* **Serena**'s *point of view*)   I feel you.

Angel *gets a call. Sees who it is and gets excited. She walks off talking into the phone to get some privacy.*

Angel   Sorry, I gotta take this. (*Into the phone.*) Hey, stranger! Wow! Where are you? I've been calling and calling. Where have you been? Talk to me.

She goes off to the side for privacy. There is a sense of urgency.

Serena (*concerned about* **Angel**)   Let me see. I like a challenge, so I will do it because I want to. Not because of my sister.

Alex   Oh no no no. I meant it. I am not interested. I don't do makeup. I am not like that.

Serena   You like looking like you just got beat up?

Alex   Some people think scars are sexy.

Serena   True! And on some folks they are. But few . . . can pull them off. And trust me, you ain't got enough swag for that.

Alex   Excuse me? Whaaaaa . . .?

Serena (imitates **Alex**)   Whaaaa . . .? Sorry, but you ain't Omar Little.

Alex   Omar Little? Who's that?

Serena   From that old show? *The Wire*? Sexy guy with big old scar on his face? (*Pause.*) Never mind. (**Serena** *studies him.*) Look, it's an option. Ok? I take in the whole personality. With you, I wouldn't even pluck your eyebrows, though God knows they could use it. You're more of a natural gold earthy type. Very little correction actually needs to be done.

Alex *starts to protest.*

Serena   But if you want to conceal it . . .

She compares a concealer and matching powder.

Here, just let me show you what I mean.

She starts to dab some on his face.

Alex   Get the heck out of here.

Serena   Don't be so closed-minded.

Alex   I am not letting you do this. Next thing you will want me to put on mascara and lipstick.

Serena   Be glad I am not charging you. If it makes you feel better, just think of it like an enhancement of your natural self . . . and definitely start using sunscreen with a color base added.

Alex   I don't use sunscreen. That's for *chicas*.

Serena   Don't come crying to me when you prematurely age. Although you already *sound* like you're 100 years old. *Muchacho*, times have changed! Where you been? Frozen in a time machine?

She pops a small mirror in his face. **Alex** *is stunned at the difference.*

Alex   Where did it go? Whoa! Wait! Where's my personality? This is crazy. It has disappeared. You know thanks, but I am just not the type to do this.

Serena   Not even sometimes? You don't like the way this looks?

Alex (*checking himself in the mirror still amazed*)   Yeah, but I am not completely down with this. I like the way I really look. Seriously. Okay, well maybe sunscreen, but that's it.

Serena   Do yourself this favor, Alex. Because you know all those "friends" on social media? Well they will be staring and comparing with you.

Alex   Let them! *¿Y que?*

Angel *has returned.*

Angel   Did she hook you up? (*Admiring* **Serena**'s *work.*) Work it, papi/(mami)!

Alex   Ha! Ain't for me. Thanks anyway. (*To* **Serena**.) But I do respect that you can do that. (*Begins to wipe off the makeup; to* **Angel** *kind of flirting.*) Besides, I think *chicas* like my face the way it is.

Angel (*blushing a little—there's a connection*)   So tell me, Alex, what's there to do here?

Alex   There's a festival starting soon. I'm going to get my *barriles*. And there's a *bombazo* tonight. You interested?

Angel   Uhhh . . . *Yeah!* I am a percussionist and dancer. Helloooo!

Alex   *BAYA!* That would be great! (*Hands her a flier; to* **Serena**.) Feel free to bring your magic tools. I bet you'll be a hit.

Alex *starts to exit still talking.*

Serena (*false enthusiasm*)   I will bring my insect repellent.

Alex   Good idea for *gringas*.

Serena (*offended*)   Excuse me?

Alex   Just kidding.

Angel (*laughing*)   No, you're not.

Serena   Immigrants here and immigrants there. What the f**k?!

Alex (*still walking away and talking*)   I am joking. I promise. You're only a *gringa* to the mosquitos. They can smell you're not from the island.

Serena   Seriously? For reals? Is that what's going on?

Alex   That and you probably smell sweet. The repellent you're using is like a *sazón* on top of your skin for our mosquitos. (*Demonstrates how a favorite PR spice is rubbed onto the top of skin is yummy.*) Ok? See you there? I didn't catch your names?

Angel   Angel.

Serena   Serena.

Alex (*pronounces her name in Spanish with love*)   *Serena.*

Seren   It's Sereenaaa . . . The Queen—aaahh!

Alex   That totally makes sense! You are the Orisha Goddess of the Ocean! The nurturer.

Angel   Hahaha . . . the nurturer? Now that's funny! (*With a light-hearted teasing.*) She nurtures the mirror.

Alex   And of course, she's a little vain. But you are *La Serena.* Sometimes it is not obvious who we really are and sometimes we even try to fight it for some reason.

Angel   She fights it real good too.

Alex *gives the Yoruban ritualistic salutation of crossing arms across the upper chest with open palms facing in towards the chest. It is a slight nod of the head, like a prayer, gratitude, reverence to thank the Orisha Yemalla.*

Alex   *¡Maferefun Yemalla!*

Serena *is intrigued by what it all means, but pretends to act nonchalant.* **Alex** *exits.*

Angel (*teasing* **Serena**)   *¡Maferefun Yemalla!* You?! A nurturer?! Hahaha.

Serena   Hey! What's so crazy about that? I got mad nurturing skills in me. Okaaay . . .?

Angel   Sure you do! That's why you came running to PR to help.

Serena   I never said I didn't want to help.

Angel   Oh really . . .?!

Serena   I just didn't want to move here. Is that a crime? I wanted to make money so I could send it here. You think I am clueless or something?

Angel   No, Sissy, you're not. Just different.

Serena   Anyway, Alex is a weirdo. He kind of got under my skin.

Angel   I don't know. . . (*Liking him and his flirting.*) I kind of dig his vibe.

Serena   You would. What's up with you anyway? Your bae giving you trouble, so you're falling in love again already?

Angel   Naw. Everything's alright. Just stuff. You know. In fact, Jazz has been hanging out with the Institute for Social Justice. I took her to that fundraiser and now she's really into it.

Serena   Yeah. So?

Angel   So . . . I kind of really like her.

Serena   Oh pleeease. You barely know her.

Angel   I know right? Help me understand this.

Serena   Maybe you've been drinking contaminated water from all the fracking I hear is going on around here?

Angel   That's not funny.

Serena   Really? Awww . . . I thought you would love that joke.

Angel   Well I don't. Don't play like that. That's serious stuff, Sissy. I've been doing some research. Did you know that 95 percent of the food here is imported? 95 percent! And now after Maria there's a whole lot of nasty opportunistic outsiders trying to take advantage of buying up land? But there's folks that ain't having it. Like the organization Vive Borikén. And all this amazing work being done, like eco-friendly parks and reclaiming agriculture. You need to wake up!

Serena (*impressed but still giving some attitude*)   I guess so. (*Still trying to act nonchalant, but she does care.*) Since we're stuck here a minute anyway!

Angel   I don't feel stuck! (*notices the musicians starting to set up*)   I mean, just look around!

Serena   Alright, but let's go change. (*Indicates* **Angel**'*s appearance.*) And ummm . . . You could elevate that. You didn't even comb your hair this morning. Honestly, I don't know how you get so much play.

Angel   Because I am fine the way I am. Deal with it.

Serena   No, you need to take better care of yourself. It reflects your state of mind.

Angel (*ignores her*)   They're already starting.

Serena *follows* **Angel** *toward musicians.*

Serena But that's self-care. How do you not get it? (**Serena** *shows care for her sister's appearance/well-being. As they walk off their conversation trails off.*)

Sound: Celia Cruz's "El yerberito" (this song speaks to the healing power of herbs in the Santeria tradition). The congero invites people to dance. **Serena** *and* **Angel** *enter and are having a good time. As the music starts to enter* **Serena***'s body* **Alex** *is playing on a conga and encourages her to engage her higher power. The words are significant and the music starts low and builds as the drumming enters* **Serena***'s body like an ancestor spirit. There may be others dancing also, but* **Serena***'s dance should stand out as the spirit connects through her via the drumming and lyrics that put her in a trance-like state and crescendos. After the music stops,* **Serena** *is radiant, woke, reborn, elevated, and understands her life purpose.*

Blackout boom with drums.

Scene Six

Lights up. It is late evening. We see **Angel** *in her bedroom on the phone when* **Serena** *walks in. She is radiant, happy, and purposeful in attitude.*

Sounds of el Coqui and the Ocean.

Angel (*listening on the phone and worried*)   And what did they advise? Who else did you talk to? Yeah, I know them. They're good, but what do they charge? (*Sees* **Serena***.*) Hey, listen, I will call you back. Yeah, I am down. Talk to you soon. And get that info! Okay, bye!

Angel (*to* **Serena**)   Where have you been? You just disappeared on me.

Serena *is holding a small pomade jar.* **Angel** *swats at a mosquito.*

Serena   You're not going to believe this!

Angel   What?

Serena   Did you see that older woman I was speaking to at the *Bombazo*?

Angel   Yeah?

Serena   Well, she's an author, Maria Benedetti, and one of her books is on the medicinal plants of Puerto Rico. She is so cool and a powerhouse of knowledge.

Angel   Yeah? And . . .?

Serena (*super–excited, hyper*)   And . . . She introduced me to the most amazing people and they shared some information on natural mosquito repellent and oh my God it really works! And it's organic and oh my God . . . it smells so good. Smell it. I have to be a part of this, right here, in Puerto Rico. With these amazing women and I can help, with my make-up and creating all kinds of natural stuff, like pomades for our hair. I am telling you this island is lit! Well, of course not entirely lit with so many still without electricity. But hell, you know what I mean. I. Am. So lit!—

Angel   Sissy, I just got some bad news.

Serena (*dumbfounded, concerned*)   Yeah . . .? What? What's wrong?—

Angel   From Jazz, she's—

Serena   I knew you were going too fast. I told you, it's too soon to be—

Angel   It's not about her. Well, it is, but—

Serena   What is it?! Just say it already.

Angel   Her little brother, Victor, was just arrested for murder. (*Pause.*) He is only fourteen years old and they want to try him as an adult.

Serena   What the . . .?!

Angel   Wrong place at the wrong time. There was a scuffle of some sort and no one really knows who did it, but he was there and now he is at fifty years to life.

Serena   Oh my God! How did he get into that situation?

Angel   You know how many times I have been in stupid situations?

Serena   I know me too. But—

Angel   But nothing! Nothing happened because somehow it was deescalated by some divine intervention or just plain luck! But it is just so weird how the Institute for Social Justice actually has been working on this very issue. I don't think that's a coincidence. I just don't know how to put my head around all this, but I need to help him. I need to stop this crazy law of—

Serena   Wait? What are you thinking?

Angel   I have to go back and help them—

Serena   How? What can you do? You're not a lawyer?

Angel   I can volunteer. The Institute looks like they fight a good fight. Who knows? Maybe I will finally know what I want to study. Come with me, Sissy. I know you miss Dre.

Serena   I do, but I feel this connection here now. I can't explain it. And as for Dre . . . I don't know . . . we will work it out.

Angel   We need to go back home.

Serena (*pause*)   I think I am home. For the first time. (*Longer pause as the sisters struggle with what to say/think.*) I am going to miss you.

Angel (*pause*)   Me too. But I need to do this. He's a good kid and being tried as an adult. That's evil. I've already been looking into flights.

Serena (*nods, conflicted emotionally—almost sarcastically*)   So, what do you need from me?

Angel (*really studies her sister and has a realization*)   Check out their website and give me your blessing . . . (*Using the Spanish pronunciation purposefully.*) . . . *Serena.*

Serena (*it hits her core of self-awareness*)   Okay. But! . . . You have to promise me to take care of yourself.

Angel   And you?

Serena (*thinks for a minute*)   I promise to not make it *all* about staring and comparing just to make money.

Angel   That's a bet.

Serena   Bet!

Serena (*conflicted, she struggles to find her grounding and forces herself to snap out of it for her sister's sake*)   Girl, then let's start with that hair.

Serena *works on* **Angel**'s *somewhat unruly hair, plaiting it, etc.* **Angel** *tries out the repellent* **Serena** *had offered. The moment is soothing for both girls.*

Sounds of the ocean, drumming, and the coqui.

Lights fade with a special on the girls.

No mosquitos are biting.

Blackout.

End of play.

Suggested Exercises for Educators and Teaching Artists for *Stare and Compare*

Before reading or seeing the play

- Classroom Exercise:

  Divide the classroom space into four corners, with each space designating a particular category. Ask students to move the space that best fits their categorization based on the following prompt: All students who identify as the older sibling in their family would move to the upper right-hand corner; all students who identify as the middle child would move to the upper left-hand corner; all students who identify as the youngest sibling would move the lower right-hand corner; and all students who identify as an only child would move to the lower left-hand corner. Give each group two minutes to come up with three things the entire group has in common.

  Next, develop tableaux and three-line plays about sibling rivalry with the students. Divide the class into pairs. Ask the students to imagine that they are siblings who are rivaling over something. The students may decide what that is. Next, they should create a frozen image, or tableau, that depicts the rivalry. (Give them five minutes to create these tableaux.) Have each pair perform their tableau, one at a time. Give the class a chance to study the tableau and to guess what the conflict might be. Next, let the "sculpture" come alive in three lines of dialogue: the first line sets up the rivalry; the second line responds to it; and the third line resolves it. The teacher should initiate this dialogue first by assigning students to be Character A and Character B. Repeat the dialogue so that in the first round Character A speaks first, and in the second round Character B speaks first.

  Note: In a good improvisation, players should always accept the circumstances that other players offer, and respond with "Yes, and . . ." The second line, therefore, should not contradict or negate the first but accept it and build upon it. Example:

  Character A Why did you copy my homework?
  Character B I didn't copy your homework. *(This negates the first "offer.")*
  Character A Yes you did. *(So now we're stuck in an undramatic loop with no resolution.)*
  Vs.
  Character A Why did you copy my homework?
  Character B Because you always get straight A's. *(This develops the story.)*
  Character A I'm going to tell Mom. *(This provides a dramatic resolution.)*
  Discuss each improvisation: What did the individual needs and desires in the rivalries reveal about the characters' personal values? How were the siblings' characters different and/or similar to one another?

- Classroom Exercise:

Give the students five minutes to do a freewrite (they will need paper and a writing instrument). The freewrite should respond to the following prompt: Where and how do you connect with your cultural identity? How do you depart from it? Note: Encourage students to write continuously for the whole five minutes, even if they go off topic. The idea is for them to not censor themselves. Let them know that the freewrite will not be graded.

Next, break the class into small groups. Those who are willing should share what they wrote. Each group should note three common themes between their writings. Next, each group should improvise a short scene of a family meeting. The family must decide whether or not to make a significant change in their life to support their culture. Which characters stand for it and which stand against it and why? Have the groups perform their scenes for the rest of the class.

After seeing or reading the play

- Classroom Discussion:

Divide the class into small groups or pairs to discuss: What character did you identify with and why, Angel or Serena?

- Class Project:

Research and create a display board with the following items (visual images are encouraged):

shekere, maracas, Bomba, barriles, subidor, buledor, claves, Hurricane Maria, el coqui, salsa dancing, Monsanto (herbicide company), Omar Little, Serena (Yemaya), *Vive Borikén* (personalized, authentic co-cultural tours), Celia Cruz's "*El Yerberito.*" Also look up the organization 150 Years Is Enough. In addition to adding information about this organization to the display, consider watching and discussing their video: https://www.njisj.org/150_years_is_enough

- Homework Exercise:

Ask students to write a one-page reflection on the following: Have you ever encountered anything spiritually inspiring or other-worldly that caused you to rethink your behavior or attitude about your life, and/or that made you feel connected to your ancestry? Describe the encounter: Where were you? What did you see, feel, smell, hear, and touch? What time of day or night was it? What happened? How did the encounter make you feel? How long did it last? What did you do as a result?

- Bonus Round:

Guide the students into writing short plays or monologues based on the encounter described in their reflection.

Permissions for Performance

All rights whatsoever in these plays are strictly reserved and application for performance etc. should be made before rehearsals by professionals and by amateurs to the following:

For *No Child...* please contact: APA, 3, Columbus Circle, 23rd Floor, New York, NY 10019, USA

For *Ghosts of Skunk Hollow* please contact: Bloomsbury Publishing Plc, 50 Bedford Square, London, WC1B 3DP, email: permissions@bloomsbury.com

For *Gunshots at 2 p.m.* please contact: Bloomsbury Publishing Plc, 50 Bedford Square, London, WC1B 3DP, email: permissions@bloomsbury.com

For *This Time with Feeling* please contact: ICM, 65 E. 55th St., New York, NY 10022, tel: 212 556 5600

For *777* please contact: ICM, 65 E. 55th St., New York, NY 10022, tel: 212 556 5600

For *Marathon and Mucilage* please contact: Bloomsbury Publishing Plc, 50 Bedford Square, London, WC1B 3DP, email: permissions@bloomsbury.com

For *Homecoming Dance* please contact: Bloomsbury Publishing Plc, 50 Bedford Square, London, WC1B 3DP, email: permissions@bloomsbury.com

For *Snap the Sun* please contact: A3 Artists Agency, The Empire State Building, 350 Fifth Ave., 38th Floor, New York, NY 10118, email: contactny@a3artistsagency.com

For *The Bottom Line* please contact: Bloomsbury Publishing Plc, 50 Bedford Square, London, WC1B 3DP, email: permissions@bloomsbury.com

For *The Aftermath* please contact: Bloomsbury Publishing Plc, 50 Bedford Square, London, WC1B 3DP, email: permissions@bloomsbury.com

For *Charisma and the Crossroads* please contact: Bloomsbury Publishing Plc, 50 Bedford Square, London, WC1B 3DP, email: permissions@bloomsbury.com

For *Southwestern High* please contact: Elaine Devlin Literary, Inc. of 411 Lafayette Street, 6th Floor, New York, NY 10003, USA

For *Stare and Compare* please contact: Bloomsbury Publishing Plc, 50 Bedford Square, London, WC1B 3DP, email: permissions@bloomsbury.com